Ceri Jones & Tania Bastow

with Jon Hird

Inside Out

Student's Book

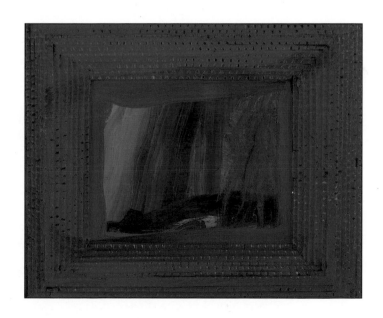

MACMILLAN

1 Identity

1 Do you recognise these famous people?

A
NAME	
DATE OF BIRTH	25.8.1930
NATIONALITY	SCOTTISH
OCCUPATION	LIFEGUARD

B
NAME	
DATE OF BIRTH	1.6.1926
NATIONALITY	AMERICAN
OCCUPATION	FACTORY WORKER

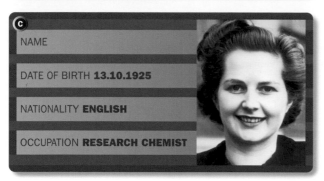

C
NAME	
DATE OF BIRTH	13.10.1925
NATIONALITY	ENGLISH
OCCUPATION	RESEARCH CHEMIST

D
NAME	
DATE OF BIRTH	19.8.1946
NATIONALITY	AMERICAN
OCCUPATION	UNIVERSITY LECTURER

2 Check your answers on page 132.

3 Work with a partner and discuss these questions:

a) What documents do you usually use to identify yourself?
b) Do you always carry ID? Is this required by law in your country?
c) When are you usually asked to show your ID?
d) What information does your ID give about you?
e) Do you have any ID on you at the moment?
f) Do you like the photo? When was it taken?

Born & bred

1 Work in small groups and answer these questions:

a) Where is your home town? Were you born there? If yes, were your parents born there too?
b) When someone asks you where you come from what do you say? If that person was a foreigner and obviously didn't know your country very well, would your answer be the same?
c) Which is most important to you in defining who you are: your town, your country, your language, your job or something else? Why?

2 🔲 01 Listen to Steve, David and Valeria answering some of the questions above. Make short notes on their answers. Which questions did they answer?

3 Compare your answers with a partner and discuss these questions:

a) Which person do you identify most closely with? Why?
b) Were any of their answers similar to the ones your group gave?

Close up

Types of
adverbials

Language reference p6

1 Look at the sentences below. Underline all the *adverbials*.

  a) I always stress the fact that I'm Scottish and not English.
  b) I live in the North of England.
  c) I've lived there since I left home.
  d) I went there to study medicine.
  e) I really like living there.

2 Work with a partner and look at these six extracts from the recording. Two or three adverbials have been removed from each. Put the adverbials in the correct place in the sentences. They are given in the order you hear them.

For example:
                             so much
… that's a difficult one because I've travelled around/. Still, Toronto I suppose. I mean, I've lived
for more than twenty years
there/, and that's where I was born.
so much / for more than twenty years

  a) He's become Canadian and he's proud of that …
    just / after thirty-five years of living there / really

  b) … people take it for granted that I'm English, or maybe they're using the word English to mean British.
    sometimes / when I'm abroad / just

  c) There is a Welsh TV channel and weekly papers and stuff, but it's not such a strong presence I suppose. I mean, it is possible to ignore it. It is possible to live and not be a Welsh speaker …
    just / totally / in Wales

  d) … I've lived here and so have my family. My family have lived in the same house.
    all my life / actually / for seven generations

  e) … I like the idea that I'm the seventh generation of notaries in the family and that a woman can carry on what was a male tradition.
    really / basically / until very recently

3 🔘 02 Listen again and check your answers.

4 Look at the adverbials that were removed in 2. Put them into the categories below.

  a) describes how often something happens
  b) intensifies an adjective
  c) emphasises the verb
  d) describes where the action happens
  e) describes when the action happens
  f) indicates how long an action continued for
  g) commenting on the noun phrase

Position of
adverbials

Language reference p6

1 Work with a partner. Look at the sentences below. Where would you normally place the adverb *always* in each of them?

  • We define ourselves according to our place of birth.
  • We have defined ourselves according to our place of birth.
  • We would have defined ourselves according to our place of birth.
  • We wouldn't have defined ourselves according to our place of birth.

2 Look at this sentence again and answer the questions.

(1) We (2) define (3) ourselves (4) according to our place of birth (5).

a) In which position, 1–5, would you normally add these adverbials to this sentence?
- when we are children
- often
- if we live there
- to some extent
- on the whole
- probably

b) Which adverbials would you not use in position 2?
c) In which position can you never add an adverbial?

3 Modify the model sentence to fit your own opinion as closely as possible.

4 Look at these pairs of sentences. The adverbials in *italics* are in different positions. How does this change the meaning of the sentence?

For example:
A *Actually* he's performing in the play tomorrow. (and not doing something else)
B He's *actually* performing in the play tomorrow. (and not just sitting in the audience)

1A *Only* Kate knows how to look after horses.
1B Kate *only* knows how to look after horses.

2A *Honestly*, I can't speak to her any more.
2B I can't speak to her *honestly* any more.

3A *Earlier*, I had wanted Rich to come to the meeting.
3B I had wanted Rich to come to the meeting *earlier*.

5 Interview another student and write a profile of them for a class magazine. Use at least five adverbials.

Language reference: adverbials

An adverbial can be a word (*usually, really, probably, softly*) or a phrase (*at home, once a week, to get a good job, when I was a child*). You generally use an adverbial to provide additional information about a verb or an adjective.

Types of adverbials

Adverbials fulfil a number of functions.

1 You can use them to add information about the verb by

a) describing how often something happens
*I speak to my mother on the phone **every other day**.*
b) describing where the action happens
*I was mugged **on the way home**.*
c) describing when the action happens
*The dinner will probably be ready **by then**.*
d) telling us how long an action continued for
*He'd been dreaming about it **for months**.*

2 You can use them to give extra information about adjectives, for example, by grading them.

*He was **extremely** happy to see her.*
*It was **fairly** hot for the time of year.*

3 You can use them to comment on a clause or focus attention on one part of it.

***Generally speaking**, the trains are very quick and efficient.*
***Frankly**, I didn't believe a word they said.*
*I've **actually** lived here for five years now.*

Position of adverbials

You can use adverbials in three positions in a sentence.

1 Initial position

***On the whole** I prefer to eat home-made food.*

2 You tend to use one-word adverbials of frequency, emphasis and probability in the mid position.

a) between the subject and the main verb:
*I **never** trusted him.*
b) between an auxiliary and the main verb:
*I've **always** loved travelling by train.*
c) In negative sentences the adverb can be placed either between the subject and a negative auxiliary:
*I **really** don't think you should be doing that.*

or directly after the negative auxiliary:
*I don't **really** think you should be doing that.*

Adverbs of probability usually follow the first pattern and adverbs of frequency usually follow the second:
*They **probably** didn't mean to offend you.*
*I don't **always** get along with him.*

3 You tend to use longer adverbial phrases and adverbs of manner in the final position.

*They finished the job **as quickly as they could**.*

Changing the position of the adverb can change the meaning of the sentence:

***Only** Sarah has Pierre's e-mail address. (no-one else has it)*
*Sarah **only** has Pierre's e-mail address. (and nothing else)*

I am who I am

Anecdote

LANGUAGE TOOLBOX

Stressing importance

I suppose it really means a lot to me ...

It's quite an important part of my life ...

It's kind of central to who I am, I suppose ...

Running out of things to say

Let me see ...

I think that's it.

There's not much else to say really.

I'm not sure what else I can tell you.

I'm sure you know what I mean.

1 Which do you identify most strongly with: your job, your home town or your family? You are going to describe the importance of one of these three things to a partner. Choose which one you are going to describe and read the questions below. Think about what you are going to say and the language you will use.

Your job

- ☐ What do you do?
- ☐ How long have you done it for?
- ☐ Did you need to study a lot to do it?
- ☐ Have you always wanted to do this job?
- ☐ Does anybody else in your family do the same job?
- ☐ What do you most enjoy about your job?
- ☐ Is there anything you don't enjoy?
- ☐ Do you think you will continue in the same job for the rest of your working life?
- ☐ Is there anything else you'd like to add?

Your home town

- ☐ Do you still live there? If yes, do you think you will ever leave? If not, would you like to go back there to live sometime?
- ☐ How long have you lived there/did you live there?
- ☐ Has your family lived there for generations or do your parents come from somewhere else?
- ☐ What's your favourite place in the town? Why?
- ☐ At what time of year is the town at its best? And its worst?
- ☐ Is it famous for anything? Do tourists come to visit it?
- ☐ Is there anything else you'd like to add?

Your family

- ☐ Do you come from a big family?
- ☐ How many brothers or sisters do you have?
- ☐ Do you have any children?
- ☐ Who do you get on with best of all?
- ☐ Is there anyone in your family you don't get on with?
- ☐ Are you a close-knit family?
- ☐ What kind of things do you do together?
- ☐ How much time do you spend together?
- ☐ Do you prefer spending time with your family or with your friends?
- ☐ Do you go on holiday with your family?
- ☐ Is there anything else you'd like to add?

2 Work with a partner. Tell them about the thing you identify most strongly with.

As you listen to your partner's anecdote, make a note of any questions you'd like to ask.

When your partner has finished, ask your questions.

The gender gap

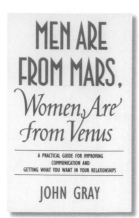

1 Work in small groups and discuss these questions. Which question generates the most discussion?

a) If you were a member of the opposite sex how would your life be different?
b) To what extent does our society expect men and women to fulfil different roles?
c) Do you think men and women think differently or perceive the world differently?

2 You are going to read an extract from a book that explores the differences between men and women. Work with a partner. Read the blurb from the book cover and answer the questions which follow.

> Once upon a time Martians and Venusians met, fell in love, and had happy relationships together because they respected and accepted their differences. Then they came to Earth and amnesia set in: they forgot they were from different planets.
>
> Using this metaphor to illustrate the commonly occurring conflicts between men and women, Dr John Gray explains how these differences can come between the sexes and prohibit mutually fulfilling loving relationships. Based on years of successful counselling of couples and individuals, he gives advice on how to counteract these differences in communication styles, emotional needs, and modes of behaviour to promote a greater understanding between individual partners.

(Excerpt from *Men Are From Mars, Women Are From Venus* by John Gray, Ph.D.)

a) Have you read the book? If you have, did you enjoy it? If you haven't read it, have you heard of it? What kind of book is it? Who was it written for? What do you think the main argument is?
b) The book is based on the premise that men and women are very different. The author mentions three categories of differences: communication styles, emotional needs and modes of behaviour. What do you think the differences are?
c) Which of the following do you think he associates with men and which with women?

uniforms	self-help books	romance	sports	clothes	shopping
gadgets and gizmos	spirituality	communication	power		

3 Work with a partner. You are going to read two extracts in which the author highlights the main differences between the two sexes.

Student A read about life on Mars on page 132.
Student B read about life on Venus on page 134.

4 Use your notes to tell your partner about your extract and then discuss these questions:

a) Do you identify with the description given of your sex?
b) Are men and women really different?

Lexis 1 Do these sentences refer to men or women?

a) _____ value power, efficiency, and achievement.
b) The issue of competence is very important to _____ .
c) _____ value love, communication, beauty and relationships.
d) _____ experience fulfilment through sharing and relating.
e) _____ feel satisfaction when they win a race, achieve a goal, or solve a problem.
f) _____ take pride in being considerate of the needs and feelings of others.
g) _____ are always doing things to prove themselves and develop their power and skills.

2 Find words or phrases in the sentences in 1 to match the definitions below.

a) the knowledge and abilities that enable you to do something well, which can often be learnt
b) something which someone has succeeded in doing, especially after a lot of effort
c) the general ability to do something well or efficiently
d) the quality of being able to do a task successfully without wasting time or effort
e) the pleasure you feel when you have done something well
f) the feeling you have when a hope, dream or ambition has been realised
g) thoughtful towards other people
h) to think that something is important and to appreciate it

3 Create a table and complete it with the verb, noun, adjective and adverb forms for your answers to 2 where appropriate.

For example:

noun	verb	adjective	adverb
skills	–	skilful / skilled	skilfully

4 Complete these sentences using words from 3.

a) I always try to take other people's points of view into ____ before making a decision.
b) I find helping others very ____ .
c) Honesty is the thing I ____ most in a friend.
d) I always feel really ____ when I manage to reach a deadline.
e) Passing my degree has been my greatest ____ so far.
f) I really admire people who are super- ____ and always manage to do everything on time.
g) My job is the one thing that gives me real ____ .
h) Using a computer is probably one of the most important ____ I've learnt in my present job.
i) Feeling ____ about doing my job gives me confidence.

5 Do you agree with the sentences in 4? If not, change them so they are true for you.

6 Work with a partner and compare your answers.

Close up

1 🔲 03 Listen to Martha and Liz discussing the book *Men Are From Mars, Women Are From Venus* and answer the following questions:

    a) Have they both read the whole book?
    b) What do they think of it?
    c) Which passages from the book do they discuss?

2 Work with a partner. Look at the statements below. Are they true or false according to the conversation you've just heard?

Martha and Liz

    a) Neither of them has read the book, they've only had a chance *to look at* it *very quickly and superficially*.
    b) Both think the Mars/Venus metaphor is a good way *to communicate* the idea of the difference between the sexes.
    c) The book claims that men prefer *to find solutions to* their problems by talking to someone.
    d) The book suggests that men tend *to reflect on* their problems.
    e) The book suggests that women tend *not to show* their feelings.
    f) The book suggests that women do not like *to discuss* their problems.
    g) The book suggests that men's refusal to talk about their problems tends *to depress* women.
    h) The main solution the author is able *to propose* is to learn to understand and *to tolerate* our differences.

3 Listen again and check your answers.

4 Look at the sentences in 2 again. Match the phrases in *italics* to the phrasal verbs below.

    1 to sort out   4 to flick through   7 to talk through
    2 to bottle up   5 to think through   8 to put across
    3 to put up with   6 to get down   9 to come up with

5 Work with a partner. Look at the three types of phrasal verbs which take objects shown below and answer the questions.

Type 1
Two of the sentences below are not correct. Which are they?
a) She flicked the book through.   c) She flicked it through.
b) She flicked through the book.   d) She flicked through it.

Language reference p12

Type 2
One of the sentences below is not correct. Which is it?
a) The metaphor puts the idea across well.   c) The metaphor puts it across well.
b) The metaphor puts across the idea well.   d) The metaphor puts across it well.

Type 3
What is the correct word order for these sentences?
a) differences we others' put should each with to learn up.
b) author with what up solution did the come?

6 Answer these questions:

    a) What are the rules for word order in types 1 and 2?
    b) Are type 3 verbs similar to type 1 or type 2?

7 Look at the other phrasal verbs in 4. Are they type 1, 2 or 3?

'I can't stand him, really, but I quite like dressing him up.'

8 Complete the sentences below with a phrasal verb from 4. Put the object (in brackets) in the right position.

a) I try not to _____ , it's always much better to talk about them with a friend. (my feelings)

b) I hate asking people for help. I'd much rather _____ on my own. (my problems)

c) I don't often buy a newspaper, but sometimes I _____ at the bar. (one)

d) I'm not a very confident speaker. Sometimes I'm not sure I've managed to _____ very effectively. (my ideas)

e) My motto is 'if you can't change it, then you'll just have to _____'. (it)

f) I tend to be a little too impulsive and don't _____ enough. (things)

g) I hate arguments, I'd much rather _____ quietly and calmly. (things)

h) My sister's a really happy, positive person, nothing ever _____ . (her)

9 Are the sentences in 8 true for you? If not, change them so that they are true. Compare your answers with a partner.

My girl

Madness

Madness are a popular British band who reached the peak of their career in the 1980s. They had many hits including **House Of Fun, Baggy Trousers** and **It Must Be Love.**

1 Work with a partner. Make a list of five common complaints girlfriends and boyfriends make about each other. Do the complaints differ according to sex?

2 You're going to listen to a song about an argument between a couple. Look at these expressions from the song. What do you think the problem between them is?

> had enough   on my own   why can't I explain
> we argued just the other night   I don't care
> see the film tonight   lovely to me   on the telephone
> doesn't understand   talked it out   mad at me

3 🔲 04 Listen to the song and put the expressions in the order you hear them.

4 Were your predictions correct? What is the boy complaining about? What is the girl upset about?

5   Work with a partner. Act out their telephone conversation.

Student A look at page 133.
Student B look at page 135.

6   ▣ 05 Listen to the conversation. Was it very different from yours?

7   Work with your partner. Here are some extracts from their telephone conversation. Do you remember who said each line, the boy or his girlfriend?

  a)   … a bit stressed out, had a hard day at work, you know, the usual.
  b)   So, what about the film then?
  c)   … do you mind if we go another night?
  d)   What's going on?
  e)   I just don't fancy it tonight …
  f)   Have I done something wrong?
  g)   But not tonight, eh? The football's more interesting …
  h)   Shall I come and pick you up?
  i)   Let's just drop it.
  j)   Whatever. Just please yourself.

8   Listen again and check your answers.

9   What do you think he should do now?

Getting angry   **1**   Work with a partner. Look at these two extracts from the telephone conversation and discuss the questions that follow.

  A   But not tonight, eh? The football's more interesting I suppose.
  B   No, forget it! I wouldn't want you to go out of your way or anything!

  a)   Does the girl mean what she says?
  b)   How does she convey her anger?

2   ▣ 06 Listen to the two extracts being repeated, first in a normal tone and then angrily. What is the difference?

3   Look at tapescript 05 on page 144. Find other phrases where the girl uses an angry tone of voice. Work with a partner and read the conversation aloud.

Language reference: phrasal verbs with objects

There are three basic types of phrasal verbs which take an object.

Type 1: not separable

verb + particle + object
*They **flicked through** the newspaper.*
*The research group **looked into** it quite thoroughly.*

Type 2: separable

1   verb + object + particle
   *We **picked** the rest of the party **up** at the corner.*
   *He'll be **bringing** the issue **up** in the next meeting.*

2   verb + particle + object
   *We **brought up** the subject of Harry's birthday party.*
   *John and Linda have **broken off** their engagement.*

If the object is a pronoun, only the first order is possible: verb + object pronoun + particle
*I'm trying to sort **it** out.* ✓
*I'm trying to sort out **it**.* ✗

The second order is favoured if the noun phrase is particularly long:
*He bottled up **all his negative feelings against his mother-in-law** until he could stand it no longer.*

Note: Distinguishing between type 1 and type 2 is never easy, but a good dictionary will tell you which pattern any verb follows.

Type 3: two particles

verb + particle + particle + object
In this type of phrasal verb the particles are not separable.
*I had to **come up with** a solution quickly.*
*I've always **looked up to** my father.*

Mistaken identity

1 Work with a partner. Read this passage and decide whether the statements that follow are true, false or unknown.

> A young man drove a car into a car park. He had just thought how badly lit it was when a man appeared next to the car and said, 'Give me the keys.' The owner of the car reluctantly handed over a large bunch of keys. The car was driven away at speed. Shortly afterwards, a police officer arrived.

a) The car was driven into the car park.
b) The young man parked the car.
c) A man demanded the car keys.
d) The driver handed over the keys.
e) The car was stolen.
f) The police were called shortly after the incident.
g) A policeman arrived.
h) Three people are involved in the story.

2 Check your answers on page 137.

3 The text is *not* describing a car robbery. What do you think the situation might be? Work with your partner and think of a story which fits with all the facts given in the passage.

4 Tell your story to the class. Which story was the most original?

5 Work with a partner. Look at the three photographs below. What do you think is happening in each one?

6 Turn to page 132 and read about the three situations. Were you right?

7 Have you ever interpreted a situation incorrectly or jumped to the wrong conclusions? Discuss your answer with a partner.

2 Taste

1 Four people were asked 'If you were a food, what food would you be?' Which of the four do you think gave each of the answers below? Why?

| 1 Melody, an art teacher and mother | 2 Nicholas, an army officer | 3 David, a sailor | 4 Zena, a pensioner |

a) 'Baked beans, because they're full of protein and good for you.'
b) 'A cauliflower, because it's flowery and intricate.'
c) 'A bar of dark chocolate, because it's smooth and velvety like me!'
d) 'Nuts, because they're hard but worth opening for what's inside!'

2 Check your answers on page 132.

3 If you were a food, what would you be? Why? Discuss your answer with a partner.

4 Were there any foods you particularly loved or hated as a child? Do you still love/hate them?

Food associations

1 What kind of food or drink would you associate with the following situations? Why?

a) being in love
b) waiting at an airport
c) rainy days
d) summer
e) the end of a hard day
f) your grandmother's house

2 Work with a partner and discuss your answers. Are your partner's associations very different from yours?

3 📼 07 Listen to six people giving their answers to 1. Answer these questions for each person:

a) Which situation are they talking about?
b) What food do they associate with that situation?

Close up

Language reference p16

Describing nouns

1 How were the foods described by the speakers? Complete the *noun phrases*.

a) b_ _ _ coffee i____ a p____ c____

b) big bowls of f____ salad w____ h____-m____ d____

c) huge plates of r____ lamb s____ w____ m____ p____

d) the b____ gravy y____ h____ e____ t____

e) c____ m ____ c____ biscuits d____ i____ c____

f) s____ s____ strawberries w____ f____ c____

g) some kind of m____ convenience food t____ d____ n____ a____ c____

2 Listen again and check your answers.

3 Work with a partner. Look at the descriptions below. They are all noun phrases with the same subject. What is it?

1 bitter vending machine coffee in a plastic cup
2 the espresso coffee that you can get in the bar round the corner
3 a cup of strong, black coffee with two or three sugars
4 fresh filter coffee percolated slowly into its own individual cup
5 hot, milky coffee steaming in a mug
6 some iced coffee in a long glass

a) Which description best describes the last cup of coffee you drank?

b) How many different adjectives are used to describe *coffee*?

c) Find a noun which is used to modify *coffee*.

d) Which descriptions follow the pattern *coffee* + preposition + noun phrase?

e) Which descriptions contain a determiner to modify *coffee*?

f) Which descriptions include relative clauses? Which relative clauses are incomplete? Which words have been omitted?

4 Find an example of each of these structures in the noun phrases in 1.

a) nouns which modify other nouns   d) complete relative clauses
b) preposition + noun phrase   e) incomplete relative clauses
c) adjectives   f) determiners

Which structures go before the noun? Which structures go after it?

5 Complete these descriptions with the words and phrases provided.

a) ____ ____ ____ fruit
   mouth-watering / caramelised / a selection of

b) ____ ____ ____ ____ gateau
   chocolate / a / multi-layered / tempting

c) ____ ____ ____ apple crumble ____
   just like your grandmother used to make / a helping of / home-made / superb

d) ____ ____ ____ crayfish ____ ____
   a white wine sauce / fresh-water / served in / a bowl of / fabulous

e) ____ ____ ____ pancake ____ ____ ____ ____
   savoury / stuffed with / stir-fried / delicious / exquisite / an / vegetables

6 Compare your answers with a partner. Which would you most like to eat?

1 Work with a partner. Look at the adjectives in the box and answer the questions which follow.

> mouth-watering   caramelised   savoury   delicious   exquisite   home-made
> superb   fabulous   tempting

a) Which adjectives express an opinion?
b) Which express a fact?
c) Look at the order of the adjectives in 5 on page 15. Do the 'opinion' or the 'fact' adjectives come first?

2 What is your favourite dish? Write a complex noun phrase describing it. Repeat it, in the wrong order, to your partner. Ask your partner to repeat it back in the right order.

A game

Round one

1 Look at this simple sentence. Identify the two noun phrases.

The girl was eating an apple.

2 Work in teams. Each team takes it in turns to expand the sentence by adding more information to the noun phrases. Teams get a point for each correct modification. The game finishes when no further modifications can be made or the sentence is in danger of becoming unintelligible.

Round two

Here is another sentence. Continue to work in teams. Expand the sentence as much as possible in three minutes. The team with the longest and most coherent sentence wins.

The student asked a question.

Language reference: describing nouns

The noun phrase

A noun phrase can include

- nouns: *coffee*
- determiners (e.g. *a cup of, some, three, this*): *a cup of coffee*
- adjectives*: *a cup of black coffee*
- descriptive details: *a cup of black coffee with sugar*

*In English, many nouns can function as adjectives.
a **fish** restaurant   **vending machine** coffee

Nouns and adjectives usually come before the noun. Longer phrases giving more descriptive detail go after the noun.

Descriptive details

The description after the noun can be either

- a prepositional phrase (preposition + noun phrase):
  *the restaurant **round the corner***

- a relative clause:
  *the restaurant **which your cousin recommended***
- a past participle clause:
  *the restaurant **recommended by the Michelin guide***
- or a present participle clause:
  *the restaurant **advertising for staff***

When the relative pronoun (*which/that/who*) is the object of the relative clause you can omit it.
We're having dinner at the restaurant (that) my brother went to last week.

Order of adjectives

Adjectives expressing an opinion usually come before adjectives (or nouns) which express a fact.
*that **wonderful new** restaurant*
*that **awful fast food** place*

A taste for travel

1  08 Listen to Anne, Kim, Bill and Steve talking about their eating experiences abroad. Did they like the food in the countries they visited?

2 Listen again and list the food vocabulary you hear each person use.

3 Compare your list with a partner. Which countries do you think they are talking about? Check your answers on page 137.

4 Work with a partner and discuss these questions:

a) Have you ever eaten food from these countries?
b) If you have, do you agree with the speakers' opinions? If you haven't, would you like to try it? Why/Why not?

Anne, Kim, Bill and Steve

Expressing enthusiasm & reservations

1 Look at these extracts from the recording. Which words do the speakers stress to express their enthusiasm or reservations?

a) Mmm, it's superb, really hot and spicy …
b) Well, it took a bit of getting used to actually.
c) Well, to tell you the truth, I didn't really like it that much.
d) … and mmm, I don't really like cabbage that much …
e) … no, it isn't really my favourite.
f) It isn't particularly elaborate, but it's good.

2 09 Listen and check your answers.

3 Look at the extracts in 1. Match the words and sounds on the left to the situations in which they are used on the right.

a) Mmm   1 introducing a negative comment
b) Well   2 stressing good qualities or softening criticism
c) really/particularly   3 expressing enthusiasm or reservation

How does the sound of *Mmm* change according to its meaning?

4 Work with a partner. Look at the two short exchanges below. Use the expressions above and add your own ideas to make the conversations sound a) more enthusiastic b) less enthusiastic.

A: How was the trip then?   A: So, how was the food last night?
B: Interesting.   B: Unusual.

5 Ask your partner about

a) the last time they ate out.   b) the last film they saw.   c) their last English lesson.

Did they enjoy themselves?

The demise of a great little restaurant

1 Read the introduction to this restaurant review and answer the questions.

a) When did the writer first visit the restaurant?
b) How is it different from other restaurants? List as many unusual things about it as you can.
c) Why do you think the writer liked it so much?
d) Would you like to eat there?

review

I first reviewed Le Palmier ten years ago. At the time I wrote that it was one of the most unusual and enjoyable seafood restaurants I had ever visited – not least because of its location on Croix St Michel, a
5 tiny island just off the coast near St Laurent. Back then it was run by a married couple, Marianne and Didier. He was the cook and fisherman, while she tended the vegetable gardens and ran the restaurant. There was only one waiter, their son Alex.
10 Access to the island was by a small launch with room for no more than five passengers. There were no advance bookings. You simply turned up at the jetty in St Laurent and waited. Eventually Marianne would come along in the launch and pick you up.
15 Sometimes you had to wait for an hour or more. To make the wait more agreeable, their daughter, Dominique, had set up a tiny bar on the jetty. It was really just a kiosk with a couple of tables where you could take a glass of white wine (from vines grown on
20 the island) and enjoy the scenery.
The trip to the island took ten minutes. As the coastline receded, Marianne would tell you what was on the day's menu and what was going on in the village. She always seemed very well informed. Or,
25 perhaps, very imaginative.
Le Palmier was in the only building on the island; a three storey house looking over the water to the mainland. On the upper floors lived the family. Their rooms had balconies filled with glorious
30 geraniums and bougainvillaea. The restaurant occupied the ground floor, opening out onto a seaside terrace. A striped canopy provided shelter from the sun. There were only four tables, each one covered with a crisp, white linen tablecloth and
35 provided with a basket of wonderful home-made bread.
The menu was, frankly, limited, but while choice was restricted, there were rarely any complaints about price, which was absurdly low, or about
40 quality. Basically, you ate whatever Didier had caught in the waters of the bay that morning. On my first visit, I had squid for the first time in my life. It was barbecued with red peppers and served with fresh salad from the restaurant gardens to the sound of *La*
45 *Traviata*. Didier was singing in the kitchen. For dessert I chose pears in red wine.
This summer, my wife and I went to St Laurent as an anniversary celebration, my first visit in several years.

2 Compare your answers with a partner.

3 When the writer went back ten years later, the restaurant had undergone a lot of changes. Work with a partner. Before you read the rest of the review, discuss these questions:

What changes do you think had taken place? Why do you think these changes took place?

4 Work with a partner and read the rest of the review.

Student A look at page 137.
Student B look at page 139.

5 Discuss these questions with your partner:

a) Would you prefer to eat at Le Palmier as it was or as it is now? Why?
b) What was the writer's attitude towards the changes?
c) Were any of the changes, in your opinion, for the better?
d) Do you know of anywhere that has undergone similar changes?

Lexis Work with a partner who read the same text as you and follow the instructions below.

1 Prepare to teach four of these words from your part of the review to a student who read the other part.

Student A

thriving	exquisite	blared out	pricey	clientele	sped off

Student B

concrete	thrust	homely	batter	entrepreneur	reverie

a) Read the text again and find the words.
b) Discuss their meanings with your partner. Think about the best way to explain them.

2 Work with a different partner and teach them the words.

3 Ask your partner to write sentences containing the new words.

4 Check that the words have been used correctly in the sentences.

Test yourself

Past tenses 1 Look at this extract taken from the restaurant review. Choose the most appropriate form of the verbs.

> Basically, you (1) **ate / were eating** whatever Didier (2) **was catching / had caught** in the waters of the bay that morning. On my first visit, I (3) **had / was having** squid for the first time in my life. It (4) **barbecued / was barbecued** with red peppers and (5) **served / had been served** with fresh salad from the restaurant gardens to the sound of *La Traviata*: Didier (6) **was singing / sang** in the kitchen. (Introduction, lines 40–45)

2 Complete these extracts with the correct form of the verbs in brackets.

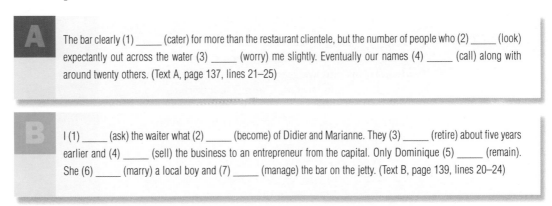

A The bar clearly (1) _____ (cater) for more than the restaurant clientele, but the number of people who (2) _____ (look) expectantly out across the water (3) _____ (worry) me slightly. Eventually our names (4) _____ (call) along with around twenty others. (Text A, page 137, lines 21–25)

B I (1) _____ (ask) the waiter what (2) _____ (become) of Didier and Marianne. They (3) _____ (retire) about five years earlier and (4) _____ (sell) the business to an entrepreneur from the capital. Only Dominique (5) _____ (remain). She (6) _____ (marry) a local boy and (7) _____ (manage) the bar on the jetty. (Text B, page 139, lines 20–24)

3 Check your answers with the review. Discuss any differences you find with a partner.

4 Choose one of the openings below and think about something that has happened to you recently.

a) I had just got in when …
b) I was walking down the road when …
c) I was in my car …
d) It was three o'clock in the morning …
e) You'll never believe who I saw the other day …
f) I'd just been …

5 Tell your partner about it.

Close up

Language reference p20

Fronting

1 The sentences below have been taken from the restaurant review. Put the words in the correct order without looking back.

a) floors family the lived upper on the. (Introduction, line 28)
b) chat to gone Marianne was with opportunity the. (Text A, line 37)
c) ran between tables waiters the. (Text B, lines 3–4)

2 Check your sentences with the review and answer these questions:

a) Are they different?
b) Why is the word order different from usual?

3 Complete these sentences about a place you remember from your past.

a) Gone is the …
b) Many were the …

4 Work with a partner. Compare your sentences and explain the changes that have taken place.

Language reference: fronting

Fronting is when you start a sentence with something other than the subject.
You use it to create dramatic effect.

Usual word order		**Fronting**
The family lived on the upper floors.	→	On the upper floors lived the family.
The days when we could sit back and do nothing are gone.	→	Gone are the days when we could sit back and do nothing.
The rain came down.	→	Down came the rain.

Fronting is usually used in writing. It is not commonly used in everyday speech.

Food for thought

Anecdote

1 You are going to tell your partner about one of your favourite restaurants. Decide which restaurant you are going to describe. Think back to the last time you ate there. Look at the questions below and think about what you're going to say and the language you will need.

☐ Where is the restaurant?
☐ What kind of restaurant is it?
☐ When did you last go there?
☐ Who did you go with?
☐ Was it a special occasion?
☐ What did you eat?
☐ How often do you go there?
☐ Do you always go with the same people?
☐ Do you always eat the same thing there?
☐ What do you like most about the restaurant?
☐ Who first introduced you to it?
☐ When do you think you'll next go back?
☐ Would you recommend it to your partner?
☐ Is there anything else you'd like to add?

2 Tell your partner about the restaurant.

3 Answer these questions:

a) Which of the following did your partner talk about?
- the food
- the service
- the decor
- the atmosphere
- the company

b) Which was most important to your partner?

c) Which is most important to you?

*'Hmm, it's all so tempting …
Cassoulet, Jugged Hare, perhaps
the venison … Oh, what the hell,
I'll have the fish!'*

Writing

1 Write a review of your favourite restaurant for a local English-language newspaper. Before you start, look at the questions below and think about what you are going to write and the language you will need.

a) Think about what kind of person the restaurant would appeal to and how best to attract this kind of person.

b) Decide what information you are going to include. Look at the list below:
- the address and phone number
- the opening times
- some information about the people who run the place
- the menu
- some typical dishes
- a description of a particular dish
- a description of the decor
- a description of the atmosphere
- a personal recommendation (A dish? A good time or day to go?)
- some information about the history of the place (How long it's been open? The history of the building?)
- anything else you'd like to add

2 Decide what order to present the information in.

3 Write your review of about 200 words.

Taste

Collocations

1 How many words can you form from the root word *taste*?

2 Complete these sentences with your answers to 1.

A	He has developed a ____ for expensive champagne.
B	Katherine has marvellous ____ in clothes.
C	The new bar is very lively, with very ____ food and a good selection of drinks.
D	We found a charming little hotel with ____ furnished bedrooms and lots of facilities.
E	She wore a silk dress in a ____ shade of pink.
F	For years he's worked as a tea-____ in China.
G	The beauty of wine-____ is that you learn to appreciate different flavours.
H	This milk ____ as though it's gone off.
I	You can't beat the ____ of fresh raspberries, straight out of the garden.
J	If you have a ____ for top class food, you'll certainly appreciate this new restaurant.
K	It would probably ____ a lot better if it didn't have so much salt in it.
L	The city has something for all ____ , from an impressive museum to a windsurfing lake.
M	The joke was in very poor ____ and quite a few people were offended.

3 The word *taste* has two basic meanings. What are they?

4 Which of the two meanings do these words and expressions have?

a) to taste
b) to be tasty
c) to be tasteful
d) to have poor taste
e) a taste of …

5 Complete these sentences with prepositions.

a) He has developed a taste _____ French films.
b) They have incredibly poor taste _____ clothes.

6 Which sentence in 5 talks about choice? Which refers to preference?

7 Choose the correct preposition in these expressions:

a) peculiar taste in/for books
b) a taste in/for exotic travel
c) a taste in/for dangerous sports
d) excellent taste in/for shoes
e) very good taste in/for music

8 Think of people you know who have these tastes. Tell a partner about them.

A question of taste

1 Work with a partner. Write a short definition of *good taste*. Use no more than twenty words.

2 Share your definition with the rest of the class. Which one do you like best?

3 🔊 10 Listen to Sarah, David and Angela discussing good taste. Make notes about what they each think good taste is.

4 Compare your notes with a partner. Were your ideas similar to the speakers'?

5 What other quality did they mention? What did the speakers understand by this quality?

6 Listen again and check your answers. Do you agree with their definitions of this quality?

Agreeing & disagreeing

1 Look at these extracts from the discussion. Words are missing from each extract. The missing expressions are used to express agreement or disagreement. Decide which type of expression is missing in each gap.

a) Sarah: … I can't believe he bought her plastic flowers for her birthday. I mean, that is so tacky. That is such bad taste.
Angela: (1) _____ . It's the thought that counts.
David: (2) _____ ! Plastic flowers don't count!

b) Sarah: Yes, I mean, taste is a very personal thing.
Angela: Yes. Beauty is in the eye of the beholder and that sort of thing.
Sarah: (3) _____ . Everyone's different and so I suppose …

c) Angela: … wearing a big gold medallion, or something.
David: (4) _____ ! Things like that are awful, aren't they?
Angela: Socks!
David: Socks and sandals, and white socks and black shoes, definitely!
Sarah: (5) _____ , some people like them.

d) **Sarah:** It's knowing what's appropriate that's good taste.

David: (6) _____ . It's also about being able to judge the quality of things. Good quality stuff is usually quite tasteful. And yes, Sarah, you're right – it's about choosing the right thing at the right time too.

Angela: That reminds me of Rebecca the other day at Jo's wedding. Talk about the wrong clothes at the wrong time!

Sarah: What, wearing that blue dress thing?

Angela: Yeah, it was obviously expensive, but talk about bad taste.

David: (7) _____ . She looked completely out of place.

Sarah: Well, (8) _____ . But Rebecca, you know, Rebecca has class …

e) **Angela:** But class is about knowing how to behave, not how to dress.

Sarah: (9) _____ , not these days. Class means being yourself and not caring what other people think.

David: Yes, but I think there's more to it than that. I think it's that you know how to behave in every circumstance, no matter how difficult the situation might be and how to deal with it. That's class.

Angela: (10) _____ . That feeling you can take everything in your stride …

2 🔊 11 Listen and make a note of the expressions actually used.

3 What other expressions for agreeing and disagreeing do you know? Do you use similar expressions in your own language?

Intonation **1** 🔊 12 Listen to the six *yes* and *no*'s from the discussion. Decide whether the speaker

a) is uncertain about what is being said.
b) is in total agreement with what is being said.
c) categorically disagrees with what is being said.

2 How does the intonation change according to the meaning the speaker wants to convey?

3 🔊 13 Work with a partner. Listen to six sentences and respond with *yes* or *no* so that your partner can tell if you agree, disagree or are uncertain.

In good taste?

1 Look at this list of actions and decide which of the following you consider:

a) completely unacceptable
b) acceptable in certain circumstances
c) totally acceptable at all times

- chewing gum
- leaving your mobile telephone on when you're at a restaurant
- kissing in public
- putting your hands in your pockets
- swearing
- losing your temper in public
- asking people how much something they are wearing cost
- eating in the street

2 Compare your views with a partner and answer these questions:

a) Would your parents have given the same answers?
b) Are your answers influenced more by what your parents taught you, what you were taught at school or what you have experienced in life?

3 City

1 How much do you know about cities around the world? Do this quiz and find out.

quiz

1 What proportion of the world's population lives in cities?

a) Over 80%   c) About a third
b) About two thirds   d) About half

2 Which is the world's largest capital city?

a) Tokyo   c) Mexico City
b) Seoul   d) New Delhi

3 Which is Europe's noisiest capital?

a) Athens   c) Rome
b) Madrid   d) Paris

4 Which is the world's oldest capital city?

a) Baghdad   c) Cairo
b) Damascus d) Amman

5 Which is the world's highest capital city?

a) La Paz (Bolivia)   c) Quito (Ecuador)
b) Lima (Peru)   d) Kathmandu (Nepal)

6 Which was the first city to reach a population of 1 million?

a) Mexico City   c) London
b) New York   d) Rome

2   14 Listen and check your answers.

Close up

Hedging   **1** Look at these extracts from the radio programme and complete the sentences.

a) It _____ _____ that there is a steady movement towards urban areas …

b) … there is still some _____ as to which is the world's largest capital.

c) … it is _____ _____ that Athens is the European capital which suffers from the worst noise pollution levels.

d) It's _____ _____ whether this information is based on popular opinion or on statistical data from Greek authorities however.

e) Sources _____ to suggest that the Syrians are right …

f) There is _____ _____ _____ about which of the world's capital cities is the highest.

> Language reference p25

2   15 Listen and check your answers.

3 Work with a partner. Which of the statements in 1 does the speaker believe is based on

a) very strong evidence?   c) weak evidence?
b) fairly strong evidence? d) unreliable evidence?

4 Use the expressions in 1 to write sentences about the following data.

Two new reports have just been published in which people living in rural and urban areas were asked about how happy they are with where they live. Below are some of the results.

	REPORT 1	REPORT 2
People who enjoy living in cities	79%	72%
People who live in a city but would prefer to live in a rural area	35%	43%
People who live in the city but spend as much time as possible outside the city	47%	29%
People who live in rural areas but would prefer to live in a city	62%	36%
Percentage of these who are under 30	84%	–
Percentage of these who are over 50	13%	–
Number of people in the sample	?	?

5 Which group(s) would you have come into? Compare your answer with a partner.

6 Look at these four newspaper headlines. What do you think the story is behind each one? Discuss your ideas with a partner.

> **A** LIFE HEALTHIER AT 800 METRES ABOVE SEA LEVEL
>
> **C** FOOTBALL CAUSES SOCIAL UNREST
>
> **D** SEDENTARY LIFESTYLE CHANGING SHAPE OF OUR BODIES
>
> **B** Most prefer to live in cities if given choice

7 ▶ 16 Listen to two people discussing one of the stories. Which story are they talking about? Were your ideas about the story right?

8 Listen again and make notes about the facts of the story.

9 Work with a partner. Write the story as you think it would have appeared in the 'News in Brief' section of the newspaper. Compare your story with the version on page 133.

Language reference: hedging

Sometimes you do not want to state a fact too categorically as you are not sure that you can prove that it is true. You can use a range of expressions to distance yourself from facts and opinions. This is called *hedging*.

Hedging with verbs

You can use *appear* and *seem (that)* to create a distance between yourself and what is said.

*It **seems that** the President may soon stand down.*
*It **appears that** the news reports are true.*
*The weather **appears** to be changing.*
*The outcome **seems** to be inevitable.*

To add further distance you can use the modal verb *would*.

*It **would appear that** you have already made up your minds.*
*They **would appear** to be hostile.*
*It **would seem that** you are in the wrong.*
*It **would seem that** you are avoiding me.*

Hedging with the passive voice

You can use passive forms of the verb to show that an opinion is not necessarily your own.

*It **is** widely **recognised** that the future of advertising is on the Net.*
*There **are not believed** to be any survivors.*
*It **is not known** whether he will accept the offer.*

Hedging with noun phrases

You can use the following noun phrases to hedge around a subject.

*There **is little doubt that** she took her own life.*
*There **is some doubt that** the country can control its inflation.*
*There **is no doubt that** he knows what he's doing.*
*There **is little evidence of** your ability to manage change.*

Where in the world?

1 Work with a partner. Discuss the following questions:

a) What is the capital of your country famous for? Does it attract a lot of visitors?
b) Which capital city would you most like to spend a weekend in?
c) Do you live in a city, a town, a village or out in the country? Have you always lived there? Do you like it? Why/Why not?

2 The following extracts from guide books describe five of the world's most famous cities. Work in small groups. Read the descriptions and decide which city is being described in each text.

❶ lonely planet

There is little point in portraying it as something it is not. Its beauty is not as awe-inspiring as other cities. It is not even particularly old, and much of what may have
5 constituted its historical legacy has over the centuries been all too quickly sacrificed to make way for the new. It is a largely modern city, a product of the 19th and 20th centuries, and the expanses of its outer
10 dormitory suburbs and peripheral high-rise apartment jungles are an oppressive introduction for anyone driving into the city for the first time.
   It may lack the historical richness and
15 sophistication of other European capitals, but it oozes a life and character that, given the opportunity to work its magic (it doesn't take long), cannot leave you indifferent. Leaving aside the great art museums, the splendour
20 of the main square and the Royal Palace, and the elegance of the city park, the essence of this city is in the life pulsing through its streets. In no other European capital will you find the city centre so thronged so late into
25 the night as here, especially if you go out at weekends. Everyone seems to stay out late, as though some unwritten law forbade sleeping before dawn. In this sense it is a city more to be lived than seen. ●

❷ lonely planet

The city is like a history lesson come to life. As you walk among the long stone palaces or across the Charles Bridge, with the Vltava flowing below and
5 pointed towers all around, you'll feel as if history had stopped back in the 18th century. Goethe called it the prettiest gem in the stone crown of the world. A millennium earlier in 965 the Arab-
10 Jewish merchant Ibrahim Ibn Jacob described it as a town of 'stone and lime'. For these reasons the city is on the UNESCO World Heritage list.
   Today it is a city of over a million
15 inhabitants, the seat of government and leading centre of much of the country's intellectual and cultural life. Unlike other capitals in this region, which were major battlefields during WW2, it escaped
20 almost unscathed and after the war, lack

of modernisation prevented haphazard modern development. Since 1989, however, the city centre has been swamped by capitalism as street
25 vendors, cafés and restaurants take over pavements, streets and parks as they did prior to 1948.
   How you feel about the city's current tourist glut may depend on where you're
30 coming from. If you're arriving from Western Europe it may all seem quite normal, but if you've been elsewhere in Eastern Europe for a while, you'll be in for a bit of a shock. As you're being
35 jostled by the hawkers and hordes of tourists, you may begin to feel that it has become a tacky tourist trap, but try to overcome that feeling and enjoy this great European art centre for all it's
40 worth. ●

❹ lonely planet

The sheer level of energy is the most striking aspect of this capital city. It's true the larger picture can be somewhat depressing – shoebox
5 housing estates and office blocks traversed by overhead expressways crowded with traffic. But this is the country's success story in action. The average suburb hasn't fallen
10 prey to supermarket culture though: streets are lined with tiny specialist shops and bustling restaurants, most of which stay open late into the night. Close to the soaring office
15 blocks exist pockets of another time – an old wooden house, a kimono shop, a small inn, an old lady in a traditional dress sweeping the pavement outside her home with a
20 straw broom. More than anything else, this is a place where the urgent rhythms of consumer culture collide with the quieter moments that linger from older traditions. It's a living city
25 and you'll never run out of things to explore. ●

❺ lonely planet

They don't come any bigger than this – king of the hill, top of the heap. No other city is arrogant enough to dub itself Capital of the World and no
5 other city could carry it off. It is a densely packed mass of humanity – seven million people in 309sq miles (800sq km) – and all this living on top of one another makes the
10 inhabitants a special kind of person. Although it's hard to put a finger on what makes it buzz, it's the city's hyperactive rush that really draws people here.
15   In a city that is so much a part of the global subconscious, it's pretty hard to pick a few highlights – wherever you go you'll feel like you've been there before.
20 Bookshops, food, theatre, shopping, people: it doesn't really matter what you do or where you go because the city itself is an in-your-face, exhilarating experience. ●

❸ lonely planet

This is a cosmopolitan mixture of the Third and First worlds, of chauffeurs and beggars, of the establishment, the avowedly working class and the avant-garde. Unlike
5 comparable European cities, much of it looks unplanned and grubby, but that is part of its appeal. Visiting the city is like being let loose on a giant-sized Monopoly board clogged with traffic. Even though you probably won't
10 know where the hell you are, at least the names will look reassuringly familiar. The city is so enormous, visitors will need to make maximum use of the underground train system: unfortunately, this dislocates
15 the city's geography and makes it hard to get your bearings. ●

(Texts from *Lonely Planet* publications)

Turn to page 132 if you need help.

3 Read back through the extracts and underline the information which helped you decide which city was being described.

4 Work with a partner and discuss these questions:

a) Which description appeals to you most? Why? Choose two or three phrases which you find evocative.
b) Have you been to any of these cities? Do the extracts reflect your experiences?
c) Do the extracts make you want to visit any of these cities?

Lexis

1 Match definitions a–h to the adjectives 1–8 on the right. Then decide which of the adjectives you would use to describe the noun phrases in the box below.

a) rather dirty
b) full of people who are very busy or lively (especially a place)
c) not organised, not arranged according to a plan
d) very tall or high in the sky (especially buildings or trees)
e) so loud, big or noticeable that you just can't ignore it
f) cheap and badly made or vulgar
g) giving a feeling of respect and amazement
h) blocked so that nothing can pass through (especially a place)

1 awe-inspiring
2 haphazard
3 tacky
4 grubby
5 clogged
6 bustling
7 soaring
8 in-your-face

plastic souvenirs   tree tops   arteries   beauty   advertising campaigns
children's hands   approach to work   market   seaside postcards
tower blocks   waterways   scenery   action movies   old trainers
coastal resorts   collection of people

2 Find the adjectives in the extracts. What are they describing?

3 Work with a partner. Look at the verbs below. Without looking back at the extracts, match each one with an appropriate phrase from the list on the right

a) (extract 1, line 7)   to make   a finger on (something)
b) (extract 1, line 17)   to work   prey to (something)
c) (extract 3, line 15)   to get   on top of one another
d) (extract 4, line 9)   to fall   its magic
e) (extract 5, line 8)   to live   your bearings
f) (extract 5, line 11)   to put   way for the new

4 Check your answers with the extracts and make sure you understand the meanings of the phrases. Use a dictionary if necessary.

5 Complete these sentences using the phrases in 3. Make any changes to the phrases that are necessary.

a) No matter how stressed you feel, once you let the beauty of the beach and the warmth of the sun _____ on you, you will begin to wind down and relax.
b) The old town is built on the edge of a cliff overlooking the gorge, using up every bit of spare space. Some houses are even built into the cliff face and people _____ in a warren of narrow cobbled streets.
c) The medieval clock tower offers a landmark which is visible wherever you are in the town, making it very easy _____ .
d) It is difficult _____ exactly what makes this grey, industrial town such a popular tourist destination.
e) It's very easy _____ the charm of the market stall holders and people often end up spending much more than they'd expected to.
f) Far too often historic town centres are carved up and charming old buildings torn down _____ .

6 Can any of the words and phrases in 1 and 3 be used to describe your home town or a place you know well? Discuss your thoughts with a partner.

Close up

Negative & limiting adverbials

1 Work with a partner. Look at the adverbial phrases in the box and decide which of them have negative or limiting meanings.

> under no circumstances   quite often   only after a long night   never
> not until he'd finished   seldom   at once   frequently   only then   usually
> only after a long wait   not a word   rarely   even in the summer   on no account

(Language reference p29)

2 Look at these sentences and answer the questions which follow.

1A *In no other European capital* **will you find** the city centre so thronged so late into the night.

1B **You won't find** the city centre so thronged so late into the night *in any other European capital.*

2A *Not until I actually lived there* **did I understand** just how great the lifestyle is.

2B **I didn't understand** just how great the lifestyle is *until I actually lived there.*

a) Which sentence appears in the extract about Madrid on page 26?
b) Look at the *adverbial phrases* in the sentences. Which is the more common position for the adverbial? Why has the adverbial phrase been moved in the A sentences?
c) Which sentences, the As or Bs, would be more likely to be spoken?
d) What happens to the word order when the adverbial phrase is placed at the beginning of the sentence?

3 Rewrite the sentences below, starting with the word or words given.

For example:
You will rarely see such a superb example of modern architecture.
Rarely *will you see such a superb example of modern architecture.*

a) I rarely visit a city more than once, but this place is really special.
Rarely …
b) I had never seen anything so breathtakingly beautiful before.
Never before …
c) You should not go out alone at night under any circumstances.
Under no circumstances …
d) You will only be able to see and feel the heart of this beautiful old town by wandering down its narrow side streets.
Only …
e) You will only begin to understand the special charm of this place after you have spent an evening there.
Only after you …
f) You can't really understand exactly how beautiful the view is until you climb to the top.
Not until …

4 Think of a town, city or village to fit each sentence.

Writing

1 You are going to write a short description of a famous town or city in your country.

a) Choose the town or city you are going to write about.
b) Decide what kind of tourist or visitor you are writing for. (Young backpackers? Families? Culture vultures?)
c) Decide on three or four main points to include in your description.
d) Write a short description (about 200 words) in the style of a guide book. Include at least one inversion and three of the words and expressions from the lexis exercises on page 27. Do NOT include the name of the town or city.

2 When you have finished writing, work in groups of three or four. Read your description to the group. Listen to the descriptions and try to guess which town or city they are describing. What information helped you get the answer?

Language reference: negative & limiting adverbials

Sometimes you can place a negative or limiting adverbial in the front position in a sentence to create emphasis. This effect is most frequently found in writing.

Word order

In this type of sentence, the *subject + auxiliary* word order is inverted.
I have never seen anything quite so breathtaking.
Never have I seen anything quite so breathtaking.

The same thing happens with the verb *be*.
It is not only one of the oldest cities on Earth, but also one of the most beautiful.
Not only is it one of the oldest cities on Earth, it is also one of the most beautiful.

In the present simple and past simple, use *do/does* or *did*.
We rarely visit that part of town.
Rarely do we visit that part of town.

Negative adverbials

Not a + noun
Not a word did she say to anyone.

Not until + verb phrase
Not until I got home did I realise how lucky I'd been.

Not until + noun phrase
Not until the end did I realise how lucky I'd been.

Under no circumstances
Under no circumstances are you to leave before you finish the exercise.

On no account
On no account can they claim to be the best.

Never
Never had I seen such a beautiful sight.

No sooner ... than
No sooner had I arrived than the doorbell rang.

Limiting adverbials

Only + by + -ing
Only by bribing the police officer was he able to get away.

Only + conjunction + verb phrase
Only if he promised to help would she tell him where he had left his keys.
Only after they had finished their lunch were they allowed outside to play.
Only when I took the test did I realise how little I knew!

Little
Little did they know that we were following them.

Rarely / seldom
Rarely had I seen such a beautiful sight.

Barely / hardly / scarcely ... when
Barely had I arrived when the doorbell rang.

Anecdote

1 You are going to describe a visit to a city which made an impression on you. Decide which city you are going to talk about and then look at the questions below. Decide which are relevant to the city you are going to talk about. Think about what you are going to say and what language you will use.

☐ When did you first visit the city? Have you visited it more than once? If so, when was the last time you were there?

☐ What was your overall impression of the place? Is there any one particular image that sticks in your mind? How would you describe the general atmosphere of the city?

☐ Why did you go there? On holiday? For work? To study? Was it your decision or did you go on a trip with friends or your family?

☐ How long did you stay? Where did you stay? What were the people like? What was the weather like?

☐ What did you do? The usual touristy things? Did you sit and watch the world go by or did you walk for miles and miles?

☐ Would you like to go back? Have you made any plans to go back? Would you recommend it to a friend?

☐ Is there anything else you'd like to mention?

2 Tell your partner about the city. Give as much detail as possible.

3 Have you visited the city your partner described? If yes, were your impressions the same? If not, would you like to visit it after hearing your partner's description? Why/Why not?

'This is Mr Trimp from the Town and Country Planning Department. He's here to demonstrate the proposals for the old town.'

One big party

1 Have you heard of Leicester Square? Where is it? Why is it well known?

2 You're going to read an article about Leicester Square. Match the questions from the first part of the article on the left with the answers on the right.

a) Where is it?
b) What is it?
c) On a bad day?
d) What's with the funny spelling?

1 OK, it's spelt funny, but it's pronounced *Lester*.
2 A loud, brash, sweaty mass of seething humanity.
3 On a good day, it's a huge meeting place for the world.
4 Between Piccadilly and Covent Garden, just north of Trafalgar Square.

3 Read the article and answer these questions:

a) What type of entertainment does Leicester Square offer?
b) What type of people go to Leicester Square?
c) What money-saving tips does the writer mention?

LEICESTER**SQUARE**

(1) ____ Leicester Square is one of the busiest spots in London. Buskers entertain the crowds with anything from an impromptu song to a political rant, tourists pay good money to have their faces ridiculed by cruel cartoonists and ⁵suburban kids queue to dance the night away at the Hippodrome, Equinox or Maximus.

(2) ____ , the whole pedestrianised area can seem like one big, youthful party.

The Square is a popular meeting place for friends ¹⁰(3) ____ and for tourists who seem to enjoy congregating outside the tube station. The cinemas claim to be the biggest and best but (4) ____ tickets are the most expensive in town. It will cost you almost double the price of a normal seat to see a blockbuster at the Empire, for example. For ¹⁵good value movie magic check out the Prince Charles cinema on Leicester Place, (5) ____ !

People-watching is one of Leicester Square's great attractions as representatives from virtually every country on little old planet Earth walk past (6) ____ . Ordinary people ²⁰are interesting enough but if you're really lucky you get the chance to eyeball visiting stars who attend the regular movie premières.

Despite its movie-made image of constant fog, London does get hot from time to time. Luckily for Leicester Square ²⁵visitors, there's a handily placed ice cream emporium where you can gorge yourself on Triple Choc Brownie until one in the morning. For main-meal feed-ups, (7) ____ avoid the overpriced chain-store eateries that front the Square and head instead for nearby Chinatown. The choice can be ³⁰overwhelming with little to differentiate one prim Cantonese restaurant from another. Watching out for where the Chinese themselves eat is probably the best indicator of quality. Eternally popular choices include a number of small, family-run places with menus listing up to 40 dim sum ³⁵dishes and other traditional offerings.

(8) ____ , Leicester Square is something of a 'must' for tourists and Londoners alike. All you need to enjoy it fully is plenty of time and a bit of patience!

4 Below are eight words and phrases which were in the original text. Insert them into the appropriate spaces 1–8.

a) Especially on Friday and Saturday nights
b) and simply gawp at each other
c) looking for a drink and chat after a hard day's slog
d) where tickets for a good selection of cult films start at the same price as a cup of coffee in the Square

e) All in all
f) your best bet is to
g) By night
h) consequently

5 Work with a partner. Student A turn to page 133. Student B turn to page 135.

6 Work in small groups and discuss the following questions:

a) What is the busiest place in the evening where you live? What do people do there? Are there buskers or eateries? Which places would you recommend?
b) Do you like to go out in the evenings? Where do you go? What do you do? When was the last time you went out for the evening? Tell your group where you went and what you did.

City life

1 Work with a partner and discuss this question:

Is life in the city more dangerous than life in the country?

Draw up a list of the main dangers of city life.

2 ▪▪ 17 Listen to two friends talking about the city they live in. As you listen, answer the following questions:

a) Do they think they live in a particularly dangerous city?
b) How many dangers from your list do they mention?
c) Do they mention any other dangers?

3 Compare your answers with a partner and discuss these questions:

a) What precautions do they suggest you should take when walking home at night?
b) In what places do they suggest you should take special care with your bag or wallet? Why?
c) There seems to have been an increase in crime recently. What sort of crime?
d) Have the speakers been victims of crime themselves? What about their friends?
e) What exactly happened to the group of tourists?
f) What do they think the police could do to improve the situation?

4 Listen again and check your answers.

Adding emphasis

1 Which word from the box can be used to mean the following?

a) extremely
b) now you come to mention it
c) only
d) very
e) to tell you the truth
f) at that very moment
g) to be honest
h) very recently
i) simply
j) totally

just
really
actually

2 Look at these short extracts from the conversation. Complete them with *just*, *really* or *actually*.

a) ... there are certain areas that you ____ know you wouldn't go into ...
b) ... ____ there have been a couple of stories in the papers recently about this spate of muggings that's been going on.
c) ... her wallet was snatched from her bag ____ as the train was coming into the station ...
d) You've got to be ____ careful there because there is a big crowd and a lot of pickpockets ...
e) You don't ____ know what's going on ...
f) ... I know that is a terrible thing to say, but it's ____ money.
g) I think she thought they were going to stab her husband ____ .
h) ... but the sad thing was that they had only ____ arrived ...
i) She didn't lose anything ____ valuable ...
j) I think they need to know if a crime's happened ____ .

3 ▪▪ 18 Listen and check your answers. Where does the stress fall?

4 Write a paragraph using *just*, *really* and *actually* at least once each. Show it to a partner to work out their meanings. Practise reading the paragraph with emphasis.

Discussion

Work in small groups. Discuss one of these sets of questions:

• Is your home town a dangerous place to live in? Do you need to take precautions when you go out at night? Would you go out alone after ten o'clock? If you were a member of the opposite sex do you think your answers would be the same?
• Do you take extra precautions when you travel? Why/Why not? Are cities more dangerous if you're a tourist? Why/Why not?
• Which of the following safety measures are used in your town: police patrols at night, close-circuit TV cameras in public places, security guards on public transport, street lighting all night? What other measures can be taken to make our cities safer?

An urban poem

Lexis **1** Work with a partner. Look at the following words and phrases taken from the poem you are about to read. Answer the questions which follow.

> a mute   a mate   to hug someone   a gut   to joy-ride   mucky
> to pinch something   to boot something or someone   daft   to nick something
> to flog something

    a)   There are two nouns which refer to people. Which one means *a partner*? Which one means *a person who cannot speak*?
    b)   One noun refers to a part of the body. Which part?
    c)   Which two verbs mean *to steal*?
    d)   Which verb means *to kick violently*?
    e)   Which verb describes a much more tender action?
    f)   Which verb means *to sell*?
    g)   Which verb means *to steal a car and drive it around just for fun*?
    h)   There are two adjectives. One means *stupid* and one means *dirty*. Which is which?

2 Some of the words above are particularly informal. They have been included in the questions below in **bold**. Discuss your answers to the questions with a partner.

    a)   Have you ever had anything **nicked** from your car?
    b)   Did you ever **pinch** fruit or sweets when you were a kid?
    c)   What would you do if you saw someone **booting** one of your **mates**?
    d)   Have you ever **flogged** anything at a second-hand stall?
    e)   When was the last time you got really **mucky**?
    f)   Have you done anything **daft** lately?

Reading **1** Work in small groups. Look at the poem below and answer the questions.

    a)   The verses have been jumbled up. Decide on an appropriate order.
    b)   Do you think the character in the poem is male or female? Which lines in the poem support your argument?

a *It took some time. Reassembled in the yard,*
he didn't look the same. I took a run
and booted him. Again. Again. My breath ripped out
in rags. It seems daft now. Then I was standing
alone amongst lumps of snow, sick of the world.

b *Boredom. Mostly I'm so bored I could eat myself.*
One time, I stole a guitar and thought I might
learn to play. I nicked a bust of Shakespeare once,
flogged it, but the snowman was strangest.
You don't understand a word I'm saying, do you?

c *Better off dead than giving in, not taking*
what you want. He weighed a ton; his torso,
frozen stiff, hugged to my chest, a fierce chill
piercing my gut. Part of the thrill was knowing
that children would cry in the morning. Life's tough.

d *The most unusual thing I ever stole? A snowman.*
Midnight. He looked magnificent; a tall, white mute
beneath the winter moon. I wanted him, a mate
with a mind as cold as the slice of ice
within my own brain. I started with the head.

e *Sometimes I steal things I don't need. I joy-ride cars*
to nowhere, break into houses just to have a look.
I'm a mucky ghost, leave a mess, maybe pinch a camera.
I watch my gloved hand twisting the doorknob.
A stranger's bedroom. Mirrors. I sigh like this – Aah.

(Poem by Carol Ann Duffy, from *Selling Manhattan*, 198?)

2  19 Listen to the poem being read and check your answers.

3 Discuss these questions with your group:

  a) Do you like the poem?
  b) What do you think the title of the poem is?
  c) How old do you think the character is? Find lines in the poem which support your argument.
  d) Where do you think the character lives?
  e) Why does s/he steal?
  f) Why does s/he steal a snowman?
  g) Why do people steal things they don't need?

4 Choose two phrases which you found particularly evocative. Explain why you chose them.

Carol Ann Duffy

Carol Ann Duffy was born in Glasgow in 1955. She has won a number of awards for her poems on contemporary issues. In 1999 she was shortlisted for the role of Poet Laureate.

(Edward Hopper, *New York Movie*, 1939. MOMA, New York)

Discussion Work in small groups. Look at the painting and discuss these questions:

  a) Look at the woman in the painting. What do you think she's waiting for? What is she thinking? How does she feel?
  b) What are the three things that bore you most? Was it the same when you were a child?
  c) What do you do when you're bored? Do you just put up with it or do you do something to amuse yourself?

4 *Talk*

Find someone in the class who:

- is the most talkative member of their family.
- has spoken in front of a crowd of 50 people or more.
- has a job that involves listening.
- knows the difference between *whisper* and *whistle*.
- has gossiped about someone today.
- can say *I love you* in at least four languages.
- has had a conversation in English outside the classroom recently.

conversation

The word **conversation**
is derived from
the Latin verb
conversari which means
'to keep company with'.
So, perhaps what you
talk about isn't as
important as the fact
that you are
being sociable.

Conversation piece

1 Work in small groups. Define the word *conversation*. Do not use more than 20 words.

2 When you have agreed on the wording, look at the two dictionary definitions on page 136 and discuss these questions:
a) Which definition is most similar to your own?   b) Which do you prefer?

3 Without looking back at the dictionary definitions, answer the following questions:

a) Is *conversation* countable, uncountable or both?
b) Where is the main stress in *conversation*?
c) What's the difference between *having a conversation* and *making conversation*?
d) What three words can you form from the word *conversation*? Use them to complete these sentences.
1   He's a great storyteller and an excellent ____ . He's never at a loss for words.
2   She writes almost ____ . When you read her books, you can almost hear her talking to you.
3   I don't want to learn how to read and write. ____ Japanese is enough for me.

4 Check your answers with the dictionary definitions.

5 Work with a partner and answer these questions:

a) What's the difference between *a chat, a conversation, a discussion* and *an argument*?
b) Think of three more verbs to fill the gap: to ____ (a) conversation
c) What is the missing preposition in these expressions?
1   they were deep ____ conversation
2   she was engaged ____ conversation
3   the subject came up ____ conversation

6 Look at these adjectives which can be used to describe conversations.

> animated   pointless   overheard   riveting   lengthy   memorable
> frustrating   enjoyable   meaningful   predictable   boring   ~~recent~~
> one-way   fascinating   in-depth   hilarious

a) Classify the adjectives under the headings below.
b) Add two more adjectives under each heading and compare your answers with a partner.

positive	negative	neutral
		recent

7 *Conversational* is a graded adjective. Work with a partner and answer these questions:

a) Which of the adjectives in 6 can be graded with adverbs such as *very* or *fairly*?
b) Which of the adjectives cannot be graded?
c) What about the adjectives you added?

8 Think about the last time you had a conversation in English. Work with a partner and discuss these questions. Use adjectives from 6 if appropriate.

a) Who were you talking to? Did you know them well?
b) Where were you?
c) What did you talk about?
d) Were you happy with your English?
e) Who did most of the talking, you or the other person/people?
f) How did the conversation end?

9 Find three things your conversations had in common.

'Oh hello, George.
We were just talking about you.'

The art of conversation

1 Work in small groups and discuss these questions:

a) What makes a conversation enjoyable?
b) What makes a conversation frustrating?
c) What's your definition of a good conversationalist?

2 Compare your answers with the rest of the class.

3 🔊 20 You are going to hear six people answering one of the questions in 1. As you listen, make brief notes on their answers. Use your notes to decide which question they are answering.

speaker	notes	question answered
1	take active part, people who don't hog conversation	a

4 Compare your notes with a partner. Did the people interviewed have similar opinions to those expressed by your class?

Lexis

1 Look at these extracts from the speakers' answers. Complete as many of the sentences as you can before you listen again.

a) ... it helps if there aren't some people who (1) _____ the conversation all the time and also people need to have a sense of humour about things, I think, not to take things too seriously and you need a conversation that (2) _____ ...

b) ... it's someone who's got a point that they want to (3) _____ _____ during the conversation. Someone with (4) _____ _____ _____ as opposed to someone who just talks endlessly about various subjects ...

c) ... also some people don't care about whose (5) _____ it is to talk, so they just, you know, (6) _____ _____ when you're in the middle of a thought ...

d) I really hate it when I'm with someone who just (7) _____ _____ _____ _____ in a conversation, and who doesn't give you a chance to speak at all.

e) ... like you're on (8) _____ _____ _____ and you can share the same tastes or experiences so you know where the other person's coming from.

f) I can't stand it when you have to (9) _____ _____ _____ _____ yourself, when the other person's not responding, or when they are responding but it's with (10) _____ _____ , you know, just going yeah, er, um, and that's all you're getting back, and when you have to work to (11) _____ _____ _____ _____ , that's really bad, when you're having to (12) _____ _____ for things to say ...

2 Listen again and check your answers.

3 Work in small groups. Choose one of the questions below and discuss it with your group using some of the expressions from 1.

   a) Who is the best conversationalist you know? What makes them such a good conversationalist?

   b) Can you remember a frustrating conversation you've had recently. Why was it so frustrating?

   c) What was the most enjoyable conversation you've had recently? Who were you talking to? What made it so enjoyable?

Conversational styles

1 You are going to read an article about conversational styles. Read the title and the first paragraph and answer these questions:

Do you identify with either Sara or Betty? Why?

2 Read the rest of the article and decide what the topic of each section is. Match the headings below to the numbered sections.

   a) Don't take it too personally   d) Pause to think

   b) Whose turn is it anyway?   e) You are what you say

   c) It depends where you come from

PACING&PAUSING

Sara tried to befriend her old friend Steve's new wife, but Betty never seemed to have anything to say. While Sara felt Betty didn't hold up her end of the conversation, Betty complained to Steve that Sara never gave her a chance to talk. The problem had to do with expectations about pacing and pausing.

Conversation is a turn-taking game. You talk, then I talk, then you talk again. One person starts talking when another is finished. That seems simple enough.

1

But how do you know when I'm finished? Well, when I stop. But how do you know when I'm stopping? When my voice gets softer, when I start repeating myself or when I slow down and leave a gap at the end.

But how soft does my voice have to get to mean 'That's about it' as opposed to 'This isn't the main point yet' or 'I'm a mumbler'? Does repeating myself mean 'I'm out of new things to say' or 'I'm emphasising'? And how much of a gap after a word means 'I'm stopping' as opposed to 'I'm pausing within my turn' – pausing for breath, to find the right words, for dramatic effect, or, as any conversational signal, just out of habit?

2

In the midst of a conversation, you don't take time to puzzle this out. You sense when I'm finished, or about to make a point, or chatting aimlessly, based on your years of experience talking to people. When our habits are similar, there's no problem. What you sense and what I feel are similar. But if our habits are different, you may start to talk before I'm finished – in other words, interrupt – or fail to take your turn when I am finished – leading me to observe that you're not paying attention or have nothing to say.

That's what was happening with Betty and Sara. The tiny pause Betty was waiting for never occurred when Sara was around, because before it did, Sara would sense an awkward silence and would kindly end it by filling the gap with more talk – hers. And when Betty did start to say something, she would tend to have what seemed to Sara like long pauses within her speech, giving Sara the impression that Betty had finished when she had hardly got started.

Such differences are not a matter of some people expecting long pauses and others expecting short ones. Long and short are relative; they have meaning only in comparison to something – what's expected, or someone else's pause. Someone who expects a shorter pause than the person she's speaking to will often start talking before the other has a chance to finish or to start. Someone who is waiting for a longer pause than the person she's speaking to won't be able to get a word in edgewise.

3

It may not be coincidental that Betty, who expected relatively longer pauses between turns, is British, and Sara, who expected relatively shorter pauses, is American. Although there are group and individual differences among British and among American speakers, on the average, British speakers tend to expect longer pauses between turns than do Americans.

Betty often felt interrupted by Sara. But Betty herself became an interrupter and found herself doing all the talking when she met a visitor from Finland. Whereas she expected longer pauses between turns than Sara, she expected shorter pauses than the Finn. And Sara, who became interrupting and dominating in conversation with Betty, had a hard time getting a word in edgewise with some speakers from Latin America or Israel.

4

Differences among speakers from different countries are most pronounced and most easily identifiable. But there are also ethnic, regional, class, age and gender differences among speakers from each country. And when members of one group can't get a conversation going with members of a certain other group, the result is often the stereotype that people from the other group are taciturn, uncooperative or dull-witted. The British, for example, think of Scandinavians as being taciturn, but among Scandinavians, the Finns have a reputation for being slow and dull. Conversely, Americans from faster-speaking regions, like New York, are thought of as pushy, overbearing and aggressive.

5

The general phenomenon, then, is that the small, automatic mechanisms for conversation, like pacing and pausing, lead people to draw conclusions not about conversational style but about personality and abilities. These habitual differences are often the basis for dangerous stereotyping. And these social phenomena can have very personal consequences. For example, a woman from the southwestern part of the United States went to live in an Eastern city to take up a job in personnel. When the personnel department got together for meetings, she kept searching for the right time to break in – and never found it. Although back home she was considered outgoing and confident, in Washington she was perceived as shy and retiring. When she was evaluated at the end of a year, she was told to take an assertiveness-training course because of her inability to speak up.

That's why slight differences in conversational style – tiny little things like microseconds of pause – can have an enormous impact on your life. These little signals make up the mechanics of conversation, and when they're even slightly off, the conversation is thrown off – or even cut off. The result in this case was a judgement of psychological problems – even in the mind of the woman herself, who really wondered what was wrong with her and signed up for assertiveness training. ■

(Adapted from *That's Not What I Meant* by Deborah Tannen, 1992)

3 Answer these questions:

a) What exactly was causing the problems between Sara and Betty?

b) Where were the two women from? Why is this significant?

c) How would you summarise the article to someone who hasn't read it?

4 Work with a partner and compare your answers.

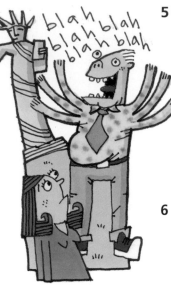

5 Without looking back, decide whether these statements are true or false according to the article.

a)   Betty didn't really have much to say to Sara.
b)   The British tend to be quieter than Americans.
c)   Israelis speak more quickly than most North Americans.
d)   The Finns have a reputation for being boring.
e)   New Yorkers take short pauses and tend not to wait for people to take their turn.
f)   People from the east coast of America tend to speak a little more slowly than those from the south west.
g)   The way different nationalities speak contributes to the formation of national stereotypes.

6 Check your answers with the article and then discuss these questions with your partner:

a)   The article is taken from a book. What type of reader is it written for?
b)   Have you ever considered this topic before? Do you agree with the argument presented in the article?
c)   Did the article make you think of anybody you know, or any situations you've found yourself in?

Lexis

1 Match these words and phrases from the article with their definitions. Look back at the article if you need to check the meanings of the words.

a)   never seemed to have anything to say (line 3)
b)   didn't hold up her end of the conversation (line 5)
c)   never gave her a chance to talk (line 7)
d)   a mumbler (line 23)
e)   chatting aimlessly (line 35)
f)   interrupt (line 41)
g)   an awkward silence (line 50)
h)   had a hard time getting a word in edgewise (line 91)
i)   can't get a conversation going (line 100)
j)   inability to speak up (line 136)

1   talking about nothing in particular
2   unable to find a common subject of interest
3   say something which makes someone else stop what they are saying or doing
4   didn't contribute enough to the conversation
5   when neither person knows what to say so no-one says anything
6   dominated the conversation
7   lack of confidence at taking part in a conversation
8   was unable to express her point of view as she was not allowed time to speak
9   someone who doesn't speak clearly
10   was usually rather quiet

2 Check your answers with a partner.

3 Work with a partner and discuss these questions:

a)   Look back at the words and phrases a–j in 1. Which might be associated with Betty and which with Sara? Are there any which you would not associate with either?
b)   Does the way people in your country speak vary from town to town or region to region?
c)   Are you typical of your region or country?

Test yourself

***wh*- words**

1 Which word(s) in the box below refer(s) to

a)   a point or period in time?
b)   a place?
c)   a reason?
d)   a relationship of possession or belonging?
e)   the way something is done?
f)   a person?
g)   a thing (2 words)?

| who | what | where | when | whose | which | why | how |

2 Use the words in the box to complete these sentences.

A (1) ____ you're talking to people (2) ____ don't really want to hear (3) ____ you've got to say, or (4) ___ keep interrupting you all the time and don't seem to care at all about (5) ____ turn it is to talk, it can be very disheartening.

B (6) ____ all you get is monosyllabic answers and you really don't know (7) ____ to keep the conversation going, you really have to hunt around for something to say, something (8) ____'ll interest them and get them talking, and sometimes you wonder (9) ____ you even bother.

3 In how many places could you have used *that*?

4 Use words from 1 to complete the following questions:

    a) ____ fault is it when a conversation breaks down?
    b) Do you sometimes start talking without thinking about ____ you're going to say?
    c) ____ is the best conversationalist you know?
    d) Have you ever been in a situation ____ you've been lost for words?
    e) ____ was the last time you said something and then wondered ____ you'd bothered?
    f) ____ do you feel about talking to strangers?

5 Discuss the questions with a partner.

Eavesdropping

Secretly listening to other people's conversations is called *eavesdropping*. Work in small groups and discuss these questions:

a) In what kind of situations is it difficult not to eavesdrop?
b) What was the last conversation you eavesdropped on? Where were you? Who was talking? What were they talking about? Did they notice that you were listening to them?

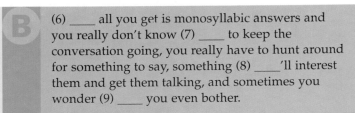

Listening **1** ▄▄ 21 You are going to eavesdrop on three conversations. As you listen, decide which conversation takes place

    a) in a university canteen.   b) at a party.   c) in a pub.

2 In which conversation

    a) did the speakers use to do something together?
    b) have the speakers just started doing something together?
    c) do the speakers share a similar problem?

3 Check your answers with a partner and discuss what the speakers are talking about in each conversation.

Lexis **1** Work with a partner. Look at the following expressions. They have all been taken from the conversations. Match them to definitions 1–6 on the right.

    a) all sweetness and light   1 a snack or a light meal
    b) something catches my eye   2 have a short rest or break
    c) have a sit down   3 to be neighbours
    d) a bite to eat   4 complain angrily about something
    e) shout and rant   5 I have my attention drawn to something
    f) to live next door   6 smiling and happy

2 Which conversation does each expression come from? Listen again if necessary and check your answers.

3 Use the expressions in 1 on page 39 to complete these questions. Make any changes that are necessary.

    a) Do you usually have a full meal at lunch time or do you just have _____ ?
    b) Is your boss normally bad-tempered or is he or she _____ ?
    c) Do you get on well with the people who _____ to you?
    d) Do you get a chance to _____ at all during the day or are you always rushing around?
    e) Is there anything that makes you really angry and makes you want to _____ ?
    f) If a really expensive item of clothing _____ in a shop window, do you go in and try it on or decide it's too expensive and walk away?

4 Choose three of the questions and ask your partner.

Close up

General tendencies

1 Look at these short extracts from the first two conversations. Write out the full form of the verbs in brackets.

a) ... he (1) _____ (shout and rant) for a while and then half an hour later he (2) _____ (forget) all about it. And then he (3) _____ (be) all sweetness and light after that.

b) ... he (4) _____ (buy) everybody a drink at the end of the night and he (5) _____ (order) in some pizza for everybody and then we (6) _____ (all sit round) and have a nice drink and a chat, and a bite to eat.

c) ... I (7) _____ (go) and make a cup of coffee and then I (8) _____ (just have) a sit down with my cup of coffee rather than work ...

2 Compare your answers with a partner.

(Language reference p41)

3 🔊 22 Listen and check your answers. Were your answers different from the recording? If yes, do you think your answers are also correct?

4 Which modal verb is used in the extracts? What time is this modal verb usually associated with?

5 Look at these sentences and answer the questions which follow.

    A He shouts and rants for a while and then he's forgotten all about it.
    B He'll shout and rant for a while and then he'll have forgotten all about it.

    a) Do the sentences refer to the present, the future or no time in particular?
    b) Which sentence is presenting a fact? Which mentions a tendency?

6 Complete the text below with the verbs in brackets. Use *will* where possible.

If I (1) _____ (have) a really difficult task to do, say writing a particularly complex report or tackling a particularly difficult question, rather than getting down to it straightaway I (2) _____ (find) all kinds of little tasks to distract me. I (3) _____ (decide) that now is the perfect time to write all those letters to long lost friends, or I (4) _____ (start) cleaning the house from top to bottom. Sometimes I (5) _____ (do) some cooking, convincing myself that I (6) _____ (actually/save) time for later by preparing all that food now. At other times I (7) _____ (spend) ages just staring out of the window and waiting for inspiration!

7 Work with a partner and discuss these questions:

    a) Can you think of any other displacement activities people indulge in when they don't want to do something?
    b) Do you get things done straightaway or do you tend to procrastinate?
    c) If you are a procrastinator, what delaying tactics do you employ? If you aren't, do you know anybody who is? Describe how they put things off.

Tendencies in the past

1 Look at this extract from the third conversation. Write out the full form of the verbs in brackets.

Adam: Yes, the bus (1) _____ (wait) for me because he knew I (2) _____ (always be) a minute late.

Nick: And we (3) _____ (sit) at the back of the bus.

Adam: We (4) _____ . (*short answer*)

Nick: We had our little club for two.

Adam: That's right. And you, you (5) _____ (always forget) to do your homework and you (6) _____ (have to) crib off mine.

Nick: Yes. Got me where I am today! And do you remember you started me off smoking? Remember we (7) _____ (go) down by the river and smoke at lunchtimes?

2 Compare your answers with a partner.

Language reference p41

3 🔊 23 Listen and check your answers. Were there any differences?

4 Work with a partner and discuss these questions:

a) Which forms of the verb did you use in 1?
b) Did you use *would* at all? If not, what verb form did you use in its place?
c) What time does *would* refer to in the extract?
d) Does *would* refer here to specific events or general tendencies?

5 Can *would* be replaced with the past simple in the following sentences? If not, say why.

a) My grandfather would sit down with us and talk for hours on end, making up fabulous stories about characters he had invented on the spur of the moment. I wish I could remember them, then I would be able to tell them to my children.

b) Our next door neighbour was a terrible gossip. She would talk for hours and hours. If we'd given her the opportunity she would have gone on indefinitely!

c) David used to be really shy as a child. He would be quite happy sitting quietly in the corner, playing contentedly by himself and he hated having to talk to strangers.

d) Sally was my best friend at university. She was the life and soul of the party. She would always know the latest jokes and could tell them really well. Life in the flat would have been very dull without her!

6 Do you know anyone like the people described above? Ask your partner.

Language reference: tendencies

You can use the modal verbs *will* and *would* to talk about tendencies in general and tendencies in the past respectively.

General tendencies

When you want to talk about facts that you think are generally true you use the present simple.

*The earth **revolves** around the sun.*
*The sun **rises** in the east and **sets** in the west.*
*The UK **consists** of four nations: Northern Ireland, Scotland, Wales and England.*

When you want to talk about things that generally tend to happen without suggesting that they always, inevitably happen, you can use the modal auxiliary verb *will*.

*Men **will** often prefer to start a conversation about sports or the news, whilst women **will** talk about their feelings or their relationships.*
*You can tell her something one minute and she'**ll** have forgotten it the next.*

Tendencies in the past

You can use *would* to talk about habits, tendencies or characteristic behaviour in the past.

*When I was young my father **would** sit down with me in the kitchen every day after school and help me with my homework. On Saturday mornings we **would** go to the movies together and he **would** let me go to the sweet shop on the way home. When we got back to the house my mother **would** be waiting for us and we **would** all have lunch together.*

You cannot use *would* to refer to a specific event in the past. You use the past simple for this.

*My father **would help** me with my homework last night.* ✗
*My father **helped** me with my homework last night.* ✓
*We **would see** a great film at the cinema last weekend.* ✗
*We **saw** a great film at the cinema last weekend.* ✓

Ann

I love them dearly but ...

1 🎞 24 Listen to Ann talking about some of the members of her family and answer the following questions:

a) Which members of the family does she mention? Make a note of their names and their relationship to her.

b) What habits and characteristics of theirs does she mention?

2 Work with a partner and check your answers. Then discuss these questions:

a) What do you think Ann's children might say about her? Do you think she may have some annoying habits or characteristics?

b) Does she remind you of anyone in your family?

Anecdote

1 You are going to tell your partner about a member of your family or a person you know, or used to know, very well. Look at the questions below. Which are you going to answer in your description? Think about the language you will need to use.

- ☐ How long have you known this person?
- ☐ What is their relationship to you?
- ☐ Have they got any annoying or endearing habits?
- ☐ Is there anything they used to do in the past but don't do anymore?
- ☐ What attracts you to this person?
- ☐ Have you had/do you have any disagreements?
- ☐ What is their conversational style like?
- ☐ How do they approach life?
- ☐ Do you have anything in common?
- ☐ Is there anything else you'd like to add?

2 Tell your partner about the person.

3 When you have finished, look back at the questions listed above. Which did your partner include in their description? Did they mention anything else? Did your two descriptions have anything in common?

Talk

Lexis

1 Work with a partner. Look at the list below. It shows some of the most common uses and forms of the word *talk*. Which part of speech is used in each sentence – noun (countable or uncountable?), verb or adjective?

A	Sitting next to Fiona was a small man who was **talking** intently to the woman on his left. *verb*
B	My mother has **talked** of little else since meeting you.
C	The next stage in the process will be **talks** between the American and Russian Foreign Secretaries.
D	I was already hearing **talk** about the merger of the two companies.
E	If you want to **talk** to me, call me 'Sir'!
F	Morris gave a riveting **talk** on his visit to East Africa.
G	He's not very **talkative** but you certainly feel his presence.
H	She has become the **talk** of the town since her very public affair with the minister.
I	If we're lucky she'll stop **talking** to us altogether.
J	Simon was always late home, despite always **talking** about family and responsibility.
K	I'm going to cover three areas in this brief **talk**, which most of you should find relevant.
L	After dinner we listened to Fred's hilarious **talk** about how to avoid becoming a millionaire.
M	After the meeting the main **talking** point was the threat of redundancy.
N	You can't **talk**! You never do any exercise, and you smoke too much!
O	All that **talk** of food made me feel extremely hungry.
P	There's fresh **talk** of a strike at the car factory.

2 Use the sentences in 1 to help you answer these questions.

   a) Complete these expressions with an appropriate preposition:
     1   to talk _____ someone _____ something
     2   to give a talk _____ something
   b) What does *She was the talk of the town* mean?
   c) In what situation would you say *You can't talk!*?
   d) Complete these sentences using one of the forms of *talk*:
     1   Are there any international peace _____ going on at the moment?
     2   When did you last go to a public _____ ? What was it on?
     3   Who's the most _____ person you know?
     4   What's the main _____ point in the news these days?
   e) What is the difference between these three nouns: *talks, a talk* and *talk*?

3 Work with a partner. Discuss the questions in 2d.

A tall tale

Stress   **1** You are going to hear a comedian telling a story containing these four items:

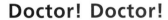

Work with a partner. Discuss how you think the items might be linked. Tell your story to the class.

2   25 Listen to the story. Is it different from your version? Did you find it funny? Why/Why not?

3 One of the important things about telling a joke successfully is getting the timing and pace of delivery right. Turn to page 133 to take a closer look at how this joke is told.

Doctor! Doctor!

1 Below are the first lines of three jokes. Match them with the other lines which have been jumbled up.

   a) A man goes to see his doctor and says, 'Doctor! Doctor! I can't stop shaking.'
   b) A man says to his doctor, 'Doctor! Doctor! Will I be able to play the violin after the operation?'
   c) A man speaks frantically into the phone, 'Doctor! Doctor! My wife is pregnant and her contractions are only two minutes apart!'

   1   'No, you idiot!' the man shouts. 'This is her husband.'
   2   And the man replies, 'Not really, I spill most of it!'
   3   'Great!' the man says. 'I never could before!'
   4   'Is this her first child?' the doctor asks.
   5   The doctor asks him, 'Do you drink a lot?'
   6   'Yes, of course,' replies the doctor.

2 Check your answers with a partner and then practise reading the jokes aloud. Pay particular attention to pace and timing.

3 Work with a partner and discuss your answers to these questions:

   a) Which is your favourite joke in 1? Which made you laugh? Which made you groan?
   b) Do you have 'Doctor! Doctor!' jokes in your language? What kind of jokes are common at the moment? Can they be translated or do they depend on a play on words?

5 Luck

1 Lucky charms vary from country to country. Match the lucky charms with the countries in the box.

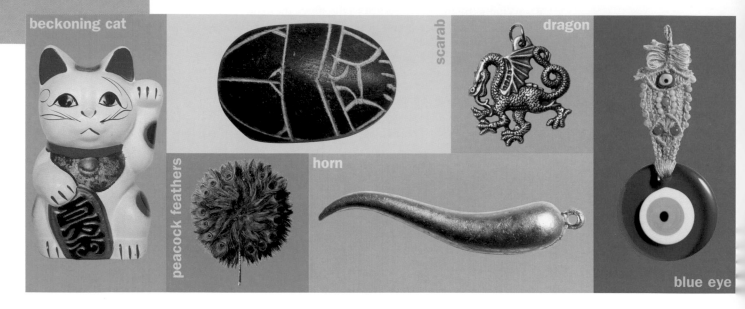

beckoning cat

scarab

dragon

peacock feathers

horn

blue eye

Turkey	Egypt	Italy	China	Japan	India

2 ▶ 26 Listen and check your answers.

3 Work with a partner and answer these questions:

a) What are considered lucky charms in your country? What is considered unlucky?

b) Have you got a lucky charm? Are you lucky? Have you ever won anything? If so, what?

c) Do you play your country's national lottery? If you do, how do you choose your numbers? What's the most you've ever won? If you don't play, why not?

d) What would you do if you won 'the Big One'?

Winning the big one

1 Read the article by Carinthia West which was published in *Tatler* magazine, and answer these questions:

a) How does the writer usually choose her lottery numbers?

b) Where is Carinthia from? Where had she been for the weekend?

c) Which do you think is the best subtitle for the article?
Life's a bitch
Dreams can come true
Hitting the jackpot

2 Compare your answers with a partner.

INTERIOR TATLER

THE ART ISSUE

Party with the art world From Hockney to Hoxton

Badminton The last social stately

Roaring Forte Why Rocco's beautiful young wife won't be tamed

Sophie Dahl HITS THE BIG TIME

Tatler

Tatler is a British magazine which contains articles on high society; which restaurants to eat in, the right people to meet, and the most fashionable clothes to be wearing.

HOW I WON THE LOTTERY

(and also managed to top up the money by selling my story to the Tatler)

Winning the Lottery is one of those things that only happens to other people. That's what I thought as I peered yet again at the winning numbers published in *The Mail on Sunday* and then once more at the ticket stub clenched in my hand. I might have been in a front-row seat on the Centre Court, so fast was my head flicking between the two, checking over and over again the fact that I held the winning numbers in my hand. It couldn't be true, but it was. I had picked five of the six Lottery numbers. I had hit the jackpot! I let out what can only be described as a bloodcurdling war whoop – and then remembered where I was.

I was sitting in the 23rd row of the 3pm Isle of Wight ferry, heading back to London after a jolly weekend. The day before, I had popped into a Spar supermarket just outside Ryde for some milk. I had been in a hurry, but my eye caught the Saturday Lottery display at the entrance to the shop, and having only seconds to spare, I abandoned my usual tactic of waiting for numbers to float down to me by divine inspiration ('Carinthia,' booms an Olympian voice, 'I see a 10, a 24, and possibly a 36'), or even that old standby of my birthday, the ideal age for a partner, my bra size, the number of my godchildren, and so on, and just dashed off the first six numbers my pen touched (for the record: 4, 11, 14, 30, 32 and 43). The ticket went into the pocket of my coat, and I forgot about it.

So there I sat on the ferry, scrabbling about for my gloves, when my fingers touched the ticket. With nothing better to do than read about some Spice Girl and her new sporting 'friend', I turned to the page with the numbers published on it. Cue the war whoop.

Seventy passengers in anoraks and baseball caps turned to stare. I was about to shout 'I've won the Lottery!' when I realised how easy it would be for me to go overboard. I could see the headlines: 'Mysterious drowning off Portsmouth ferry. Seventy strangers share Lottery Win'. Suddenly, perfectly ordinary people turned into a snarling pack of wolves. My war whoop tailed off and I tried to pretend that I'd read something frightfully funny in the newspaper (this is rather hard when you are reading *The Mail on Sunday*), and I subtly transferred the ticket (by now burning in my hand like green kryptonite) to a position of safety under my bottom.

I was still 20 minutes from port, and you never know what might happen. It's amazing what the mind can do. Five minutes earlier, I was your regular law-abiding citizen. Now I was plotting like a hardened criminal, prepared to protect that piece of paper and already planning spending sprees in Harvey Nicks, dawn raids on Hermes and Gucci, and Gulfstream getaways to Rio.

But you know what girls are like. I had to tell someone, and I knew exactly who. My mobile phone, amazingly, works in the middle of the Solent (but not at Hyde Park Corner), so I rang my friend Mr Evans in Wales. I wanted to know how much I'd won, and he studies Lottery wins assiduously. I slunk furtively down behind my paper and whispered my amazing news. 'Five numbers, is it, Cariad?' he said in his lilting Welsh voice. 'Just a minute, while I look it up.'

He was gone long enough for more visions to flit through my mind: Lear jets this time, and top-of-the-range Mercedes and summer homes in Sardinia. 'Are you sitting down?' he said when he returned, sounding super-excited. 'You lucky girl, you've won £1,700. Think what you can do with that.' He went on to explain that because the bonus ball was included in my winning five I'd just missed the £14 million jackpot, but he was sure I was on a winning streak and it was only a matter of time before I would win 'the Big One'.

When I lived in Los Angeles in the Eighties and people talked about 'the Big One', they meant the giant earthquake that was due to hit. I felt as if I'd been hit by it as I switched off the mobile phone and sensed the smile slipping off my face. The green kryptonite stopped burning and began to feel like an uncomfortable, crumpled bump underneath me – and the other passengers started reaching for their bags and giving me a wide berth.

My ship was coming in, all right, but holed beneath the waterline, covered in barnacles, and with the rigging looking like something out of a bodice-ripper. I felt a bit silly. My shining hour was gone, my coach had turned into a pumpkin, and although £1,700 is not to be sneezed at, there will be no BMW for me – more like a BMX – and the diamond-encrusted Cartier collar for my new Border collie will have to wait.

Oh, well, I'm still the only person I know who's ever won the Lottery. And anyway, 'spend-spend-spend Carinthia' just doesn't sound quite right. ■

(Carinthia West. © *Tatler* / The Condé Nast Publications Ltd.)

---

3 Work with a partner. Discuss these questions:

a) How did she feel when she found out that she had won? And when she found out *how much* she had won?

b) What would she have spent the money on if she had won the jackpot? Would you have bought the same things?

c) What do you think she will buy with the money she did win? What would you do with that amount of money?

d) What do you think Carinthia is like? What social class do you think she belongs to? Why?

Lexis

1 The writer assumes the reader has the same background knowledge as herself. Do this quiz and see how much you have in common with Carinthia.

1 The Centre Court (line 8) refers to …
a) an important court of law.
b) a famous theatre.
c) a tennis court at Wimbledon.

2 A Spice Girl (line 36) is …
a) a girl who likes excitement.
b) a member of the pop group 'The Spice Girls'.
c) a female British spy.

3 Green kryptonite (line 51) is …
a) a type of Indian food.
b) the only effective weapon against Superman.
c) explosive material.

4 Harvey Nicks (line 59) is …
a) an expensive department store in London.
b) a burger bar.
c) a village near London.

5 The Solent (line 64) is …
a) the water between the Isle of Wight and the British mainland.
b) the centre of British telecommunications.
c) a place on a ferry.

6 My coach had turned into a pumpkin (line 96) Here the writer is …
a) talking about vegetables.
b) referring to the story of Cinderella.
c) referring to a common problem people have with their coaches.

7 A BMX (line 98) is …
a) a cheap version of the BMW.
b) a train service.
c) a bike.

8 A Border collie (line 100) is …
a) a designer shirt.
b) a breed of dog.
c) a woman who helps with the cooking and cleaning.

2 Check your answers on page 132.

3 The writer uses a selection of descriptive verbs. Find the verbs in the text which mean:

a) to look at very closely (paragraph 1)
b) to hold very tightly (paragraph 1)
c) to move in a disorganised manner (paragraph 3)
d) to become less or die down (paragraph 4)
e) to move quietly and secretly (paragraph 6)
f) to move quickly (paragraph 6)
g) to leave quietly or slowly (paragraph 7)

4 Which verbs in 3 can involve

a) the eyes?
b) the hands?
c) the whole body?
d) the voice?

5 Use the verbs in 3 in an appropriate form to complete these sentences.

a) When he noticed his ex-wife come into the room, he _____ back into the corner and hoped she wouldn't spot him.
b) The teacher threw a handful of sweets up into the air and the children, squealing with delight, _____ trying to get as many as possible.
c) He _____ early last Friday without telling the boss.
d) She _____ her fists until her knuckles turned white.
e) The supporters' shouts of excitement _____ as the other team scored the winning goal.
f) I have a very nosy neighbour. She's always _____ over the fence to see what I'm doing.
g) At the party she _____ from one room to the other like a butterfly.

6 Tell your partner about the last time you did two of the actions in 5.

Close up

Unreal conditionals

1 🔊 **27** Listen to a conversation between Sarah and Angela, who have just read Carinthia's article. Answer these questions:

a) Which parts of the article did they enjoy in particular?
b) Do they play the lottery?
c) Has either of them ever won anything?

2 Compare your answers with a partner.

3 Look at these extracts from the conversation and complete the sentences.

Sarah and Angela

EXTRACT 1

Sarah: ... it's a good story.
Angela: Yeah, and all that stuff about what (1) _____ if (2) _____ 'the Big One'.
Sarah: Yeah, I really like that bit about how (3) _____ her dog's life, like (4) _____ a diamond-encrusted collar right now ...
Angela: Nah, I think it's more likely that (5) _____ a snazzy little red sports car!

EXTRACT 2

Sarah: I got really close to winning once. If (6) _____ my brother's birthday instead of mine (7) _____ .
Angela: How much (8) _____ if (9) _____ ?
Sarah: Oh, millions no doubt! I (10) _____ a new house, a car, a luxury yacht and I (11) _____ as a secretary any more, I can tell you!

---

4 Listen again and check your answers.

Language reference p48

5 Work with a partner and answer the questions below.

Extract 1
a) Is a real or an unreal situation being described?
b) Find one possible past result of the situation.
c) Find two possible present results.

Extract 2
a) Is a real or an unreal situation being described?
b) Find one possible past result of the situation.
c) Find one possible present result.

6 Write out the correct form of the verbs in brackets.

a) If I _____ (stay in) last night, I _____ (not/be) so tired today.
b) If I _____ (not/work) late last night, I _____ (go) to the cinema.
c) If I _____ (go) to bed earlier, I _____ (not/get up) so late.
d) If I _____ (sleep) a little bit more, I _____ (not/yawn) now.

7 Look at the sentences again. What other modal verbs can you use instead of *would*?

8 Are any of the sentences in 6 true for you? If not, change them to make them true and compare your sentences with a partner.

9 Look at these sentences and answer the questions which follow.

Had the writer chosen her numbers differently, her life might have changed dramatically.
Had I complained to the manager, I would have had my money refunded.

a) How are these sentences different in structure from the ones in 6 on page 47?
b) Which structure is more formal?

10 Complete these sentences so they are true for you.

a) Had I …
b) Had I had …
c) Had I been …

Language reference: unreal conditionals

The *if* clause (describing an unreal situation)

When you want to describe a past situation which is unreal, or imagine how a past situation might have been different, you backshift the verb in the *if* clause.

What really happened (real past)		What might have happened (unreal past)
She **won** a small amount of money in the lottery.	→	**If** she **had won** the jackpot …
She **wasn't paying** attention.	→	**If** she **had been paying** a little more attention …

Substituting *if*

Instead of using *if* to introduce the unreal situation, you can invert the subject and verb.

If she had won the jackpot … → **Had** she won the jackpot …
If your work had been more satisfactory … → **Had** your work been more satisfactory …

This is more typical of formal language, especially if it is written.

The main clause

Describing possible present consequences
You use *would (do)* or *would be (doing)* to describe the **possible present consequences** of the unreal past situation.

*If she **had won** the lottery she **wouldn't be working** for the Tatler any more.*
*If she **had been paying** more attention she **wouldn't be** in such a mess.*

Describing possible past consequences
You use *would have (done)* or *would have been (doing)* to describe the **possible past consequences** of the unreal past situation.

*If she **had won** the lottery she **would have bought** a snazzy red sports car.*
*She **wouldn't have been daydreaming** in class if the lesson **had been** a little more interesting.*

The *if* clause and the main clause can be used in either order.

A lucky break

1 Look at the pictures. What do you think the story is that connects them?

2 🔲 28 Listen to Louise telling her story. How similar was your story?

3 Answer these questions about the story:

a) Who first noticed the thieves?
b) How were the thieves caught?
c) Whose idea was it?
d) How do you think the thieves felt?

Close up

Wishes & regrets

1 Match the first part of the sentences on the left with the endings on the right.

a) I bet the thieves wished they'd   1   kept an eye on her coat while she was in the bar.
b) Kelly wishes she'd   2   spent so long chatting.
c) The girls wished they hadn't   3   turned the phone off.

What do you notice about the verb structure which follows these wishes and regrets?

2 What other wishes or regrets might the people in the story have had?

Language reference p50

3 Match the two halves of the sentences in the three groups below.

1

a	I wish I loved you	1	but hard as I try, I can't.
b	I wish I didn't love you	2	but I don't.
c	I wish I could love you	3	but the fact is, I do.

2

a	I wish you had left	1	because you're getting on my nerves.
b	I wish you would leave	2	so early.
c	I wish you weren't leaving	3	before my mother arrived.

3

a	I wish I had told you	1	but I promised I wouldn't tell anyone.
b	I wish I could tell you	2	but I didn't know you'd be so upset.
c	I wish I hadn't told you	3	but I was scared you'd get angry with me.

4 Look at the sentences again and answer these questions.

a) Which three sentences express a definite wish to change the past?
b) Which two sentences express a definite wish to change the present?
c) Which four sentences express a desire to change the near future or the present?

5 Which verb forms are used in cases a–c in 4?

6 Finish these sentences so they are true for you. Discuss your sentences with a partner.

a) I wish I (past simple) …
b) I wish I had …
c) I wish … (past continuous)
d) I wish … would …
e) I wish … could …

Regrets

1 Which of these sentences are incorrect? Make changes to them so they are correct.

Language reference p50

a) I regret leaving my job last year.
b) If only I spent so much money at the weekend.
c) I regret to have that argument with my best friend.
d) I regret not having learnt to play a musical instrument.
e) If only I'd got up so late this morning.
f) I regret not going to Spain on holiday last year.
g) I regret having lent my car to my brother.
h) I regret not to take my driving test.
i) If only I'd got through my work more quickly.

2 Are any of the regrets in 1 true for you? Tell your partner about them.

Game **Wishful thinking**

Work in small groups. Think of a famous person, cartoon or fairytale character. Write down three possible wishes or regrets that this person or character might have made. Read your wishes to the rest of the class to guess who it is.

Language reference: wishes & regrets

You backshift the verb after *wish* to express the following unreal (and wished for) situations.

Regrets about past situations

| I **didn't tell** you the truth. | → | I wish that I'**d told** you the truth. |
| I **wasn't** really **concentrating**. | → | I wish I'**d been concentrating**. |

Regrets about present situations

| I **don't have** enough time to study. | → | I wish I **had** more time to study. |
| You'**re working** very hard at the moment. | → | I wish that you **weren't working** so hard. |

A desire to change the future

| They'**re coming** to visit us next weekend. | → | I wish they **weren't coming** to visit us next weekend. |
| I'**m going** to fail my exam again. | → | I wish I **wasn't going to** fail my exam again. |

Could is also used to emphasise the inability to change a situation in the present or future.
I wish I loved you. (but I don't)
I wish I **could** love you. (but I can't)

You can also use *would* to describe a desired change in the present or future. It emphasises a sense of longing or irritation.

| It **isn't** raining. | → | I wish it **would rain**. |
| You **smoke** in the house. | → | I wish that you **wouldn't smoke** in the house. |

In informal clauses with *wish, that* is normally omitted.

Other ways of expressing regret

if only + past perfect
If only I'd studied English when I was younger.
If only I hadn't eaten the whole pizza!

regret + -*ing*
The verb which follows *regret* is always in the -*ing* form whether it is an auxiliary verb or not.
I regret choosing French when I was at school.
I regret not having studied English when I was younger.

Notes:
You use *wish* + *to*-infinitive to express a formal intention. This form is usually used in writing.
We **wish to inform** you that the offices will be closed on Mondays until further notice.
We **wish to congratulate** you on your recent success.
We **wish to thank** all those who participated in the recent conference.

You can also use the verb *regret* + *to*-infinitive in a formal context to say that you are sorry about something. It is often used to break bad news.
We **regret to inform** you that you have failed your exams.
I regret to announce that Paul will be leaving the company at the end of the month.

Wish fulfilment

Lexis **1** Look at this list of song titles with *wish* in them. Have you heard of any of the songs or artists? Which title do you like best? Which is the most romantic title? Which is the saddest title?

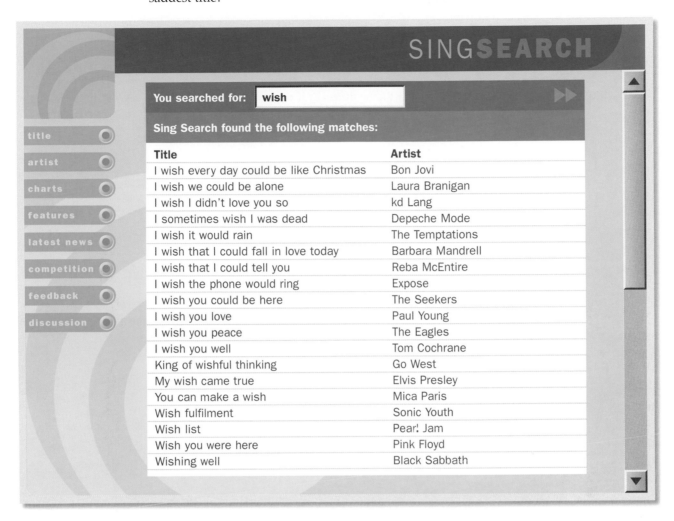

SINGSEARCH

You searched for: **wish**

Sing Search found the following matches:

Title	Artist
I wish every day could be like Christmas	Bon Jovi
I wish we could be alone	Laura Branigan
I wish I didn't love you so	kd Lang
I sometimes wish I was dead	Depeche Mode
I wish it would rain	The Temptations
I wish that I could fall in love today	Barbara Mandrell
I wish that I could tell you	Reba McEntire
I wish the phone would ring	Expose
I wish you could be here	The Seekers
I wish you love	Paul Young
I wish you peace	The Eagles
I wish you well	Tom Cochrane
King of wishful thinking	Go West
My wish came true	Elvis Presley
You can make a wish	Mica Paris
Wish fulfilment	Sonic Youth
Wish list	Pearl Jam
Wish you were here	Pink Floyd
Wishing well	Black Sabbath

title
artist
charts
features
latest news
competition
feedback
discussion

2 Work with a partner. Look through the list again and answer these questions:

a) What part of speech is *wish* and the words formed from it in each title?
b) Find two adjectives formed from the root *wish*. What nouns do they collocate with?
c) The noun *wish* is used to describe other nouns. Find two examples.
d) Find an example of each of these patterns:
   I wish + clause
   I wish you + adverb
   I wish you + noun

3 Write some song titles using the prompts below. Use your imagination!

a) wish/phone/ring
b) wish/fly/eagle
c) wish/tell/truth
d) wish/all the money in the world
e) wish/somewhere else
f) wish/you/me

4 Complete these questions with an appropriate verb and discuss them with your partner.

a) In the UK it is traditional to ＿＿＿ a wish when you blow out candles on a birthday cake. Do you have the same, or similar, traditions in your country?
b) If you could ＿＿＿ three wishes now, what would they be?
c) Have any of your wishes ever ＿＿＿ true?

Anecdote

1 You're going to tell your partner about an event or an important period in your life that has influenced the way you are today. Before you tell your partner, think about these questions and the language you will use.

- ☐ What was it? An accident? A holiday abroad? A chance meeting? A stroke of luck or an unfortunate incident? An event at school or university? A new job?
- ☐ How long ago was it?
- ☐ What happened exactly?
- ☐ Why was it so important?
- ☐ How did it influence you? Did it influence you for the better or for the worse?
- ☐ Do you wish it had never happened or are you glad that it did?
- ☐ How would your life be different if this event had not occurred? Would you have the same friends/job/character? Would your lifestyle be different?
- ☐ Is there anything else you'd like to add?

2 Tell your partner about the event.

3 Did your anecdotes have anything in common?

The day of the triffids

1 Work with a partner. Look at the picture which illustrates part of the story you are going to hear. What do you think the story is about?

2 ▪▪ **29** Listen to some extracts from the book, *The Day of the Triffids*. Decide whether these sentences are true or false.

a) The storyteller's whole body was in bandages.
b) The storyteller knew something was wrong because he couldn't hear any traffic.
c) The storyteller was in a mental hospital.
d) Somebody in the street was singing.
e) On Tuesday 7th May the Earth passed through some comet debris.
f) The storyteller really enjoyed the fireworks.
g) The storyteller opened the curtains for the patients in the surgical ward.
h) A Triffid is a carnivorous animal capable of killing a man.

3 Work in small groups and answer these questions:

a) How did the comet debris bring about 'the end of the world'?
b) How did the writer survive it?
c) Why did he think that he might have been transferred to a mental hospital?
d) When did he realise that all the other patients were blind?
e) What made Triffids different from other plants?

4 Listen again and check your answers.

5 Work with a partner. Discuss these questions:

a) What would some of the major consequences of practically everyone going blind be? The storyteller described it as 'the end of the world'. Do you think he was exaggerating?
b) Approximately 99% of the population were blinded. Imagine that you and your partner were two of the lucky ones who weren't. How would you have spent that first Wednesday?

Three months on ...

The Day of the Triffids starts off with the end of the world as we know it. This is caused by comet debris which blinds practically everyone. To add to everyone's difficulties the Earth is also plagued by man-eating Triffids.

Work with a partner. Write the narrator's diary for the first three months of life after 'the end of the world'. Before you start writing discuss the points below with your partner. Write about 100 words for each month.

The first month
Have you met other sighted people? How did you meet them? What do they do? Do you or they have skills that will be useful in this 'new' life?
What has happened to the people who were blinded by the comet debris?
What is everyday life like? What about food, water, electricity? Do you still use money?
How are you dealing with the Triffids?
Are you still living in the same town or city or have you had to move? Why?

The second month
Do you still get on with the other sighted people you've met? Do you share the same objectives for the future? What are they?
Have your food supplies run short? What are your plans for long-term food supplies?
Are the Triffids increasing in number or have you found a way of reducing their numbers?
What medical problems have you had?

The third month
What do you do every day? Are your lives beginning to get into a routine?
What do the blind people do?
How are you feeling? Are you optimistic for the future? What do you think the future holds?

6 Mind

1 How much do you know about your brain? Answer true or false to these quiz questions and find out.

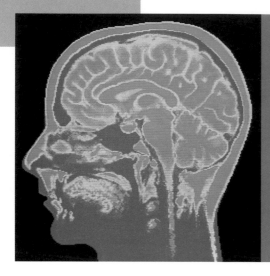

A	On average, the adult brain weighs 2.8kg in a man and 2.2kg in a woman.
B	The brain floats in a liquid in the skull.
C	50% of the average human brain is water.
D	Your brain is uniformly pink in colour.
E	The human adult brain uses up to 25% of the blood's oxygen supply.
F	We only use 10% of our brains.
G	Your brain cannot feel pain.
H	Your brain is more active watching TV than it is sleeping.
I	We yawn more when our brains are not being stimulated.
J	The human brain continues to send out electrical signals for up to 37 hours following death.

2 Check your answers on page 133.

Mind matters

1 Work with a partner. Discuss these questions:

a) Have you read or heard about this book or Dr Oliver Sacks?

b) What do you think the case called *The Man Who Mistook His Wife for a Hat* is about?

2 Read these four extracts from the case and match these headings to them.

a) The doctor's examination   c) The diagnosis

b) The doctor's first impression   d) The patient

> *The Man Who Mistook His Wife for a Hat* is the title of a book concerning malfunctions of the brain. It was written by the neurologist Dr Oliver Sacks. The title of the book is also the title of one of the cases.

The Man Who Mistook His Wife for a Hat

1

Dr P. was a musician of distinction, well-known for many years as a singer, and then at the local School of Music, as a teacher. It was here, in relation to his students, that certain strange problems were first observed. Sometimes a student would present himself, and Dr P. would not recognise him; or, specifically, would not recognise his face. The moment the student spoke, he would be recognised by his voice. Such incidents multiplied, causing embarrassment, perplexity, fear – and, sometimes, comedy. For not
5 only did Dr P. increasingly fail to see faces, but he saw faces when there were no faces to see: genially, when in the street, he might pat the heads of water-hydrants and parking-meters, taking these to be the heads of children; he would amiably address carved knobs on the furniture and be astounded when they did not reply.

The notion of there being 'something the matter' did not emerge until some three years later, when diabetes developed. Well aware that diabetes could affect his eyes, Dr P. consulted an ophthalmologist, who took a careful history and examined his eyes
10 closely. 'There's nothing the matter with your eyes,' the doctor concluded. 'But there is trouble with the visual parts of your brain. You don't need my help, you must see a neurologist.' And so, as a result of this referral Dr P. came to me.

2

It was obvious within a few seconds of meeting him that there was no trace of dementia in the ordinary sense. He was a man of great cultivation and charm, who talked well and fluently, with imagination and humour. I couldn't think why he had been referred to our clinic.

15   And yet there was something a bit odd. He faced me as he spoke, was oriented towards me, and yet there was something the matter – it was difficult to formulate. He faced me with his ears, I came to think, but not with his eyes. These, instead of looking, gazing, at me, 'taking me in', in the normal way, made sudden strange fixations – on my nose, on my right ear, down to my chin, up to my right eye – as if noting (even studying) these individual features, but not seeing my whole face, its changing expressions, 'me', as a whole. I am not sure I fully realised this at the time – there was just a teasing strangeness, some failure in the normal

20 interplay of gaze and expression. He saw me, he scanned me and yet …

    'What seems to be the matter?' I asked him at length.

    'Nothing that I know of,' he replied with a smile, 'but people seem to think there's something wrong with my eyes.'

    'But you don't recognise any visual problems?'

    'No, not directly, but I occasionally make mistakes.'

3

25 He saw all right, but what did he see? I opened out a copy of the National Geographic Magazine, and asked him to describe some pictures in it.

    His responses here were very curious. His eyes would dart from one thing to another, picking up tiny features, individual features, as they had done with my face. A striking brightness, a colour, a shape would arrest his attention and elicit comment – but in no case did he get the scene-as-a-whole.

30   'What is this?' I asked, holding up a glove.

    'May I examine it?' he asked, and, taking it from me, he proceeded to examine it.

    'A continuous surface,' he announced at last, 'infolded on itself. It appears to have' – he hesitated – 'five outpouchings, if this is the word.'

    'Yes,' I said cautiously. 'You have given me a description. Now tell me what it is.'

35   'A container of some sort?'

    'Yes,' I said, 'and what would it contain?'

    'It would contain its contents!' said Dr P., with a laugh. 'There are many possibilities. It could be a change-purse, for example, for coins of five sizes. It could …'

    I interrupted the barmy flow. 'Does it not look familiar? Do you think it might contain, might fit, a part of your body?'

40   No light of recognition dawned on his face.

    No child would have the power to see and speak of 'a continuous surface … infolded on itself', but any child, any infant, would immediately know a glove as a glove, see it as familiar, as going with a hand. Dr P. didn't. He saw nothing as familiar. Visually, he was lost in a world of lifeless abstractions.

4

'Well, Dr Sacks,' he said to me. 'You find me an interesting case, I perceive. Can you tell me what you find wrong, make

45 recommendations?'

    'I can't tell you what I find wrong,' I replied, 'but I'll say what I find right. You are a wonderful musician, and music is your life. What I would prescribe, in a case such as yours, is a life which consists entirely of music. Music has been the centre, now make it the whole, of your life.'

(Extracts from *The Man Who Mistook His Wife for a Hat* by Oliver Sacks, 1985)

3   **Work with a partner and discuss these questions:**

a)   What were Dr P.'s first symptoms?

b)   Why did Dr P. consult an ophthalmologist? Why was the ophthalmologist unable to help him?

c)   What did Dr Sacks notice about Dr P.'s eyes when they first met?

d)   Was Dr P. aware that he didn't see normally? Why/Why not?

e)   How *did* Dr P. see?

f)   How do you think Dr P. would describe a book or a pair of glasses? What might he mistake them for?

g)   What advice did Dr Sacks give the patient? Is this the kind of advice you would expect from a doctor? Why did he give him this advice?

h)   Look at these titles of other case histories from the book. What do you think the problem was in these cases?
The Lost Mariner
The Phantom Finger
The Dog Beneath The Skin
You can find out by reading the file cards on page 134.

Lexis

1 Find words in sentences 1–8 below with the following meanings:

a) looking steadily at something for a long time
b) noticed
c) move suddenly and quickly
d) understand something by looking at it
e) know what something is when you see it again
f) looked at or over something carefully or quickly
g) to look closely or analytically at something
h) become aware of something using your eyes

1 It was here, in relation to his students, that certain strange problems were first observed. (line 2)
2 … Dr P. would not recognise him; or, specifically, would not recognise his face. (line 3)
3 … instead of looking, gazing, at me, 'taking me in', in the normal way … (lines 16–17)
4 He saw me, he scanned me and yet … (line 20)
5 He saw all right, but what did he see? (line 25)
6 His eyes would dart from one thing to another … (line 27)
7 … taking it from me, he proceeded to examine it. (line 31)
8 You find me an interesting case, I perceive. (line 44)

2 *Observe, recognise* and *see* have more than one meaning. Look at these sentences and match the verbs with the meanings in the box.

a) I recognise I'm not perfect.
b) I see what you mean.
c) They have recognised the importance of your contribution.
d) If you travel abroad it is important to observe the customs of the country you are visiting.
e) Are you still seeing Peter?
f) 'That wasn't very clever,' he observed.
g) The police observed the criminals from the house across the road.
h) As I see it, she's making a big mistake.

> to watch   to understand   to follow or obey a law/rule   to admit
> to comment/remark   to have an opinion on something
> to meet someone socially or date someone   to acknowledge

3 How would you translate *observe, recognise* and *see* into your own language? Do the translations have multiple meanings?

4 Write a paragraph using *observe, recognise* and *see*. Use each word once. Show it to a partner and ask them to work out the meanings of the verbs you have used.

The five senses

1 Work with a partner and discuss these questions:

a) What are the five senses?
b) Which do you think is most important to you in your everyday life?
c) Which would you be able to cope best without?
d) Which sense triggers the most memories?
e) Have you ever lost the use of one of your senses temporarily?
f) Do you think any of your senses is especially well-developed?

2 🔊 30 Listen to Mike, Maria, Helen, Nick and Petra each answering one of the questions in 1. Make notes on their answers. Which senses are they talking about? Which question is each person answering?

3 Compare your notes with your partner. Were the speakers' answers similar to yours?

Close up

Verbs of the senses

Language reference p58

1 Work with a partner. Look at the verbs in the box. Which refer to an ability? Which refer to an action? Which can refer to both?

smell	feel	see	look	hear	listen	taste	touch

2 Complete these extracts from the speakers' answers using correct forms of the verbs in the box. You may need to add a modal verb or a negative.

a) Yes, the most important one is sight I suppose … I mean, if you're blind, if you (1) _____ , then although you can lead a full life and all that, I think it does make you more vulnerable, more dependent on other people …

b) … I would really hate it if I (2) _____ what things or people looked like … or the expression on a person's face when they're talking to you. I mean, you wouldn't even know if they (3) _____ at you or whether they looked interested in what you were saying.

c) … I read this article about a man who'd gone deaf and then his hearing was restored to him, and he spoke about how isolating it can be if you (4) _____ .

d) … he really missed (5) _____ to music, that was the worst part he said. That and not being able to (6) _____ his wife's voice.

e) … I (7) _____ the palm trees, (8) _____ the food, (9) _____ the sun on my skin …

f) … they used an international signing language which was based on touch – they would (10) _____ each other and sign on each other's palms, and they (11) _____ each other talking – and it showed them going to a drum concert too – like a traditional Japanese drum concert – and they (12) _____ the music, I mean they (13) _____ the vibrations of the drums, even though they (14) _____ them.

g) … I'm really sensitive to things like gas leaks and anything that (15) _____ bad …

h) … I (16) _____ really strong things, like coffee or if something's burning in the kitchen, but I (17) _____ other things like perfume so I don't know how much to put on. And I really miss the subtler smells in the kitchen. It affects my taste too. Everything (18) _____ so bland.

3 31 Listen and check your answers.

4 Were your answers different from those in the speakers' answers? If yes, do you think your answers are also correct?

5 Look at the verbs in *italics* in the following sentences. Which describe:

- an ability or a sensation?
- an action?

a) He's amazing, he can *hear* a tune just the once and then reproduce it perfectly.

b) When *I'm watching* a film at the cinema I like to sit in the middle of a row so that I can *see* more clearly.

c) When you've got a heavy cold you can't really *taste* things properly.

d) When it's windy you can't always *feel* how hot the sun is on your skin and it's very easy to get sunburnt.

e) 'Don't *touch* that plate – it's just come out of the oven.'

f) The teacher got really angry because none of the children *were listening* to what he was saying.

g) It was a terrible fire; they could *feel* the hot air and *smell* the smoke a kilometre away.

h) Always *smell* wine before *tasting* it.

i) If you turn the volume down a little, you'll be able to *hear* it much more clearly.

j) He *didn't look* before crossing the road and was almost knocked over by a bus!

6 Look at the sentences again and discuss these questions with your partner:

a) Which verbs are used to describe an ability or a sensation?

b) Which verbs are used to describe an action?

c) Find the modal auxiliaries and any other phrases with similar meanings. Are they used with descriptions of ability, descriptions of action, or both?

7 Complete these sentences with the correct form of an appropriate verb from 6 on page 57.

a) Sometimes I found it difficult to concentrate in class. I used to switch off, ____ out of the window and I ____ to a word the teacher said.

b) Sometimes groupwork can be really difficult, I just ____ what people are saying when there are a lot of people talking at the same time.

c) If I was short-sighted, I'd have laser treatment on my eyes, so that I ____ without having to wear glasses.

d) I find that I can remember a word much better if I ____ it written down.

e) When I ____ freshly cut grass I always think of the end of summer term and exams.

f) When I was a kid I hated cabbage. I just couldn't eat it. If there was even the slightest trace of it, say in a soup or something, I ____ it straight away and absolutely refused to eat it.

g) I used to ____ perfectly when I was younger, but now I need to wear glasses to read or when I go to the cinema.

h) I love summer evenings when you can sit outside and you ____ the heat of the sun still on your skin.

8 Are these sentences true for you? Discuss them with a partner.

9 Work with a partner. Look at the pairs of sentences below.

a) Discuss the difference in meaning of the verbs in *italics*.
b) Which verbs are stative and which are dynamic?

1A I *can see* John. He's just over there, standing next to the bar.
1B I'm *seeing* John tomorrow. I'll let him know what we've decided.

2A I *could hear* strange sounds coming from downstairs, so I decided to go and investigate.
2B I've *been hearing* great things about you recently. You must be doing really well.

3A I'm *not feeling* very well, I think I'm going to go and lie down for a while.
3B That heater's really good! I *can feel* the heat from here.

4A I'm *just tasting* the soup to see if I need to add any more salt.
4B I really *can't taste* the difference between butter and margarine.

5A She was in the garden *smelling* the roses when she was stung by a bee.
5B We lived near a chocolate factory. It was great. You *could smell* it all around you.

Language reference: verbs of the senses

You can talk about your senses in two ways:
- using stative verbs, to refer to abilities or sensations
- using dynamic verbs, to refer to voluntary actions

Stative verbs	Dynamic verbs
see	look (at)/watch
feel	touch/feel
hear	listen (to)
smell	smell
taste	taste

can, could & be able to

You can often use stative verbs with *can*, *could* or *be able to*.

I *can see* much better when I'm wearing my glasses.
I *could smell* the smoke, but I *couldn't see* the fire.
I would love to *be able to hear* as well as I *could* when I was younger.

Continuous forms

You rarely use verbs with stative meanings in continuous forms. When they are used in continuous forms, the meanings usually change and they become dynamic.

I'm seeing the car over there. ✗
I'm seeing the doctor tomorrow about my back. ✓
(meaning = meeting)

I'm feeling your hand on my shoulder. ✗
I'm feeling much better today. ✓
(meaning = talking about your state of health)

I'm smelling gas. ✗
He's smelling her new perfume. ✓
(meaning = investigating)

I'm tasting too much salt in this dish. ✗
They're tasting the dessert to see if they like it. ✓
(meaning = testing)

I'm hearing beautiful music coming from the flat upstairs. ✗
She's been hearing good reports about his work. ✓
(meaning = being told about something)

Verbs with **dynamic** meanings refer to action or change.
*I **spent** the weekend in Barcelona.*
*She's **gained** a lot of weight recently.*

Verbs with **stative** meanings refer to a state or condition. They are not usually used in continuous forms or imperatives.
*I **love** my husband.*
*He **believes** that his method is right.*

Pet psychology

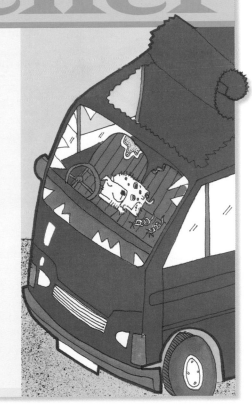

Discussion Work in small groups and discuss these questions:

a) Have you ever had a pet? What was it? What was its name?

b) What's the most unusual pet you've heard of? Why do you think people keep such animals?

c) Do you think pets serve a useful function? If so, what?

d) Do you think people get too attached to their pets?

Reading **1** Match the problems to the definitions.

a) nervous breakdown
b) addiction
c) separation anxiety
d) phobia
e) territorial aggression

1 hostile action taken towards trespassers
2 the condition of doing or consuming something habitually and being unable to give it up
3 a loss of mental health and strength
4 a state of uneasiness brought about by the absence of a person or thing
5 an irrational fear or hatred of something

2 Read this pet case history and decide which of the problems above Willy was suffering from.

TheCanine Cruncher

The day Mr X took delivery of his new van was the day his dog decided to start out on a new career. Previously a docile creature, Willy the cross-bred terrier turned into Lex
5 Flex, the Canine Cruncher, in the time it took his owner to eat a three course meal.

Having left his trusty companion to keep an eye on the smart new van, Mr X returned from lunch to find that his new
10 mode of transport had been completely remodelled. What had been a sturdy, dependable method of delivering frozen foods around the city centre would now not have looked out of place by a beach on a
15 hot summer's day. The roof had been torn back as if with a tin opener, an air conditioning system had been thoughtfully provided by the removal of the windscreen and the seats had been given a new look,
20 which might have been described as 'ripped and tattered'. Exhausted by all his hard work, Willy was having a quick nap when his owner reappeared.

Speechless, Mr X rushed towards his
25 hound with his arms outstretched. Waking up with a jump, Willy sat up to greet his owner and barked with excitement. However, being a modest sort of dog and not thinking it necessary for his devoted
30 owner to thank him so profusely, he bounded through the shattered windscreen and took off down the street. Mr X's voice could be heard fading into the distance behind him as he raced away. Overcome
35 with emotion, the van owner returned to survey the full extent of the new design.

These days it's not uncommon to see Mr X driving round the streets of the city looking for his absent friend. Numbed by
40 the efficiency of his new air-conditioning system, he's often spotted scouring the streets between deliveries, under the protection of a warm blanket. Rumour has it that he's bought a small shotgun to give
45 Willy when they are reunited, just as a small token of his appreciation.

3 Work with a partner and discuss the meanings of these expressions.

a) a docile creature (line 3)
b) ripped and tattered (lines 20–21)
c) a quick nap (line 22)

d) Rumour has it (lines 43–44)
e) a small token of his appreciation (lines 45–46)

4 The text contains a lot of descriptive language. However, the actual events of the story can be summarised in a few sentences. Write as short a factual account of the story as you can.

Close up

Participle clauses

1 Without looking back, make three sentences from the text, using one clause from each column.

COLUMN 1	COLUMN 2	COLUMN 3
a) Having left his trusty companion	he's often spotted scouring the streets between deliveries,	and barked with excitement.
b) Waking up with a jump,	to keep an eye on the smart new van,	under the protection of a warm blanket.
c) Numbed by the efficiency of his new air-conditioning system,	Willy sat up to greet his owner	Mr X returned from lunch to find that his new mode of transport had been completely remodelled.

2 Look back at the text and check your answers.

Language reference p61

3 Look at your answers to 1 and answer these questions:

a) Find the *participle clause* in each sentence. Which contains a
- present participle? • past participle? • perfect participle?

b) What is the subject of each participle clause?

c) Where is the subject of each participle clause?

4 Look at this pair of sentences and answer the questions.

A Exhausted by all his hard work, Willy was having a quick nap when …
B Willy was exhausted by all his hard work, so he was having a quick nap when …

a) Which sentence, A or B, is more likely to be spoken? Which was used in the text? Look back and check.

b) What has been added to B to replace the participle clause?

5 Rewrite these sentences using participle clauses.

a) When I finished university I took a year out to travel and give myself time to decide what to do next.

b) After my last English exam I went straight to bed because I was totally exhausted.

c) Because I live on my own, I don't really do a lot of cooking.

d) I have a large car, so I'm often the driver when I go out with friends in the evening.

e) I like to spend the weekends relaxing as I'm tired after a long week at work.

6 Are these sentences true for anyone in your class?

7 Work with a partner. Look at the following sentences and add 'not' *where necessary*.

a) Wanting to offend people, they decided to extend the guest list to include both family and friends.

b) Discouraged by the long climb ahead of them, they set off at dawn, chatting happily.

c) Having completed the form, please send it, with a photograph, to the address below.

d) Jean has a clear grasp of the grammar, but having spoken English for quite a few years, he lacks confidence in conversation.

e) Knowing that arriving on time would make a very bad impression, he left with plenty of time to spare.

f) Relieved at hearing that she had passed, Sandra immediately phoned her parents.

8 What do you notice about the position of *not* in the sentences in 7?

9 Rephrase your answers to 7 without using participle clauses. You may need to add linking words.

For example:
They didn't want to offend people so they decided to extend the guest list to include both family and friends.

Language reference: participle clauses

Participle clauses do not include a subject or linking words. You can form them with a:

Present participle
Being a little shy, he chose not to speak out in front of everybody.
Not having a lot of time, they decided to take a taxi.
In these cases the participle is substituting for the subject and a different form of the verb:
Because he was a little shy, he chose not to speak out in front of everybody.
Because they didn't have a lot of time, they decided to take a taxi.

Past participle
Woken by a noise, James phoned the police.
Not taken in by his charm, she refused his offer of dinner.
In these cases the participle is substituting for the subject and the verb *be*:
James was woken by a noise, so he phoned the police.

She wasn't taken in by his charm, so she refused his offer of dinner.

Perfect participle
Not having understood the question, she failed to answer it correctly.
Having mixed the chemicals together, we observed the reaction.
In these cases the perfect participle is substituting for the subject and a verb in the past perfect.
Because she hadn't understood the question, she failed to answer it correctly.
After we had mixed the chemicals together, we observed the reaction.

Note: Participle clauses are often used to avoid repetition and to shorten complex sentences. They are more commonly found in written language, such as narratives, reports and essays.

Mind

Collocations

1 Look at the expressions in **bold** in these sentences. Is *mind* a verb or a noun in each one?

a) Have a good trip. **Mind how you go** on the roads, they're terrible at this time of day.
b) They pay really well. **Mind you**, they can afford it.
c) Don't worry, we'll sort it out somehow. **Something will come to mind**.
d) Jen's invited me to go on holiday with her, but **I'm in two minds about it**.
e) What annoys me about him is the fact that he keeps **changing his mind** all the time.
f) Stop wasting time, **make up your mind!**
g) **Never mind!** I'm sure you'll do much better next time.
h) **Do you mind** if I open the window?
i) Don't worry about what other people think, just **speak your mind!**
j) **Bear in mind** that you're not as young as you used to be!

2 Match each expression in 1 with one of these meanings.

1 Say what you honestly think
2 On the other hand
3 You'll think of an idea
4 Don't worry
5 I can't decide
6 Would it bother you
7 Don't forget
8 Be careful
9 Altering his opinion
10 Make a decision

3 Do you know any other expressions with *mind*?

4 Work with a partner. Discuss these questions:

a) When were you last in two minds about something?
b) Do you mind if people smoke in restaurants?
c) When was the last time you spoke your mind? Did you offend anyone?

Word linking

1 ▭ **32** Listen to a conversation between three people. Where are they? Who do you think the boss is? Why?

2 Look at these sentences from the conversation. Complete them with expressions including *mind*.

> **a)** Look John, _____ leaving the room for a minute? There's something I need to discuss with Pete here.
> **b)** Oh, dear. I think I know what you're going to say. _____ if I smoke?
> **c)** I thought as much. _____ , it doesn't come as much of a surprise. Not after last year's fiasco.

3 Listen again and check your answers.

4 Look at the following phrases. How do the speakers pronounce the underlined sections? Practise saying the phrases.

Woul<u>d you</u> mind   <u>Do you</u> mind   Min<u>d you</u>

5 Work with a partner and discuss the following questions. Think carefully about the pronunciation of the underlined sections.

a) <u>Did you</u> do anything special last night?
b) <u>Do you</u> prefer tea or coffee?
c) <u>Do you</u> mind if people keep you waiting?
d) Would <u>you</u> mind if someone borrowed something of yours without asking?
e) <u>Did you</u> go anywhere on holiday last year?
f) What woul<u>d you</u> do if you won a lot of money on the lottery?
g) <u>Do you</u> go to the cinema often, or <u>do you</u> prefer to watch videos?
h) How woul<u>d you</u> react if a friend told you they were going to live abroad?

I'm going slightly mad

1 Look at the pictures. There's something going wrong in each one. What is it?

2 ▭ **33** Listen to the song. All the images in the pictures are included. Note the order in which they are mentioned.

3 Listen again. What other images and metaphors are used to describe the singer's state of mind? Look at tapescript 33 on page 150 if you need help.

4 What do you know about Freddie Mercury? Why do you think he wrote this song?

7 Review 1

7

NEWS IN BRIEF

Counting on the money

A woman from Dewsbury, (1) *obsessed* with Dracula and vampires since she was a child, has set up a company (2) *importing* coffins from Transylvania.

High and dry

Emergency staff at a hospital in Hampstead, London treated a man last week after he inhaled fumes from his socks, (3) ____ while drying in front of an electric heater.

Stolen moments

Women (4) ____ chips from their partner's plate is the most common cause of arguments between couples (5) ____, according to a recent poll.

Crisis point

The guest speaker at a meeting in Plymouth last night had to abandon his talk, (6) ____ How to Cope in a Crisis, when he was called home because his house was on fire.

Compact case

A Midlands police force is seeking a make-up artist to make volunteers (7) ____ in identity parades look more like the suspected criminals.

Whole in one

A man (8) ____ his wife to bingo only to stop her complaining about the amount of golf he plays won the £200,000 jackpot at a club in Bristol.

Flower power

A florist's in the Midlands is offering bunches of dead roses (9) ____ in black paper for jilted lovers to send to their former partners.

Deeply in love

A couple (10) ____ while learning to scuba dive got married in a tank full of tropical fish at Birmingham's national sea life centre.

Relative & participle clauses

1 The stories above are all taken from British newspapers. Complete the relative or participle clauses by adding a verb from the box in the correct form. You may also need to add a relative pronoun. The first two have been done for you.

> ~~import~~   catch fire   entitle   eat out   steal   take part
> ~~obsess~~   wrap   accompany   meet

2 One of the stories is not true. Which one is it? Check your answer on page 132.

Verb forms   Complete the newspaper story by putting the verbs in brackets into the correct form.

SNAKES ALIVE!

A young groom-to-be with a phobia about snakes (1) *woke* (wake) on the morning of his wedding (2) ____ (find) his room and his body covered in snakes about 30cm long. Mike Sanders, 22, who (3) ____ (marry) at 2 o'clock that afternoon, was so terrified that he (4) ____ (can/not/move) or even (5) ____ (shout out) for help, (6) ____ (believe) the slightest twitch (7) ____ (result) in his immediate death. (8) ____ (lie) in his bed, and despite the frantic knocking of his bride on the door, he (9) ____ (remain) motionless as the hour of his wedding (10) ____ (come) and (11) ____ (go). He (12) ____ (eventually/rescue) when police officers (13) ____ (break into) his house, whereupon it (14) ____ (emerge) that the snakes were plastic, certainly not poisonous, and (15) ____ (put) there by friends as a stag-night joke.

Clearly shaken a week later and still (16) ____ (not/speak) to his friends since his ordeal, Mr Sanders (17) ____ (tell) reporters, 'Snakes (18) ____ (always/be) my absolute number one hate ever since I was a child. My so-called friends were well aware that I (19) ____ (not/find) it in the slightest bit funny. I (20) ____ (not/think) I (21) ____ (ever/be able) (22) ____ (forgive) them.'

(23) ____ it ____ (not/be) for his friends' misplaced sense of fun, Mr and Mrs Sanders (24) ____ (today/celebrate) one week as man and wife.

Words of wisdom

Negative & limiting adverbials

1 Join the two halves of the famous quotes. The first one has been done for you.

1 Time is like a river made up of events. No sooner does anything appear
2 Not until it is too late
3 Only when I am unbearably unhappy
4 Not only should justice be done,
5 Never before have we had so little time
6 Not only is the universe queerer than we suppose,
7 Never has a man turned so little knowledge
8 Not only did he not suffer fools gladly,

a) to such great account.
b) do I have the true feeling of myself.
c) does one recognise the really important moments in one's life.
d) to do so much.
e) than it is swept away and something else comes into its place.
f) but it should manifestly and undoubtedly be seen to be done.
g) he did not suffer them at all.
h) but queerer than we *can* suppose.

2 Match the quotes with the people below. Check your answers on page 134.

a) Roman Emperor Marcus Aurelius Antoninus philosophising about change. *Quote 1*
b) US President Franklin D. Roosevelt in a speech to Congress in 1941.
c) Former Lord Chief Justice of the United Kingdom, Gordon Hewitt.
d) British geneticist J. B. S. Haldane contemplating extraterrestrial life.
e) Anonymous: about US Statesman Dean Gooderham Acheson.
f) Dramatist and poet T. S. Elliot talking about Shakespeare.
g) Crime writer Agatha Christie reflecting on her life.
h) Czech novelist Franz Kafka bearing his soul.

3 Are there any other well-known words of wisdom or famous quotes that you like?

Discussion bingo

1 You are going to play a game of bingo. Follow the rules below.

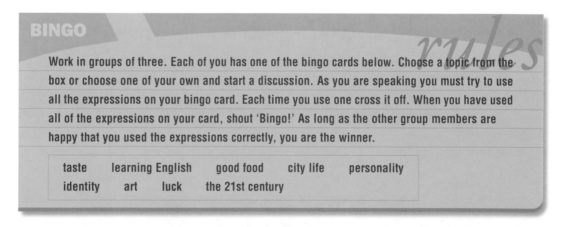

BINGO   *rules*

Work in groups of three. Each of you has one of the bingo cards below. Choose a topic from the box or choose one of your own and start a discussion. As you are speaking you must try to use all the expressions on your bingo card. Each time you use one cross it off. When you have used all of the expressions on your card, shout 'Bingo!' As long as the other group members are happy that you used the expressions correctly, you are the winner.

taste	learning English	good food	city life	personality
identity	art	luck	the 21st century	

CARD 1

Talking of …
It seems that …
When I was younger, I'd often …
Not necessarily, because …
I really regret …
Oh, come on …

CARD 2

Frankly, …
Gone are the times …
I really do wish …
There is no doubt that …
People will always …
Only when …

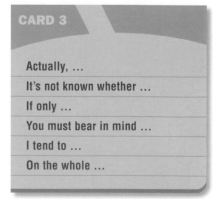

CARD 3

Actually, …
It's not known whether …
If only …
You must bear in mind …
I tend to …
On the whole …

2 Choose a different card and a different topic and play again.

All change

Position of adverbials

1 Work with a partner and read the following pairs of sentences. Explain the difference in meaning between them.

a) A I don't particularly want to go.
    B I particularly don't want to go.

b) A I think John's only got his phone number.
    B I think only John's got his phone number.

c) A I'm a hundred per cent certain she's not going.
    B I'm not a hundred per cent certain she's going.

d) A I did my work quickly and got ready to go out.
    B I did my work and quickly got ready to go out.

e) A I really like your T-shirt.
    B I like your T-shirt really.

f) A I never knew you'd been there.
    B I knew you'd never been there.

g) A Personally, I don't think he'll apologise.
    B I don't think he'll apologise personally.

h) A For a moment I didn't believe him.
    B I didn't believe him for a moment.

i) A I'm sure he'll still be here in the morning.
    B I'm still sure he'll be here in the morning.

j) A Just Sam and I went for a drink.
    B Sam and I just went for a drink.

Ian, John, Helena and Angela

2 🔊 **34** Listen to ten short dialogues which correspond to the pairs of sentences in 1. Is the second speaker's comment closer in meaning to sentence A or B in each dialogue?

3 Work with a partner. Write some similar dialogues and sentences of your own.

4 Work in small groups and read your dialogues and sentences. Ask the other members of your group to guess which of the two sentences is closest in meaning to the dialogue.

Ready, steady, go!

Phrasal verbs

1 Find twelve more phrasal verbs in the grid below. The verbs go →, ↓ and ↘.

T	L	O	O	K	I	N	T	O	H	R	S
R	H	X	B	O	T	T	L	E	U	P	Z
P	A	I	B	R	E	A	K	O	F	F	C
U	U	S	N	V	B	L	Q	O	J	G	O
T	S	T	E	K	R	K	N	M	B	E	M
U	P	O	A	C	T	T	Y	E	R	T	E
P	I	E	R	C	H	H	G	Z	I	D	U
W	C	G	D	T	R	R	R	N	N	O	P
I	K	A	U	L	O	O	P	O	G	W	W
T	U	W	I	F	H	U	S	K	U	N	I
H	P	K	J	Z	A	G	T	S	P	G	T
F	L	I	C	K	T	H	R	O	U	G	H

2 Choose four of the verbs and write sentences for them. Trade sentences with other students in the class until you have one for each verb.

Greetings from down under

1 Read Juliette's e-mail to her friends and correct her mistakes. There are at least twenty mistakes.

From: Juliette <juliette@kanga.com>
Subject: Australia
▷ Attachments: Picture of Sydney Harbour

Dear all,

As I didn't write for so long, I thought it was time I dropped all you a line or two from not-so-sunny Australia! The weather has got quite bad here unfortunately in Sydney over the last few days. I think summer is finally over! Never mind it, it'll give me the chance to do all the things I've been putting off while I've been lying on the beach taking it easy!

Life here is great – I've just found a job which is working in a café little and friendly near the harbour. Actually, Lena, it's the place recommended your friend. It only is a few hours each week, but the pay is good and there are working there some great people. The most of them are also travelling round the world like me. In fact, a few days ago I met someone thinking he met you all in Vietnam. Do you remember an English guy called Kim? He says it was somewhere in the mountains – he told me the name, but I can't remember it.

Anyway, I'm here in Australia for almost a month now. As you know, Marcella decided to for a while stay in Thailand with Yuichi. They seem totally in love! He is really nice actually. I'm sure Marcella has told you all about it by now! Anyway, I was really glad to stop moving after all the buses, trains and planes I was taking to get here from Bangkok. Well, I say 'moving'! Often the buses would stop in some remote town or village for what was feeling like hours! Nobody dared get off in case the bus suddenly left without them. At the time I wished I flew here, but looking back, it was an experience I suppose! Consequently, I spent when I first arrived a few days relaxing and wandering round the city and then I went on a trip along the coast for a couple of weeks before going to the Blue Mountains for few days. The mountains, which aren't that far from Sydney actually, absolutely are incredible – very beautiful and peaceful.

So, what about you lot? You must e-mail me back and let me know all the gossip back home. Miguel and Virginia, how's the new house? And how are you two, Lena and Stefan? By the way, are you hearing the new 'Superhead' CD yet? If not, you should check out it – it's brilliant! It was where you first met at their concert, wasn't it?

Well, I'll finish now as I've got to go and work at the café. I miss you all lots – if only you are all here with me. Now that I've stopped travelling around for a while, I'll write more often – I promise! Hope you like the picture! Write back soon.

Lots of love

Juliette xxxxxx

2 Write a letter or an e-mail to a friend telling them your news.

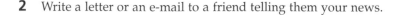

The word game

Lexis

1 The books were put on the shelves in a very *pazdrahha* way.

2 Give two words that describe a way of looking.

3 She's very *valkettai* – it's difficult to get her to shut up at times!

4 A person who has influenced you in some way

5 I think I'll just *psil* off quietly. See you tomorrow.

10 What you would do if you won the lottery jackpot.

9 I didn't catch much of what he said – he's such a *blmmuer*.

8 Your favourite smell, taste and sound

7 Give four expressions that include the word *mind*.

6 I couldn't get a word in _____! She just went on and on and …

11 His greatest *civaehenmet* was getting his book published.

12 Tell a joke!

13 I didn't like it. I thought it was in very _____ taste actually.

14 I didn't read it properly – I just *lcefkid* through it.

15 Give three words made from the word *taste*.

20 They were having a very in-_____ discussion about politics or something.

19 I don't think he *nedcgroies* how important it was.

18 An early memory

17 Her sister's got wonderful taste _____ furniture.

16 The boys stole a car and went for a _____ before crashing it.

21 Give three words that can describe a discussion or conversation.

22 The streets were _____ with traffic which made it difficult to travel around the city.

23 We've discovered a new restaurant with an *eiieuxqst* menu.

24 I didn't think they _____ their ideas across very well.

25 Your favourite restaurant

30 She had to *ascrbleb* about in her bag for her glasses when the film started.

29 Your favourite city

28 Have you heard about Jane's _____ to chocolate? She can't get enough of it!

27 Give two informal words that mean *steal*.

26 *Romuur* has it that the two companies are going to merge.

31 She _____ her fists in an effort to control her anger.

32 Something you regret

33 That's a pretty *fdta* idea!

34 Your home town

35 It's never a good idea to _____ up your feelings.

Play in small groups. You will need a dice and counters. The first player rolls the dice and moves along the board from the Start, according to the number on the dice. The player completes the task on the square they land on. If the player is successful, they can play in the next round. If not, they miss their next turn. The winner is the first player to reach the Finish.

There are four types of question:

| Rearrange a mixed-up word. | Add a missing word. | Complete a task. | Talk about something for thirty seconds without stopping. |

8 Cyberspace

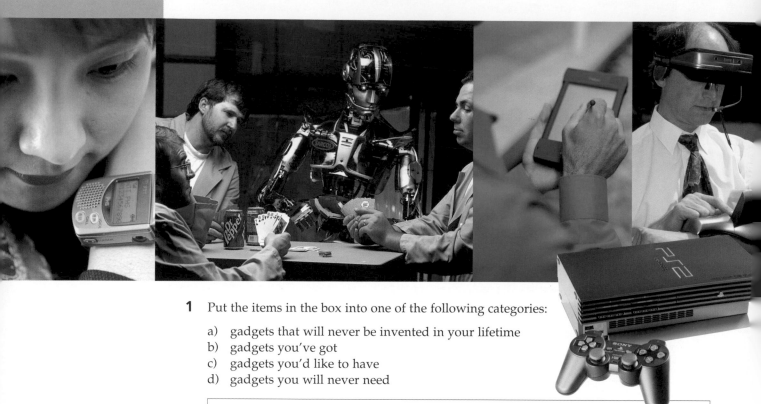

1 Put the items in the box into one of the following categories:

a) gadgets that will never be invented in your lifetime
b) gadgets you've got
c) gadgets you'd like to have
d) gadgets you will never need

> mobile phone link-up to Internet   heli-bike   TV games console (e.g. Playstation)
> miniature TV screens in wrap-around sunglasses   palmtop computer
> relaxation cocoon   CD Walkman   fully programmable housework robot
> electronic shoe-shine   voice-operated car   external memory boost for your brain
> transparent bodysuit for safer sunbathing   wrist phone with visual display unit
> language microchip implanted directly in the brain   automatic ice-cream maker
> ergonomic office chair with inbuilt massage function

2 Compare your answers with a partner and add another two items to each category.

Future perfect

1 Work with a partner and discuss these questions:

a) What do you know about Stephen Hawking?
b) Have you ever read any of his books?

2 Read the information about Stephen Hawking on page 139. Does it include any facts that you didn't already know?

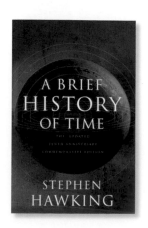

3 You are going to read an interview with Stephen Hawking, in which he is asked to predict the future of humankind in the third millennium. Before you read the text, work with a partner and make your own predictions about the following:

a) making contact with an intelligent life form from another planet
b) developments in computer technology
c) genetic engineering on plants, animals and humans
d) developments in human intelligence and knowledge

4 Read the article and find out what Stephen Hawking's predictions for the areas in 3 are.

A brief history of the future

Will we colonise the universe? Are aliens out there? Can computers outsmart us? In a unique interview, Professor Stephen Hawking, who has spent a lifetime applying his formidable intellect to the big questions, gives Nigel Farndale his predictions for the human race.

I've come here – to Cambridge University's Department of Applied Mathematics and Theoretical Physics, where Hawking holds the professorial chair once held by Isaac Newton – on the turn of the millennium to ask him what he thinks the future has in store for the human race.

If the world's population continues to grow at its present rate – doubling every 40 years – there isn't going to be enough room for us all on Earth by the year 2600. So will we, I ask, be able to spread out to other planets? His hands go into action. The only sounds in the room are the clicking of the pressure pads and the whirring of the computer. The electronic voice delivers the answer five minutes later. 'We shall probably manage a manned or, should I say, personned, flight to Mars in the next century,' Hawking says. 'But Earth is by far the most favoured planet in the solar system. Mars is small, cold and without much atmosphere, and the other planets are quite unsuitable for human beings. We either have to learn to live in space stations or travel to the next star. We won't do that in the next century.'

I ask whether we humans will keep on changing, or will we eventually reach an ultimate level of development and knowledge? Click click click. 'In the next 100 years or even in the next twenty, we may discover a complete theory of the basic laws of the universe (the so-called Theory of Everything, in which quantum theory is unified with Einstein's theory of general relativity), but there will be no limit to the complexity of biological or electronic systems we can build under these laws.'

I'm just about to ask a supplementary question when the hands start up again. A few minutes pass before Hawking adds: 'By far the most complex systems we have are our own bodies. There haven't been any significant changes in human DNA in the past 10,000 years. But soon we will be able to increase the complexity of our internal record, our DNA, without having to wait for the slow process of biological evolution. It is likely that we will be able to redesign it completely in the next 1,000 years – by increasing our brain size, for example. Of course, many will say genetic engineering on humans will be banned but I rather doubt that they will be able to prevent it. Genetic engineering on plants and animals will be allowed for economic reasons and someone is bound to try it on humans – unless we have a totalitarian world order, someone will improve humans somewhere.'

'We need to become more complex if biological systems are to keep ahead of electronic ones. At the moment computers have an advantage of speed but they show no sign of intelligence. This is not surprising as our present computers are less complex than the brain of an earthworm, a species not known for its intellectual powers. But computers' speed and complexity double every eighteen months and this will probably continue until computers have a similar complexity to the human brain.'

But will computers ever show true intelligence, whatever that might be? 'It seems to me that if very complicated chemical molecules can operate in humans to make them intelligent, then equally complicated electronic circuits can also make computers act in an intelligent way. And if they are intelligent, they can presumably design computers that have even greater intelligence and complexity.'

'On the biological side, the limit of human intelligence has been set by the size of the human brain that will pass through the birth canal,' Hawking says. 'Having watched my three children being born, I know how difficult it is to get the head out. But in the next 100 years I expect we will learn how to grow babies outside the human body so this limitation will be removed. But ultimately, increases in the size of the human brain through genetic engineering will come up against the problem that the chemical messages responsible for our mental activity are relatively slow-moving – so further increases in the complexity of the brain will be at the expense of speed. We can be quick-witted or very intelligent, but not both.'

It's time to ask the big one: will we make contact with aliens in the next millennium? He smiles. His fingers click the pressure pads. The answer comes seven minutes later. 'Even if life developed in other stellar systems, the chances of catching it at a recognisably human stage are very small. Any alien life we encounter will be much more primitive or much more advanced than us. And if it's more advanced why hasn't it spread through the galaxy and visited Earth? It could be that there is an advanced race out there which is aware of our existence but is leaving us to stew in our own primitive juices. However, I doubt they would be so considerate to a lower life form. Some people believe that the reason we have not been contacted is that when a civilisation reaches our stage of development it becomes unstable and destroys itself. But I'm an optimist. I think we have a good chance of avoiding nuclear war and Armageddon.'

(Adapted from *The Sunday Telegraph*, 2nd January 2000)

5 Work with a partner and answer these questions:

a) Does anything Stephen Hawking says surprise you?

b) Do any of his predictions scare you?

c) What would you like to know about the future? Ask your partner what they think might happen.

Lexis

1 Look at these extracts from the text. Use prepositions to complete the sentences.

a) I've come here ... on *the turn* ____ the millennium to ask him what he thinks the future *has in store* ____ the human race. (lines 1–5)

b) ... there isn't going to be enough room for us all on Earth ____ *the year* 2600. (lines 7–8)

c) ... there will be *no limit* ____ the complexity of biological or electronic systems ... (lines 30–31)

d) ____ *far the most* complex systems we have are our own bodies. (lines 33–34)

e) Genetic engineering on plants and animals will be allowed ____ *economic reasons* ... (lines 42–43)

f) We need to become more complex if biological systems are *to keep ahead* ___ electronic ones. (lines 46–47)

g) ... genetic engineering will *come up* ____ the problem that the chemical messages responsible for our mental activity are relatively slow-moving – so further increases in the complexity of the brain will be ____ *the expense* ____ speed. (lines 72–75)

h) I think we *have a good chance* ____ avoiding nuclear war ... (lines 89–90)

2 Check your answers with the text.

3 Use the expressions in *italics* and the prepositions from 1 to complete these sentences.

a) Younger people who are coming into my company are far more computer-literate than me and it takes a lot of time and energy ____ them in the promotion stakes.

b) There have been few significant changes in my lifestyle since ____ the century.

c) ____ urgent problem facing our cities is the use of private cars.

d) People born in the 21st century will ____ living to be a hundred.

e) Once I've mastered English there'll be ____ the job opportunities that open up for me!

f) I've got exams coming up soon and I know pretty well what the near future ____ me – lots of studying!

g) ____ 2020 more than half of the population will be over 60.

h) Investment in computer technology has been ____ thousands of local jobs.

i) I've been job hunting for quite a long time now and I often ____ the 'no experience, no job' trap which is so hard to get out of.

j) I'm studying English ____ . I'm sure it'll help me get a better job.

4 Compare your answers with a partner. Are any of the sentences true for you or your country?

Close up

Language reference p72

Will for predictions & assumptions

1 Work with a partner. Look at the predictions (1–7), below, that were made in the text and find examples of the following verb patterns:

a) *will* + infinitive
b) *will* + continuous
c) *will* + perfect
d) *will* + simple passive
e) *will* + perfect passive

1 By the end of this century we will have landed a spaceship on Mars.

2 We won't colonise Mars as it is far less hospitable than Earth.

3 In a hundred years' time we will be producing babies outside the womb.

4 We won't be contacted by aliens.

5 Genetic engineering on humans won't be banned this century.

6 By the end of the millennium techniques will have been developed to redesign human DNA.

7 The development of computers will continue until they are more intelligent than humans.

2 What is the difference in the meaning between the five verb forms?

3 Add the adverb *probably* to each of the predictions in 1. What do you notice about the position of *probably*?

4 Complete the following sentences using *will / will be / will have / will have been* and the appropriate form of the verb in brackets.

　　a)　By this time next week I _____ (take) five exams.
　　b)　I _____ (probably not go) to the cinema next week.
　　c)　My dinner _____ (cook) by the time I get home this evening.
　　d)　Things are very busy at work at the moment so I _____ (probably ask) to do some overtime some time over the next week or so.
　　e)　This time tomorrow I _____ (sit) on a plane on my way to New York.
　　f)　I imagine I ____ (probably have) my first child by the time I'm thirty.
　　g)　My suit _____ (probably clean) by now so I can pick it up from the dry-cleaners.

5 Change the sentences so that they are true for you. Compare your sentences with a partner.

6 Read the following assumptions about your English. Are they true for you? Compare your answers with a partner.

Now that you are at an advanced level you'll probably have been studying for quite a number of years. You'll feel fairly confident in being able to put your point across in most situations and won't have any problems talking to native speakers.

However, a native speaker with a strong regional accent will sometimes give you some trouble. You'll have been using cinema and television to give you practice in listening and no doubt you will have bought magazines and newspapers in

English to read in your spare time. You will possibly also have read a few novels or short stories. Maybe you'll have made English speaking penfriends or cyberpals and possibly you will have been invited to spend a holiday with them.

7 Look at the uses of *will* in 6, above. In each case, what time is referred to: past, present, future or a combination of times?

8 Make assumptions and predictions about your partner using the verb phrases and time expressions in the boxes below.

For example:
Maria will probably have had something to eat before coming to class.
She'll probably be tired after a long day.
She probably won't have done her homework.
She'll probably have got married by this time next year.
She'll probably be going on holiday with her parents sometime soon.

Verb phrases

have something to eat　　get married　　pass a driving test　　have children get a new job　　buy a new house　　win a sports competition meet someone famous　　go on holiday　　win the lottery　　make some new friends take an exam　　be tired　　do homework

Time expressions

before coming to class　　as soon as s/he gets home　　sometime soon　　never last summer　　by this time next year　　at some point during her/his life yesterday　　sometime during the last year or so　　after a long day

9 Show your sentences to your partner and see what they think. Were your assumptions correct? Was your partner happy about your predictions?

Language reference: *will* for predictions & assumptions

You can use *will* to show you are making a *prediction*.

(In the future) *Computers **will** be more intelligent than humans.*

You can also use it to make assumptions about the present or even the past.

(In the past) *You **will** have learnt a lot of grammatical structures.*

All the following structures are possible:

will + infinitive

Future: *Genetic engineering **won't be banned** this century.*
Present: *You'll **be** totally confident about using English on the phone by now.*

will + continuous

Future: *We'll all **be working** from home by the end of the next century.*
Present: *You'll either **be reading** this with a partner or studying it at home on your own.*

will + perfect / perfect continuous

Future: *Men **will have been sent** to Mars by the end of the next century.*
Present / past: *You'll **have studied** English for quite a number of years I imagine.*
*You'll **have been studying** in class and at home on your own.*
Past: *You'll **have taken** a holiday in an English speaking country.*

will + probably

Notice the position of *probably* in affirmative and negative sentences; usually after *will* in affirmative sentences but before *won't* in negative sentences.

*They'll **probably** want to stay for dinner.*
*They **probably** won't want to stay for dinner.*

*We'll **probably** be living in space stations.*
*We **probably** won't be living in space stations.*

*He'll **probably** have eaten already.*
*He **probably** won't have eaten already.*

Future worlds

1 Work in small groups. You are going to make predictions about the state of the world at the end of the 21st century. Choose one of the pairs of topics below to discuss in depth.

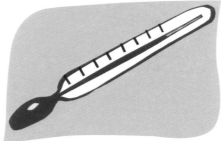

Work and industry

- Will people still be working an average 40 hours a week? If not, will they be working more or less?
- Will the majority of people be working from home? What kind of work will they be able to do from home?
- Will there be more or less unemployment? What new industries will grow and develop?
- Will landlines have become obsolete with everybody using mobile phones or will some other form of communication have taken over?
- What other changes will there be?

Health and society

- Will people be living longer? If yes, how much longer? Will we have found the secret to eternal life?
- Will we have found cures for cancer and other life threatening diseases? What other health problems will have arisen?
- Will society become more violent and dangerous? Will the gap between rich and poor narrow or increase?
- Will people become less sociable? Will it become more difficult to meet new people?
- Will the family unit still exist?
- What other changes will take place?

Leisure time and holidays

- What will people be doing in their free time? Will they have more or less free time?
- Will they still be doing the kinds of leisure activities we do today?
- Will there be new kinds of sports or hobbies?
- Will we be able to go on virtual holidays without leaving our homes?
- Will people continue to travel around the world or will there be purpose-built holiday complexes in each town offering tropical micro-climates and artificial tourist attractions?
- What other changes do you envisage?

2 Choose a secretary who will take notes on your discussion. Discuss the questions for the topics you have chosen.

Structuring the presentation

First of all we'll look at …

Then I'll move on to …

Now I'd like to present …

Now I'd like to explain …

To round up I'll …

Reporting on your discussion

There was some disagreement as regards …

We were pretty much in agreement as far as … was concerned.

We found it difficult to imagine …

We reckoned that …

One thing we felt sure about was …

On the whole we felt that …

On reflection we agreed that …

Playing for time

Now that's a very interesting question …

I'm glad you brought that point up …

I'm glad you asked me that …

3 Prepare to report back to the class on your discussion.

a) Appoint a spokesperson.

b) Help the spokesperson prepare a presentation of your ideas. Read the tips in the box. Can you think of any other useful tips?

giving a presentation

- Give your listeners a brief **outline** of your presentation at the beginning so they know what your main points will be.
- Make brief **notes** on each section. Have the notes for each section on separate cards in front of you. Don't try and read your presentation – use the notes to remind you about the main points only.
- Don't rush. **Pause to think** and gather your thoughts if you need to.
- Let your listeners know when you're moving on to a **new point**.
- Explain that you will be allowing time for **questions** at the end (either at the end of each main point, or at the end of the whole presentation) so that you don't have to deal with interruptions.
- Use the '**playing for time**' phrases from the toolbox if someone asks you a difficult question.

c) Your presentation should cover the following points:
- an introduction of the topics you chose to discuss and an explanation of why you chose these topics
- a brief outline of your discussion and any problems you encountered
- a brief outline of your conclusions
- an opportunity for the discussion to be opened to the floor and questions asked

4 Listen to the other groups reporting on their discussions. Whose vision of the future is

a) most realistic?

b) most optimistic?

c) most pessimistic?

Share your views with the class.

Video games: a new art form?

1 Work in small groups and discuss these questions:

a) Have you got a TV games console?

b) If you have, what games do you play? How many hours a week do you spend playing on it? How long have you had it?

c) If you haven't got one, have you ever used one? Would you like to have one? Why/Why not?

Trigger Happy

Steven Poole's book is an in-depth study of video games. It deals with the history of video games and how they have developed since they first appeared in the early 1970s.

2 📼 **35** You are going to hear an interview with Steven Poole, a journalist who has written a book about video games. Work with a partner and write three or four questions you would like to ask him. Listen to the interview and see if your questions are answered.

3 Work with your partner and discuss these questions:

a) Were your questions answered?
b) What did Steven Poole say about the following topics:
   1 the comparison between video games and cinema
   2 technological developments over the last 30 years or so
   3 the effect that violent games might have on children
   4 women and video games

4 Imagine you are a journalist preparing to write one of the following articles. Listen to the interview again and make notes which you think will be useful when you write the article.

a) Video games: are they polluting our minds?
b) From TV tennis to Tomb Raider: a history of video games
c) Video games – something for everyone?

5 Compare your notes with another student who's going to write the same article as you. Did you note down the same things? Keep your notes as you will need them to help you write your article later.

Close up

Using discourse markers

1 Look at these extracts from the interview. The discourse markers have been taken out of each extract. Put them in the correct place in the text.

a) So why are video games so popular? Well, they combine very fast moving, well-designed graphical images with very interesting sound design and music. (1) _____ they're interactive so the computer system poses you very interesting challenges and difficulties at very high speeds. (2) _____ the video game is a much more challenging and involving art form …

So, in this sense   But crucially

b) The very early video games like *Pong* just took place on one screen. (3) _____ the space in video games started to get larger. And then the big innovation took place in the 90s, which was the invention of full 3D. (4) _____ you started to control characters who explored fully realised, solid 3D environments.

But then   This meant that

c) A lot of people think that playing violent video games might be bad for children but I don't think that's true. (5) _____ , millions of people around the world play these games and the vast majority of them are very peaceful people and never pick up a gun in real life. The violence in video games after all is very crude, cartoon violence. Now, (6) _____ if a slightly disturbed child plays these video games too much, then he might become more violent, (7) _____ that sort of child would become more violent if he watched a film or listened to a heavy metal record …

but then it's true that   after all   it's certainly true that

d) … that's not the case in Japan or America where many more women have become interested in video games. (8) _____ , the idea that video gaming is an anti-social activity is no longer true at all. (9) _____ can you invite your friends round to your home to play a four-player game of *Micro Machines*, you can go to a bar and play games on networked PCs there …

Not only   Also

e) … a lot of people thought films were mindless entertainment (10) _____ we know that cinema is an art form and we have film critics who can analyse films and enhance our enjoyment of them, and I think in the future this will be true of video games (11) _____ .

as well   but now

Language reference p75

'Son, you're just going to have to use your imagination and pretend it's a video game.'

2 36 Compare your answers with a partner. Then listen and check.

3 Look at the discourse markers that were removed from the extracts. Which of them

    a) highlight the difference between two things?
    b) add similar information to what's already been said?
    c) draw conclusions?

4 Put the discourse markers in brackets in the correct position in the sentences.

    a) Video games provide entertainment and the opportunity to make new friends. (also)
    b) Video games are the new films. Far more money is spent on games now than on going to the cinema. (after all)
    c) Most video gamers are men. Most games have been marketed towards them. (but then it's true that)
    d) New technology allows games to have high quality sound and images. It means that the player can interact with the characters and their surroundings. (but crucially)
    e) Video games can be violent and could encourage children to act violently, but they are unlikely to be the only influence on their behaviour. (so, in this sense)

5 Choose discourse markers from the box to complete the text below.

> but now   also   as well   not only   but more importantly   as well as
> but then it's true that   so, in this sense   this means that   after all

WILL COMPUTERS BECOME THE NEW *PLEASURE DOMES?*

Twenty-five years ago we relied mainly on TVs, radios and stereo equipment to provide entertainment in our homes, (1) _____ their place is quickly being taken over by computers. (2) _____ do we use computers to lighten our load at work, increasingly we are using computers for fun (3) _____ . More and more home computers have access to the Internet. (4) _____ we can now access a huge range of leisure facilities in our homes, such as reading newspapers on screen, shopping from home, (5) _____ downloading music and films. Developments in optical fibre cables and DVD videos and CDs mean that we can now download entire albums or feature films onto our computers and soon video players and hi-fis could become totally obsolete.

6 What do you think about the ideas presented in the text?

7 Use at least five of the discourse markers you've studied, and the notes you made from the interview to write your article based on the interview with Steven Poole. Use about 200 words.

Language reference: using discourse markers

Discourse markers are used in both speech and writing to give your ideas a coherent structure and to help your listeners or readers follow what you want to say. You can use them to help explain a number of ideas. Here are some examples.

Contrasting two ideas or things

*Computers are being used for entertainment, **but more importantly** they have educational uses as well.*
*In class Tommy is very well-behaved **but outside school** he can be a little monster.*

Adding similar information

*Did you know that he can play the clarinet **as well**?*
*She's **also** been involved in developing some new computer graphics programs.*

***Not only** do they offer the best visual quality on the market, their sound is probably the best you can get.*

Note: When you use *Not only* in the initial position as above, the verb that follows it needs to be inverted. (See Unit 3, page 29.)

Drawing conclusions

***So, in this sense** video games can be considered to be a new art form.*
***This means that** we can expect to see a whole range of new games appearing on the market.*
***It's true that** more and more people are getting interested in video gaming.*
***After all,** we are living in the computer age.*

Net work

1 Do you use e-mail or the Internet? If you do, what do you use them for? Brainstorm as many uses as possible for both. If you don't, why not?

2 🔲 37 Listen to four people talking about how they use e-mail and the Net. How many uses do they mention from your list? Do they mention any others? Do you identify with any of the speakers?

Lexis **1** The extracts below are taken from the first speaker's answer. Work with a partner and complete the sentences with words associated with computers and the Internet.

a) I kind of start off (1) _____ , looking for something specific. I might want some information on a particular, on a particular subject, but I get carried away, I get diverted, I end up looking at something completely unrelated …

b) … there's some really, really, really, funky shopping (2) _____ . You can pick up all sorts of different things …

c) … I've (3) _____ I think nearly all the, all the kind of sound (4) _____ that you need, so I end up watching film (5) _____ on different products, and getting kind of, well, getting completely carried away.

2 🔲 38 Listen and check your answers.

3 Match your answers to 1 with these definitions.

a) The programmes used to operate a computer.
b) More formally known as *navigating*, this means to visit various sites on the Internet, usually moving from page to page using highlighted links.
c) Places on the Internet where companies or organisations display information about their products.
d) Short extracts, designed to give you a taste of a product and hopefully encourage you to buy it.
e) If you have copied pages or programs from the Internet onto your own computer you have done this.

4 Look at the words and phrases in the box. Would you associate them with e-mail, the Internet or both? If there are any words you don't know, find someone in the class who can explain them to you.

> server   log on   search engine   hyperlink   home page   bookmark
> attachment   graphics   online   inbox   chat room   newsgroup

5 Work with a partner. Choose three of the words from 3 and 4 and write definitions for them. Close your books and exchange your definitions with another pair of students. Can you remember the terms?

6 What role does the computer play in your everyday life? Do you think it will be the same in ten years' time? Discuss your answers with a partner.

Big brother is watching you!

Here is a description of the world's first truly interactive TV programme, *Big Brother*. Read the description and then work with a partner and answer the questions that follow.

BIG BROTHER

'Ten people. Ten weeks. One house.' Big Brother, Gran Hermano, Il Grande Fratello ... probably the world's most successful 'Real Life' TV show. In this 24-hour online soap opera ten contestants are chosen from tens of thousands of hopefuls. They live together for two and a half months in a house completely cut off from the rest of the world, with no access to TV, radio or newspapers and no means of contacting their family and friends. Mobile phones are banned and the contestants' every movement is recorded by dozens of television cameras and microphones placed throughout the house. From the kitchen to the garden. From the bedrooms to the bathroom.

The programme places the people in the house in an interesting, if difficult, position. They must get on together or the ten weeks could turn into a living hell, but they must also compete against each other to win the votes and support of the viewing public. Every week the viewers decide which one of the candidates will be evicted from the house. At the end of the ten weeks there is only one winner. So far, all the winners, and in fact many of the losing contestants, have won themselves a place in the hearts of the viewing public and have gone on to star in their own TV shows, or to be offered modelling or acting contracts. ◉

a) Hundreds of thousands of people applied to take part in the programme. Why do you think they wanted to take part? Would you like to take part in a similar programme?

b) What do you think the contestants miss most from the outside world? What would you miss most?

c) The programme has been watched by millions around the world. What do you think is the secret of its popularity?

Writing

1 Work with a partner. Look at the advert on the right and discuss what you think the producers are looking for in the ideal contestants. Think about personal qualities, practical skills, past experiences and motivation for taking part.

2 You are going to write a letter of application from the ideal candidate. It should be no longer than 200 words and should explain why you think you should be selected.

a) Decide what information you need to include in your letter.

b) Think about the points you discussed in 1 and consider which aspect of the experience is going to be most challenging for you. How will you rise to the challenge?

c) When you have finished writing the first draft, show it to a partner and see if they can help you improve on it.

3 Work in two groups. You are going to look at the applications from the other group and decide on one candidate to go on to the next round of the selection procedure.

a) Before you look at the applications, decide within the group on your selection criteria.

b) Decide which candidate gives the best overall impression.

c) When you have chosen the candidate, prepare to present your choice and to justify your decision.

**TEN PEOPLE
TEN WEEKS
ONE HOUSE
ONE WINNER**

We are making an international version of

BIG BROTHER

with prize money of

£100,000

Are you able to communicate well in English and able to give up to ten weeks of your time to the programme?
If so, send us a letter telling us why you should be picked to be one of the housemates.

Applications to be sent to
Big Brother, PO Box 258, London W1 5JZ

9 Law

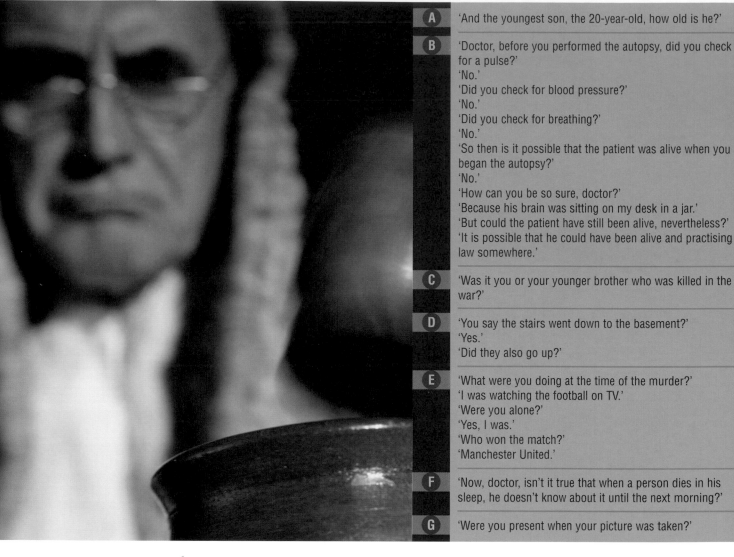

A 'And the youngest son, the 20-year-old, how old is he?'

B 'Doctor, before you performed the autopsy, did you check for a pulse?'
'No.'
'Did you check for blood pressure?'
'No.'
'Did you check for breathing?'
'No.'
'So then is it possible that the patient was alive when you began the autopsy?'
'No.'
'How can you be so sure, doctor?'
'Because his brain was sitting on my desk in a jar.'
'But could the patient have still been alive, nevertheless?'
'It is possible that he could have been alive and practising law somewhere.'

C 'Was it you or your younger brother who was killed in the war?'

D 'You say the stairs went down to the basement?'
'Yes.'
'Did they also go up?'

E 'What were you doing at the time of the murder?'
'I was watching the football on TV.'
'Were you alone?'
'Yes, I was.'
'Who won the match?'
'Manchester United.'

F 'Now, doctor, isn't it true that when a person dies in his sleep, he doesn't know about it until the next morning?'

G 'Were you present when your picture was taken?'

1 Above are some extracts from court cases. In all but one of them a silly question is asked. Which one?

2 Which one did you find the most amusing?

In the courtroom

Lexis **1** The words and phrases in the box are all connected to the theme of law. Work with a partner and put the words under one of the headings below.

| crimes | punishments | people | legal processes |

sue   libel   suspended sentence   jury   the accused   contempt of court
judge   counsel   arson   award damages   community service   manslaughter
weigh up the evidence   fraud   speeding   witness   return a verdict
cross examine   solitary confinement

2 Add another word or phrase to each category.

3 Use words and phrases from 1 to complete these sentences.

a) What's the difference between the two? Well, slander is when you say something about someone which isn't true. ____ is when you publish it, and that's when people generally take action.

b) If a person is on trial for murder the press can't refer to them as 'the murderer'. They have to say '____'.

c) You're guilty of ____ when you didn't kill the victim deliberately.

d) You ____ someone if you want to claim money from them because they have harmed you in some way.

e) The jury has to listen to the case, ____ and then ____ .

f) A ____ means that you don't actually have to go to prison unless you commit another crime.

g) '____' is a more formal term for a legal adviser.

h) ____ can be anything from teaching kids to play football to cutting the grass. Obviously, it's not paid.

4 Choose another three words or phrases from 1 and write three sentences like the ones above. Give them to a partner to complete.

5 🔲 39 Listen to three conversations. Which of the crimes in 1 are the speakers talking about?

Test yourself

Paraphrasing

1 Look at the sentences below. Which of the three conversations from 5, above, do they come from?

a) The verdict we returned was unanimous – guilty.

b) That's a lesson I won't forget in a hurry.

c) The best person to ask is Fred MacIntyre.

d) It was fascinating, seeing how a court works.

e) It's been almost three weeks since they published the article.

2 There is always more than one way of saying something. Paraphrase the sentences in 1 starting with the words given.

a) We …
b) I …
c) Fred MacIntyre …
d) Seeing …
e) They …

3 Compare your answers with a partner. Are there any differences between your sentences?

4 Paraphrase these sentences starting with the words given.

a) A recent court case was held in Wales.
   1 It was …
   2 Wales …

b) In the witness box stood a Welshman who was accused of shoplifting.
   1 A Welshman …
   2 Accused …

c) He was defended by a Welsh lawyer.
   1 Defending …
   2 The lawyer …

d) Towards the end of the trial the lawyer asked the judge if he could speak to the jury in Welsh.
   1 'May I …
   2 The lawyer …

'Mae'r erlynydd yn sais, mae'r cyfreithiwr yn sais, mae'r barnwr yn sais. Ond cymro ydi'r diffynydd, cymro ydw i a cymry ydych chi. Felly cyflawnwch eich dyletswydd.'

e) The judge agreed because he didn't wish to appear biased towards English.
   1 Not wishing …
   2 In order not to …
f) The jury returned a verdict of not guilty.
   1 A verdict …
   2 Not guilty …
g) The judge was puzzled as the defendant was obviously guilty.
   1 What puzzled the judge …
   2 The defendant …
h) The judge didn't speak Welsh so he hadn't understood what the lawyer had said.
   1 Not being able …
   2 As the judge …

The lawyer had said to the jury 'The prosecutor is English, the prosecution counsel is English, the judge is English. But the prisoner is Welsh, I'm Welsh and you're Welsh. Do your duty.'

5 Use the sentences you have written in 4 to write an account of the court case for the 'News in Brief' section of a newspaper. Make any changes or additions that you think are necessary.

6 Compare your story with the one on page 135. What differences are there?

Crime & punishment

1 Put the crimes below in order of seriousness. Decide on the punishment you think a person guilty of each crime should get.

> mugging   swearing in public   kidnapping   drink driving   graffiti
> creating and releasing computer viruses   trespassing   dropping litter

2 Compare your answers with a partner.

3 ▪▪ 40 Nine people were asked what punishment they would give people guilty of the above crimes. Listen and answer these questions:

a) Which crime is each person talking about?
b) Which speaker does *not* refer to one of the crimes above?

4 Listen again and answer these questions:

a) What punishments do the speakers suggest?
b) Which punishments do you agree with? Do you disagree with any of them? Why?

Speaker	Crime	Punishment
1	trespassing	

Discussion **1** Work in small groups and discuss these questions:

a) Do you think punishment is an effective deterrent to crime? If yes, which kind of punishment do you think is most effective? If not, how would you prevent crime?
b) Do you think crime is ever justifiable?

2 Read the cases below and discuss the questions that follow each one.

Case one

A driver swerves to avoid a little girl crossing the road. The driver goes off the road and injures a pedestrian.

Case two

A footballer trips up an opponent deliberately. The opponent breaks a leg and is unable to play football again. He sues the other footballer for a lifetime of lost earnings.

Case three

Bob adds a double vodka rather than a single to Joe's drink. Joe gets into his car and is stopped by the police on the way home. He's breathalysed, found to be over the legal alcohol limit and banned from driving for six months. Joe sues Bob for the money he has to spend on taxis over the next six months.

Case 1
a) What is the driver guilty of, if anything?
b) Who should pay for the pedestrian's medical expenses?
c) Who should pay for the damage done to the car?

Case 2
Should the footballer pay? Why/Why not?

Case 3
Should Bob pay for Joe's taxi expenses? Why/Why not?

Legal wrangles

1 Work with a partner and discuss these questions:

a) Have you ever had anything stolen? If you have, what was it? Did you get it back? Were you insured? Was the thief caught?
b) If you haven't, what would cause you the most inconvenience if it was stolen?

2 ▄▄ 41 Listen to Anne telling Tim about a time she had something stolen. Are the statements below true or false?

a) Her car was stolen by three teenagers who wanted to sell it for cash.
b) Her insurance documents had 'disappeared' from the car.
c) Her insurance didn't cover accidents after theft.
d) She had read the contract carefully before signing it.
e) She thought that the insurers had altered the original insurance document.
f) Her friend finds it difficult to believe the story.
g) Her insurance company paid up in the end.
h) She split up with her boyfriend.

Anne and Tim

Word linking **1** Work with a partner. Look at the phrases below which have been taken from the dialogue. Discuss when the <u>underlined</u> consonants are pronounced and when they are silent.

a) a bran<u>d</u> new car
b) they jus<u>t</u> didn'<u>t</u> wan<u>t</u> to pay up
c) secon<u>d</u> hand
d) Wha<u>t</u> di<u>d</u> you do?
e) I wen<u>t</u> back
f) they sai<u>d</u> i<u>t</u> didn'<u>t</u> matter
g) I was insure<u>d</u> agains<u>t</u> theft
h) I ough<u>t</u> to have done
i) I couldn'<u>t</u> be bothered
j) you coul<u>d</u> have aske<u>d</u> a friend

2 ▄▄ 42 Listen to the recording and check your answers.

3 Look at the questions below. Which final *t* and *d* sounds are silent? Work with a partner and practise reading the questions out loud.

    a) What do you think about the woman in the story?
    b) What would you have done if you'd been her?
    c) Do you read everything you sign?
    d) What was the last thing you signed?
    e) Have you ever had to go to a police station? What for?

4 Discuss your answers to the questions with your partner.

Close up

Using modals to talk about the past

1 Work with a partner. Look at the modal verb phrases in these sentences which have been taken from the conversation. Match them to the functions 1–3 below.

    a) The insurance company wouldn't pay up.
    b) I couldn't believe it when I saw it!
    c) You really should have read it before signing it.
    d) I suppose with hindsight I ought to have done.
    e) Couldn't you have asked your boyfriend to check it over for you?
    f) They're standard forms so I thought I'd be all right.
    g) They might have simply ticked the box themselves to save them having to pay out the equivalent of £8,000.
    h) I reckon they must have taken it from the car, along with all the other documents.
    i) They wouldn't have dared do something like that, surely.
    j) They certainly could have done it if they'd wanted to.
    k) You must have been upset at the time.
    l) They can't have just stolen the documents like that.

    1 reporting speech or thought
    2 speculating/making deductions
    3 commenting/criticising

2 Answer these questions:

    a) What time do all the sentences refer to?
    b) Which modal verbs are used in the three types of sentences?
    c) What form of the verb follows the modals in the three types of sentences?

Language reference p83

3 Look at the sentences below. In two of them the modal verb is being used incorrectly. Correct the sentences which are wrong.

    a) Anne mustn't have been very happy when she found her car had been stolen.
    b) Her boyfriend must have worked hard to win the case.
    c) The boys can't have known how to drive very well.
    d) Anne can have made a mistake about the insurance company.

4 Rewrite these sentences using an appropriate modal verb phrase.

For example:
I believe they stole the documents.
They must have stolen the documents.

    a) It's possible that they changed the original contract.
    b) You were a bit silly signing a contract without reading it first.
    c) I think it's possible that you're wrong.
    d) The garage owner had the opportunity to take the documents.
    e) The boys' parents refused to take any responsibility for their actions.

5 Use the words and phrases below to make three sentences which are true for you or people you know. Discuss your sentences with a partner.

should have	could have been	may	ought to	wouldn't	must have been

Language reference: using modals to talk about the past

Here are some of the ways you can use modals to talk about the past.

To report speech or thought

The modals typically used for reporting speech or thought are *would* (to report *will*) and *could* (to report *can*).

'We'll take care of things for you,' they said.
They promised they**'d take** care of things for us.

'I'll have finished the work by the end of the day,' he promised.
He promised that he **would have finished** the work by the end of the day.

'This time next week I'll be lying on a tropical beach,' I thought.
I thought **I'd be lying** on a tropical beach this time next week.

'You can come with us, there's plenty of room in the car,' she said.
She said that I **could go** with them as there was plenty of room in the car.

To speculate or make deductions

The modals typically used for speculating and making deductions are *would, could, might, must* and *can't*.

When they are used to talk about the past you use them with the perfect form of the verb.

*Surely they'**d have said** something to you before now.*
*They **couldn't have done** it, because there wasn't time.*
*It **might** just **have been** an honest mistake.*
*They **must have been** really worried about him to have called the police.*
*He **can't have known** about the appointment, it's not like him to be late.*

When you speculate or make deductions about the past, you can only use *must* in affirmative sentences, and *can* in negative sentences.

To comment or criticise

The modals typically used for commenting and criticising are *could, should* and *ought to*. When you use them to talk about the past they are used with a perfect verb form.

*You really **shouldn't have left** without apologising, you know.*
*They **could have told** us they were going to be so late; we were really worried.*
*I know I **ought to have had** the car serviced sooner.*

Law

Collocations

1 Look at the expressions in the box below. Which means …

a) suspected of having committed a crime?
b) she doesn't follow rules?
c) we are all equal in the eyes of the law?
d) take revenge without using the legal system?
e) bossing people about?
f) What I say must be respected?
g) illegal?
h) obeying and respecting the law?
i) legally?

'I'm in for forgery.'

> a law unto herself   laying down the law   against the law
> take the law into my own hands   no-one is above the law   by law
> in trouble with the law   law-abiding   my word is law

2 Complete these sentences with the expressions in 1.

a) After years as a _____ citizen, John decided to rob a bank and flee the country.
b) Policeman: You were doing 160 kilometres per hour.
   Prince: Yes, but do you know who I am?
   Policeman: Yes, but _____ .
c) There was a constable here earlier. I think Mark's _____ again!
d) I was tempted to _____ and wring his neck.
e) 'Do this! Do that! Be back by 10!' My father was always _____ .
f) You can never tell what Ruth's going to do. She's _____ .
g) I'm the boss and _____ .
h) Most Europeans are required _____ to carry ID cards.
i) In some countries it's _____ to chew gum.

Discussion

1 Work in small groups and discuss these questions:

a) Why do people take the law into their own hands?

b) Which laws are most often broken in your country?

2 Look at the proposals for laws below. Discuss with your group which would affect you personally. Which of these laws would make the world a better place?

a) No-one should work more than a 32-hour week.

b) Shops should all be open 24 hours a day.

c) Cars should be banned from city centres.

d) The dropping of chewing gum should be forbidden.

e) Mobile phones should not be used in public areas.

3 Compare the outcome of your discussion with other groups.

4 Are there any laws in your country that you would like to change or introduce?

Legal anecdotes

1 Read the anecdote below and decide which is the best title for it.

a) It pays to do your homework   b) Honesty is the best policy   c) Crime doesn't pay

A prominent Canberra barrister, Ian Byrne, appeared for an Italian who was seeking worker's compensation for an injury which he claimed he received at work.

It was alleged on his behalf that he had difficulty in moving, bending and even walking. He could not lift any heavy article, nor could he indulge in his hobbies of gardening and tennis. So severe was the injury that he was practically housebound.

Prior to the trial the respondent insurance company engaged a loss assessor to follow the applicant Italian, photograph him when he was unaware, and report with a view to giving evidence at the trial.

Eventually the application came on for hearing. Ian Byrne put his client (whom I shall call Bruno) in the witness box. He told his story of pain and suffering. He showed that he had severe limitation of movement and could not bend or carry weights because of his unfortunate injury.

At the end of his examination Ian Byrne's opponent, a somewhat inexperienced Counsel, sprang to his feet, enthusiasm gleaming in his eyes, and said 'Your Worship, I have here nearly 350 metres of film which shows this man Bruno bricklaying, lifting weights, concreting, vaulting a fence, working on his own house and even running. I would ask leave of Your Worship to run the film before I begin to cross-examine the applicant.'

The film was then run. It showed the applicant running, making a brick wall, carrying wheelbarrow loads of bricks, picking up slabs of concrete, climbing up and down ladders, digging in the garden and running behind a lawnmower. Further, it depicted the applicant's home and his small truck with his name clearly marked on the door, and also showed him wearing a red cardigan which he was wearing in the witness box. At the finish of the screening the enthusiastic Counsel for the insurance company commenced his cross-examination.

'You saw that film?'

'Yes,' said Bruno.

'There is nothing wrong with your back at all, is there?'

'Yes,' said Bruno. 'Everything that I said before is true. That was not me in the picture. That was my brother.'

'But,' exploded Counsel. 'That was your house, wasn't it?'

'Yeah,' said Bruno.

'And the same cardigan you've got on today is the one shown in the film?'

'Yeah,' said Bruno, 'I lent it to my brother. He is very good to me. He helps me round the house, he paints, he cements the paths, he mows the lawns.'

'But,' said learned Counsel, 'His Worship has seen the film and he knows it is you.'

'It is not me. It's my brother.'

In due course Ian Byrne called the brother, and when he walked into Court it was obvious to all that he was the identical twin of the applicant; and after a few questions it was obvious that he was the one in the film doing all the physical acts.

The angry Counsel for the defendant had the applicant recalled and said to him, 'You have tried to deceive the Court. You and your brother knew he was being photographed.'

'Yes,' said the applicant, 'we thought it was funny.' ■

(From *The Oxford Book Of Legal Anecdotes*)

2 Work with a partner and answer these questions:

a) Why was Bruno in court?

b) Why was he photographed?

c) What didn't the lawyer who was representing the insurance company know?

d) How do you think he felt when Bruno's brother walked into the courtroom?

1 The anecdote contains a lot of formal vocabulary. Look back at the text and find more formal words or phrases with these meanings.

a) well-known (column 1)
b) asking for (column 1)
c) before (column 1)
d) employed (column 1)
e) very bad (column 1)
f) in addition (column 2)
g) showed (column 2)
h) started (column 2)
i) later (column 3)
j) to trick (column 3)

Broadsheets

Large format newspapers which are generally aimed at the 'educated classes'. News is reported in a formal style and there are fewer photographs than would normally be found in a **tabloid**. The items reported are generally of a serious nature and cover issues of national and global interest. Examples of British broadsheets include *The Times*, *The Independent* and *The Guardian*.

Tabloids

Newspapers which contain bold headlines and large photographs. The page size is half that of a **broadsheet**. The writing style is informal; sentences are short and dramatic vocabulary is used to grab the reader's attention, especially in the headlines. Tabloids often contain horoscopes, stories about celebrities and problem pages. Stories tend to be of more national than global interest. British tabloids include *The Sun*, *The Mirror* and *The News of the World*.

2 Look at the information about tabloid and broadsheet newspapers on the left. Decide which of the newspaper extracts below are from

a) a tabloid newspaper.
b) a broadsheet newspaper.

3 Complete the extracts using the correct form of the words and phrases in 1. Decide whether to use the formal words or the more informal ones.

A

Martin Smith in court yesterday

THUG BEHIND BARS

THUG MARTIN SMITH, who has a reputation for starting fights in nightclubs, was thrown into jail yesterday for a four year stretch after smashing the nose of a (1) ____ footballer. The attack was so violent that soccer superstar Pete Thirsk needed 24 stitches.

The judge heard how Smith (2) ____ a punch up with Thirsk after a night out on the town in June. …

B

Martine Moon murdered

MARTINE MOON, internationally renowned star of film and stage, was found dead in her New York apartment last night. Sources report that the actress was found with (3) ____ injuries to her head and body. So malicious was the attack, it is reported that police who found the body were unable to identify it immediately as that of the actress. A murder investigation is underway.

Miss Moon, who had recently been (4) ____ to star in a new Hollywood blockbuster, is reported to have been found surrounded by photographs (5) ____ her with a number of male co-stars. Such was the attention she received from admirers around the world, it is thought that jealousy is the motive behind the murder. …

Martine Moon

C

Tears and anger as groom disappears

'He (6) ____ me,' sobbed Tracey Smith on what should have been the happiest day of her life. 'He told me he loved me. How could he have done this?' Only days (7) ____ the couple's wedding day Tracey's fiancé, Tony Briggs, disappeared with all the money in their joint bank account, his passport and the tickets for their honeymoon in Jamaica …

D

MORE FUNDS FOR MARS PROJECT

The government has been approached by the National Space Agency for additional funds for the Mars exploration project. It is reported that the Agency has neither been able to complete the construction of the craft which will be sent to the planet, nor has it been able to recruit suitable candidates to man it. (8) ____ , it is reported that the mission is running five years behind schedule.

Dr Philip Carr, spokesman for the project, will attend a meeting with ministers today, (9) ____ an additional £10 million, which will come mainly from the tax payer. Ministers will consider the application and announce their decision (10) ____ . A result is expected within the next week.

A government spokesman said last night …

Writing

1 Work with a partner. Choose one of the stories on page 85 to finish. Make sure you use a style of writing appropriate to either a broadsheet or a tabloid newspaper.

2 Look back at the courtroom anecdote on page 84. Rewrite the text as a story for a tabloid newspaper. Think carefully about style and lexis.

Close up

Inversion after *neither / nor, so & such*

Language reference p86

1 Look at these sentences from the newspaper reports on page 85. What do you notice about the position of the verb and the subject after *nor, so* (+ adj) and *such*?

A So malicious was the attack, it is reported that police who found the body were unable to identify it immediately as that of the actress.

B Such was the attention she received from admirers around the world, it is thought that jealousy is the motive behind the murder.

C It is reported that the Agency has neither been able to complete the construction of the craft which will be sent to the planet, nor has it been able to recruit suitable candidates to man it.

2 The sentences in 1 are all from broadsheet stories. Rewrite them as they would appear in a tabloid.

3 Match the first half of the sentences on the left with the endings on the right.

A	The north of the country doesn't have theatres	1	but he *is* very popular.
B	The government is so determined to stop young people smoking	2	that the jury failed to reach a verdict.
		3	that they have recommended the company to all their colleagues.
C	He isn't young and he isn't good looking either		
D	They were so happy with the results	4	and it doesn't have opera houses.
E	There was such an outcry over the new proposals	5	that it has banned tobacco advertising.
F	There was such confusion over who was telling the truth	6	that the government is having to reconsider its plans.

4 Rewrite the sentences using inversions. Make any other changes that are necessary.

5 Think about stories that are in the news at the moment. Write sentences about them using *so, such* and *neither/nor*.

6 Work in small groups and discuss your sentences.

Language reference: inversion after *neither / nor, so & such*

When *neither* or *nor* are used to add a further negative comment to a sentence you invert the subject and the verb:
*They weren't hungry and **nor were they** thirsty.*
*He wasn't seeking recognition and **neither did he** appreciate it when it came.*

When *so* or *such* are used at the beginning of a sentence you must invert the subject and verb:
*So disgusted **was he** by the service, he decided to complain to the manager.*
*So excited **was she** by the idea of winning a car, she spent all her money on tickets.*
Such was the weather, that even the most daring windsurfers stayed at home.

Such was his skill, even the most experienced lawyers feared him.

Note: You tend to use these structures in formal contexts and they are more usually found in writing than in speech.

You also invert the subject and the verb when *so, neither* or *nor* are used at the beginning of a short answer to show agreement or disagreement:
I hate that first day back at work after the holidays.
So do I!

I don't really understand why people complain so much about the heat.
Neither do I.

Love in the first degree

Bananarama

Bananarama formed in 1981. Their hits include **Love In The First Degree, Robert De Niro's Waiting** and **Venus.**

1 Complete the song using the words and phrases in the box. You need to use some of them more than once.

> thrown away the key   locked in a prison cell   guilty   put the blame on me
> stand accused of   hear my plea   the judge and the jury   set me free

LOVE IN THE *first* DEGREE

Last night I was dreaming I was ____
When I woke up I was screaming, calling out your name
Whoa, and ____
They all ____
They wouldn't go for my story
They wouldn't ____

Chorus:
Only you can ____
'Cos I'm ____
____ as a girl can be
Come on baby can't you see
I ____ love in the first degree

____
Of love in the first degree

Someday I believe it, you will come to my rescue
Unchain my heart you're keeping and let me start anew
The hours pass so slowly
Since they've ____
Can't you see that I'm lonely
Won't you help me please

Chorus

____ of love, ____ of love in
____ of love, ____ of love in
____ , of love in the first degree
And ____ , they all ____
They wouldn't go for my story
They wouldn't ____

2 📼 43 Listen and check your answers.

3 The song compares being in love to being in prison. Finish these sentences in an appropriate way.

a) Love is like a battlefield …   b) Life is like the sea …   c) Money is like …

4 Write another comparison of your own.

10 *Firsts*

1 Match the first half of these quotations on the left with the second half on the right.

a) Winning isn't everything,
b) Be content with your lot,
c) If at first you don't succeed,
d) If at first you don't succeed,
e) If at first you do succeed,
f) It's not the winning that's important,

1 try to hide your astonishment. (Harry F. Banks)
2 try, try again. (William Edward Hickson)
3 it's the taking part. (Anonymous)
4 it's the only thing. (Vince Lombardi)
5 one cannot be first in everything. (Aesop)
6 then cheat. (Anonymous: graffiti)

2 Which of the quotations

a) would you adopt as your motto?
b) offers the best advice?

It's not the winning ...

1 You're going to read a newspaper article about the first of a new type of motor race. Before you read it, discuss these questions with a partner:

a) What's the longest distance you've ever travelled by car?
b) Would you like to take part in a motor race? Why/Why not?

2 Read the article and find four differences between this rally and other more famous modern motor events.

AN ADVENTURE DRIVE FOR MR AND MRS *AVERAGE*

The World Cup Rally: a familiar name but a totally new concept. This adventure rally will take drivers from London to the Himalayas and back, but with a new twist. For the first time, ordinary members of the driving public can take part in an international motor rally. In fact, this race is open exclusively to amateur drivers of normal, mass production family saloons, who will not be financed by multi-million pound
5 sponsorship deals but will be paying their own way.

The idea was first proposed by Roger King, the chairman of the Society of Motor Manufacturers. The Society was worried that modern motorsports were no longer fulfilling one of their prime functions. They just weren't selling cars out of the showrooms as they used to. Something needed to be done. All the high profile car events were either for high-tech cars which had never been designed to go anywhere near a road in the first place, or for priceless vintage cars, way outside the reach of ordinary pockets, whereas the focus needed to be shifted
10 back on to the ordinary, everyday cars in the showrooms. It was decided that it was high time these ordinary production cars were brought back into the limelight with an event where ordinary motorists could fulfil the dream of a lifetime without being put off by the cost.

Famous motor events such as the Formula One championship or the Paris–Dakar rally are followed by millions of potential car buyers world wide, but their ardent fans would never consider buying the vehicles they support. If an equally interesting, high profile race could focus their attention on normal, family cars, surely this would boost sales. And what about designing an event which they could actually take part in if they
15 wanted? And so the World Cup came into being: a competition for the sort of ordinary cars that normal people drive on an everyday basis, a competition that could fire the imagination of all those armchair rally drivers and who knows, maybe tempt some of them out of their living rooms and on to the road. The rally will take participants down the old silk route to India, via the Golden Temple in Amritsar and up along a stunning, though challenging, route through the Himalayas before driving back again to London. The whole competition will be run against the clock, with the team who succeeds in completing the route in the shortest time winning.
20 The competition revives the name and spirit of the classic World Cup rallies of the nineteen-seventies, with long distance international routes over rough terrain. However, in those days the cars were not driven by ordinary drivers. The newly revived World Cup will take the rally an important step further. Whereas the drivers in the original World Cup rallies were professional rally drivers, in the new World Cup Rally, for the first time, the entrants will be ordinary car drivers, competing in their own cars and without the help of highly-skilled mechanics and the millions of pounds of high-tech sponsorship which nowadays accompanies all professional rally driving teams.
25 In all other aspects however, the rally will follow the traditions of the original World Cup rallies. The rally will start in London and follow a route across the mountains of Greece to Istanbul. From there they will drive across Iran, Pakistan and into India, where they will drive up into the Himalayas before turning round and driving all the way back to London and the Motor Show at Earls Court, where the winning cars will be put on display.
The drivers will be driving standard production cars with engines no bigger than 1.4 litres for petrol cars and 1.7 litres for diesel cars (there
30 are more than 60 different models in these two categories on sale in Britain alone) and will be accompanied by a navigator. The precise details of the route will be kept a secret and the teams will be told where they are going and which route to follow day-by-day. It is expected that a number of family teams will be taking part. For a once in a lifetime experience the cost is by no means prohibitive: £4,750. Surely that's enough to tempt anyone to take part?

3 Work with a partner and discuss these questions:

a) How many people are needed for each team?
b) What are the aims of the rally?
c) What is the aim of the article?
d) Why hasn't the average person been able to take part in this type of sport up to now?
e) Would you like to take part in this rally? Why/Why not?

Lexis **1** Match the two halves of the phrases below without looking back at the text.

a)	mass	1	the clock
b)	multi-	2	in a lifetime
c)	high	3	fans
d)	against	4	million
e)	once	5	details
f)	precise	6	production
g)	ardent	7	rally driver
h)	armchair	8	profile

2 Complete these sentences with the phrases in 1.

a) _____ of football will follow their team around the world.
b) My dad's an _____ . He never misses an event if it's on TV.
c) _____ sportsmen have a duty to show their countries in a positive light.
d) Taking part in a world-recognised event would be a _____ experience.
e) The _____ of cars means they are not usually equipped for rally driving.
f) International sports events are frequently backed by _____ pound sponsorship deals.
g) Many sportsmen train by racing _____ .
h) A marathon runner must know the _____ of the course before setting off.

3 Work with a partner and discuss these questions:

a) Do you know any ardent sports fans?
b) Have you had a once in a lifetime experience?
c) Do you enjoy working or playing sports against the clock, or does it cause too much stress?
d) Multi-million pound sponsorship deals are changing the nature of modern sports. Do you agree?

Close up

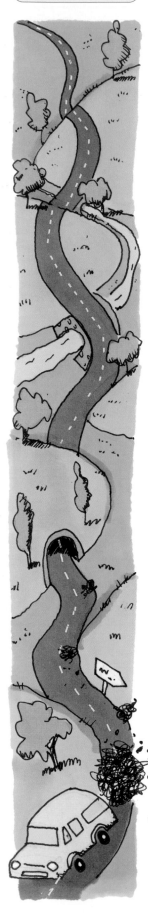

Contrast

Language reference p91

1 Look at the extracts below which have been taken from the text. In each one the new World Cup Rally is being contrasted with its predecessor.

a) What specific characteristics are being contrasted each time?
b) Underline the discourse marker of contrast in each sentence.

A The World Cup Rally: a familiar name but a totally new concept.
B … this race is open to … amateur drivers … who will not be financed by multi-million pound sponsorship deals but will be paying their own way.
C All the high profile car events were either for high-tech cars … or for priceless vintage cars, way outside the reach of ordinary pockets, whereas the focus needed to be shifted back on to the ordinary, everyday cars in the showrooms.
D However, in those days, the cars were not driven by ordinary drivers.
E Whereas the drivers in the original World Cup rallies were professional rally drivers, in the new World Cup Rally, for the first time, the entrants will be ordinary car drivers …
F In all other aspects however, the rally will follow the traditions of the original World Cup rallies.

2 Complete these sentences using *but, whereas* and *however*. In some sentences more than one answer is possible.

a) The drivers in the original World Cup rallies were professional rally drivers. ____ , in the new World Cup Rally, for the first time, the entrants will be ordinary car drivers.
b) The drivers in the original World Cup rallies were professional rally drivers ____ in the new World Cup Rally, for the first time, the entrants will be ordinary car drivers.
c) ____ the drivers in the original World Cup rallies were professional rally drivers, in the new World Cup Rally, for the first time, the entrants will be ordinary car drivers.
d) The drivers in the original World Cup rallies were professional rally drivers. For the first time, the entrants in the new World Cup Rally, ____ , will be ordinary car drivers.
e) The drivers in the original World Cup rallies were professional rally drivers, ____ , in the new World Cup Rally, for the first time, the entrants will be ordinary car drivers.

3 Look back at the sentences in 2. Use *but, whereas* or *however* to complete these rules.

a) ____ is always followed by a comma.
b) ____ can be used to start a sentence which contains two contrasting ideas, or in the mid position of a sentence.
c) ____ and ____ can be used to link two contrasting ideas within a sentence or to introduce a contrasting idea at the beginning of a new sentence.
d) ____ can be used after the subject of the second contrasting clause. ____ and ____ cannot be used in this position.

4 Complete these sentences using *but, whereas* or *however*.

a) I've never been very good at competitive sports. My brother, ____ , is great at them; he's won loads of prizes.
b) I think jogging can be very boring ____ I do it because it's a great form of exercise.
c) I know that swimming is very good for you too. ____ , I find it extremely tedious.
d) ____ individual sports can be a bit competitive, I think team sports are more fun.
e) The scariest sport I've ever done was white water rafting. I was absolutely terrified ____ I'm glad I did it.
f) I love watching football live at the ground, ____ I prefer to watch athletics on TV.

5 Change the sentences above so that they are true for you. Discuss them with a partner.

Language reference: contrast

You can use the discourse markers *but, however* and *whereas* to contrast two ideas.

But

You can use *but* to link two contrasting ideas within a sentence. When used like this it is used in a mid position.
*I like playing golf **but** I hate watching it on TV.*

You can also use *but* to introduce a contrasting idea at the beginning of a new sentence. This use is more common in informal language.
*Golf's a fun pastime and is a great way of spending some time outdoors. **But** watching it on TV can be really tedious.*

In both cases, *but* is being used **between** the two contrasting ideas.

However

You can also use *however* to link contrasting ideas.
*I'm really bad at remembering names sometimes. **However**, I hardly ever forget a face.*

The main difference between the use of *but* and *however* is that *however* is always followed by a comma and *but* is more informal.

You can also use *however* after the subject of the second contrasting clause.
*I never used to come first in anything at school. My brother, **however**, seemed to be constantly winning prizes and competitions.*
In this case *however* cannot be substituted with *but*.

Whereas

You can use *whereas* either at the beginning or in the middle of a sentence which contains two contrasting ideas.
***Whereas** most people prefer to work a 9 to 5 day, I prefer to have a more flexible timetable.*

*Most people prefer to work a 9 to 5 day, **whereas** I prefer to have a more flexible timetable.*

Notice that *whereas*, in contrast with *but* and *however*, can introduce either the first or the second of two contrasting ideas.

Firsts

Collocations

1 Match the expressions on the left with the meanings on the right.

a)	at first	1	excellent
b)	first and foremost	2	the opening performance of a play
c)	first lady	3	basic medical treatment
d)	from first to last	4	early morning
e)	first aid	5	mother tongue
f)	first class	6	at the beginning
g)	first-hand	7	more than anything else
h)	first language	8	the wife of a president
i)	first light	9	from beginning to end
j)	first night	10	information or experience gained directly

2 Use expressions with *first* from 1 to complete these sentences.

a) Have you got a ____ box at home, in case of accidents?
b) Have you ever been to a ____ at the theatre?
c) Do you know anyone who's as fluent in English as they are in their ____ ?
d) Where's the best place to have a ____ meal in your town?
e) Would you rather read about other countries and cultures in books, or experience them ____ ?
f) Can you name the ____ of the United States of America?

3 Work with a partner. Choose three or four of the questions in 2 to ask and answer.

4 Look back at the expressions in 1. In which of them can the word *first* be replaced with *second*? How does the meaning change?

5 Do you know any other expressions with *first* or *second*?

Great firsts

1 Read an account of one of Reinhold Messner's great climbs and answer these questions.

a) What 'first' was he hoping to achieve?
b) Why did he face opposition from the mountaineering world?
c) What mental and physical hardships did the climbers experience towards the end of the climb?

First Without Oxygen

Climbing Mount Everest, the tallest mountain in the world, was a challenge that eluded scores of great mountaineers until 1953, when Sir Edmund Hillary and Tenzing Norgay first reached its summit. Over the next three decades, more 'firsts' followed, including the first ascent by a woman, the first solo ascent, the first traverse (up one side of the mountain and down the other) and the first descent on skis. But all of these climbers had relied on bottled oxygen to achieve their high-altitude feats. Could Everest be conquered without it?

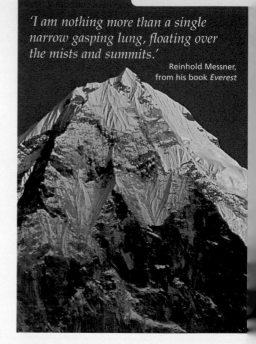

'I am nothing more than a single narrow gasping lung, floating over the mists and summits.'

Reinhold Messner, from his book *Everest*

As early as the 1920s, mountain climbers debated the pros and cons of artificial aids. One, George Leigh Mallory, argued that 'the climber does best to rely on his natural abilities, which warn him whether he is overstepping the bounds of his strength. With artificial aids, he exposes himself to the possibility of sudden collapse if the apparatus fails.' The philosophy that nothing should come between a climber and his mountain continued to have supporters fifty years later when in 1978 Reinhold Messner and Peter Habeler decided to attempt the ascent – without bottled oxygen.

Messner and Habeler quickly found themselves the subject of criticism by members of both the climbing and medical communities. They were labelled 'lunatics', who were placing themselves at risk of severe brain damage. The physiological demands of climbing Everest had been studied on previous expeditions, and found to be extreme.

Despite the controversy, Messner and Habeler continued with their plan. On May 6, Messner and Habeler set out. They reached Camp III (7,200 metres) easily and felt ready to move on to the South Col the next day. They were now reaching altitudes where they could expect to feel the effects of oxygen deprivation. Messner and Habeler had agreed on carrying two oxygen cylinders to Camp IV, in case of an emergency, and had also made a pact to turn back if either person lost his coordination or speech.

The next day, it took them only three and a half hours to reach the South Col (7,986 metres), where they camped for the afternoon and evening. At 3am on May 8, the two woke and began preparing for the day's attempt on the summit. Simply getting dressed took them two hours. Since every breath was now precious, the pair began using hand signals to communicate. Progress was slow. Trekking through the deep snow was exhausting, so they were forced to climb the more challenging rock ridges. Messner and Habeler now faced exhaustion unlike any they'd encountered before. Every few steps, they leaned on their ice axes and gasped for breath. Messner described feeling as though he were going to 'burst apart'.

Upon reaching the South Summit, the pair roped themselves together and pressed on. The wind battered them about, but they saw a break in the sky and were hopeful that the weather would improve. They had 88.12 vertical metres to go. Messner described a feeling of apathy mingled with defiance. He testified into his tape recorder that, 'breathing becomes such a serious business we scarcely have strength to go on.' He described feeling like his mind was dead – and that it was only his soul that compelled him to crawl forward.

Sometime between one and two in the afternoon on May 8, 1978, Messner and Habeler achieved what was believed to be impossible – the first ascent of Everest without oxygen. Messner described his feeling: 'In my state of spiritual abstraction, I no longer belong to myself and to my eyesight. I am nothing more than a single narrow gasping lung, floating over the mists and summits.'

David and Sue

2 Work in small groups and discuss these questions:

a) The two climbers suffered a lot of physical hardship to make the ascent. What do you think made them do it?
b) What is it that drives people to take on extreme physical challenges?

3 🔊 44 Listen to David and Sue discussing a psychological study on the topic. As you listen, answer the questions below.

a) What does the study suggest?
b) What other reasons are mentioned for people taking up mountaineering?

4 Compare your answers with a partner. Did the speakers mention any of the points you raised in your discussion in 2?

Lexis

1 Look at this extract from the conversation. Complete the sentences with appropriate words or phrases.

David   Mmm, and then there's the danger element too. I can kind of understand the (1) _____ of seeing how far you can (2) _____ , you know, (3) _____ and all that, but not to the point of (4) _____ .

Sue   Yeah, I reckon they must be really (5) _____ by something, a need to (6) _____ themselves, a need to (7) _____ something really special. I don't think that's necessarily negative, I mean we wouldn't make any (8) _____ at all, would we, if we didn't try to do the impossible …

2 ▭ 45 Listen and check your answers.

3 Complete the sentences below with words and phrases from 1. Make any changes that are necessary.

   a) In order to succeed in any sport at an international level you need to be _____ by the desire to be the best.
   b) Extreme sports allow people to _____ . If they want to risk their lives like that it's up to them.
   c) You'll only make _____ in your life if you continually test yourself against others.
   d) I don't really enjoy facing up to physical _____ . They scare me.

4 Do you agree with the sentences in 3? Discuss your answers with a partner.

5 Look at the list of great human achievements below and discuss the questions with a partner.

   - Reaching the North Pole
   - Crossing the Antarctic on foot
   - Swimming the Atlantic
   - Circumnavigating the globe in a hot air balloon
   - Apnoea diving (without oxygen) to 150m
   - Pot-holing in uncharted caves and passages
   - Sailing single-handed around the world

   a) Which do you think would be the most difficult?
   b) Which do you think would be the most dangerous?
   c) Which, if any, appeal to you?
   d) What's the greatest challenge you've faced? It may or may not have been a physical challenge.

Apnoea diving

Word stress

1 Look at the words below and underline the main stress. The first one has been done for you.

   a) <u>al</u>titude   f) achievement
   b) coordination   g) apparatus
   c) exciting   h) mountaineers
   d) challenge   i) circumnavigate
   e) emergency   j) ascent

2 ▭ 46 Listen and check your answers.

3 Work with a partner.
   Student A turn to page 137.
   Student B turn to page 139.

Pot-holing

First prize

1 ▶ 47 Listen to three conversations and match them to the pictures.

2 In which conversation are the speakers talking about

    a) coming first?
    b) doing something for the first time?

Lexis   **1** Choose the correct word to complete these expressions from the conversations.

    a) When I was a child I got my pocket money on Saturdays and I had to *eke it out / through / up* all week.
    b) Last year I *plucked out / up / down the courage* to go travelling on my own.
    c) The first thing that *springs of / to / from mind* when I think of holidays is a sandy beach.
    d) I *asked* my first girlfriend *in / around / out* when we were in the school playground!
    e) I used to *run off / in / around* everywhere in bare feet when I was young.
    f) I like to be *picked off / in / up* at the airport whenever I've been away.
    g) My parents are never at home; they're always *on / off / at* somewhere.

2 Work with a partner. Discuss the meanings of the expressions in *italics*.

3 Are any of the sentences in 1 true for you?

Close up

Patterns with   **1** Look at these sentences from the third conversation. In which sentence could *get* be
get   replaced with

    a) received?
    b) ask?
    c) were?

    1 I had to get my dad to drive me out …
    2 At the end of the night we got picked up and taken home …
    3 That's when I got my first kiss.

2 Look at these sentences. Replace *get* with one of the words in the box.

> became   was   manage   ask   have   received

(Language reference p95)

    a) I hardly ever get to go to the cinema these days.
    b) I usually get my mum to do my washing for me.
    c) The film was a bit boring to start with but then it got really exciting towards the end.
    d) I got a nasty letter from my bank manager this morning.
    e) I must get my holiday photos developed before I forget!
    f) He was really pleased when he got chosen to be the captain.

3 Look at these sentences containing *get* and rephrase them.

For example:
The problem's not too serious. We'll get it working for you by this time tomorrow.
The problem's not too serious. We'll solve it and it'll be working for you by this time tomorrow.

a) He's a great instructor, so patient. He's the one who got me skiing again after the accident.
b) I don't know if I'm going to get to finish this report before we go out.
c) Come on! It's about time we got going on this new design, isn't it?
d) Let's get painting, otherwise we won't finish before dark.
e) I got everyone listening to the band's new album and now they've all bought it!

4 Rewrite these sentences using *get*. You may have to make some changes to the sentence structure.

a) I had the chance to go abroad for the first time when I was ten.
b) I was hopeless at sports when I was at primary school; I never used to be chosen for any of the teams.
c) I convinced my brother to do my homework for me when I was younger.
d) At this time of year busloads of tourists visit our town.
e) We're having a few problems with our car; it's really difficult to start it in the mornings.
f) I saw a great film last week – it really made me think.
g) I always start to feel really nervous the night before an exam.
h) I usually have my hair cut once a month.
i) It's so hot at the moment, I'm finding it really difficult to fall asleep at night.
j) I'm quite shy when I first meet someone but once we start to talk, I'm fine.

'That reminds me – the strap broke on ours. I must get it repaired.'

5 Are any of the sentences you wrote true for you?

Language reference: patterns with *get*

You can use *get* in many different ways.

Become

When you use *get* with an adjective it means *to become*:
*Things started to **get exciting** towards the end.*

Obtain

When you use *get* with a noun it means *to obtain* or *receive*:
*I **got my degree** last summer.*

Succeed

Get + to-infinitive means *to succeed in doing something* or *to have the chance or opportunity to do something*:
*I finally **got to see** the Grand Canyon last year.*
*Apparently you can **get to be** a politician without qualifications these days.*

Start

Get + -ing means *to start doing something*:
*Let's **get going** then, or we'll be late.*

Persuade/cause

Get + object + to-infinitive means *to ask* or *persuade someone to do something*:

*She **got her brother to decorate** her flat for her.*

When you want to focus on the *activity* rather than the *result*, use *get* + object + *-ing*.
*After a long time and a lot of effort I finally **got them singing** in unison.*
*We promise we'll **get your computer system running** perfectly by this time tomorrow.*

You can also use *have* in this structure. (See Unit 12)

Get passive

You can also use *get* instead of *to be* in passive structures. This use is generally more informal and is sometimes called the *get passive*.
*He **got run over** by a car.*
*The window **got broken** by some kids playing football.*

In addition, you can use *get* instead of *have* in the structure *have something done*.
*He **got his brother arrested**.*
*I **got my photos developed**.*
*I **got my wallet stolen** when I was on holiday.*

Anecdote

1 You're going to tell your partner about a time when you came first or the first time you did something new. Decide which you'd like to tell your partner about then look at the questions below and think about what you're going to say and the language you will need.

Coming first
- ☐ What did you come first in? Was it a race, a competition or something else? Or did you win first prize in a raffle?
- ☐ How old were you at the time?
- ☐ Where were you?
- ☐ What did you have to do to win?
- ☐ Why did you enter the competition?
- ☐ Did you have to pay to enter it or have any special qualifications?
- ☐ What did you win?
- ☐ Were you pleased with your prize?
- ☐ Can you remember how you felt?
- ☐ Is there anything else you'd like to add?

Doing something for the first time
- ☐ Is this something you've done recently for the first time or is it something that you remember particularly clearly from the past?
- ☐ What did you do?
- ☐ When did you do it?
- ☐ Where were you?
- ☐ Did you have to do any preparation? If so, what did the preparation involve?
- ☐ Why did you do it?
- ☐ How did you feel?
- ☐ Would you do it again?
- ☐ Is there anything else you'd like to add?

2 Tell your partner about the occasion.

3 Find three similarities or differences between your stories.

Test yourself

Passives

1 Read through this news story quickly and answer the questions that follow.

FIRST MEETING *IMMINENT*

Plans (1) _____ (still/finalise) last night, despite significant problems in communication, for the first face-to-face meeting with intelligent life from outer space. Contact (2) _____ (first/establish) over three years ago but the information (3) _____ (only/make) public once a team of international linguistic experts had confirmed without a shadow of a doubt that Gaters were indeed friendly.

Daily bulletins (4) _____ (issue) by the ETF (Earth Task Force) on the state of communications with Gat, the Gaters' home planet. It (5) _____ (report) that Gaters have been trying to make contact with us for over 25 years now. It (6) _____ (believe) that their initial attempts failed because they overestimated the evolution of our communication systems and their earlier messages of peace and goodwill fell on deaf ears. However, they persevered and recent developments in the field of communications has meant that we are finally able to 'hear' them.

The location and date of the meeting (7) _____ (still/confirm). An unofficial source from the ETF said that a Gat spaceship had left Gat seven and a half weeks ago. It (8) _____ (previously/state) that it would take approximately eight weeks for a spaceship travelling at the speed of light to arrive which would mean that a visit (9) _____ (expect) any time from 27th June onwards. There has been much speculation concerning the Gaters' physical appearance but no information (10) _____ (release) on this point.

a) Are the Gaters more or less developed than us?
b) Where will the meeting take place?
c) Do you think this news story (or a similar one) is ever likely to be published?

2 Complete the story using the verbs in brackets in an appropriate passive form.

3 Rewrite the following sentences starting with the words given and a passive.

For example:
It is said that this week's lottery jackpot will be £9,000,000.
This week's *lottery jackpot is said to be £9,000,000.*

a) It is expected that Brazil will win the next World Cup.
   Brazil …
b) It has been reported that unemployment has risen steeply.
   Unemployment …
c) It has been estimated that 1,000 people have lost their homes due to the recent floods.
   1,000 people …
d) There were assumed to be only ten people injured following last night's rail accident.
   It is …
e) The actress is reported to have been offered a role in Cedric Scheybeler's new film.
   It is …

4 Have any similar stories been reported in the news recently?

Making the first move

1 Initiator, follower or ditherer, which are you? Read the following descriptions. Which do you think best describes you? Discuss your answer with a partner.

THE INITIATOR	THE FOLLOWER	THE DITHERER
You're never afraid of making the first move. If you want something, you go for it. You don't worry about conventions, you do what suits you and if other people come along for the ride, then fine.	You're one of life's cautious types. You don't realise that you could break new ground if you wanted to. You prefer to do things that have already been tried and tested rather than take risks. You know that doing something that works will give you good results, and that will make you look good. Trying something new may not work out as well.	Shall I, shan't I? That's often what other people hear you say. It's not a question of making the first move or hanging round to follow but whether you should or shouldn't. You never know what to do for the best and sometimes opportunities just slip through your hands while you hesitate. Go on – take the plunge once in a while. You might be pleasantly surprised by the results!

2 Read the first two questions in a quiz designed to determine which of the personality types you are.

a) What would your answers bc?
b) What would a typical initiator, follower and ditherer's answers be?

① You meet someone you like at a party and talk to them for a short time. You'd like to see them again. Would you

a. go up to them and give them your phone number and suggest meeting up sometime?
b. go over to say goodbye as you leave and hope they'll suggest meeting up again?
c. think about going over, then change your mind and just smile as you leave?

② You're interested in taking up a new sport, but don't want to do it alone. Would you

a. mention it to some of your friends and hope they'll organise a trip?
b. arrange and pay for a weekend course and then persuade your friends to go along?
c. buy magazines and books about it, find out about it on the Net, talk about it, but never actually get round to doing anything?

3 Compare your answers with your partner.

4 Work in small groups and write another four questions for the quiz. Choose new situations and think of three alternative answers that would suit the personality types.

5 Work with a partner from a different group. Ask and answer all your new quiz questions.

6 Having done the quiz, have you changed your mind about your personality type?

11 Stories

Work with a partner. Look at the pictures and discuss these questions:

a) Do you know the characters in the pictures?
b) What do you know about their stories?
c) How do the characters in these pictures, which were all drawn between 1860 and 1923, differ from the images that are familiar today?
d) What country do you associate them with?
e) Are there any famous stories or legends associated with your country?

Story telling

1 Work in small groups and discuss these questions:

a) What makes a good story?
b) What makes a good storyteller?
c) Do you know anyone who's a particularly good storyteller? What kind of stories does he or she tell?
d) When did you last hear a good story? What was it about?
e) Do you prefer reading stories or listening to them?

2 You're going to hear an interview with Helen East, a professional storyteller. Look at the list below and think about which areas you would be most interested in hearing about.

a) her background
b) her first job as a storyteller
c) why she became a storyteller
d) the project she's currently involved in
e) the job of a professional storyteller
f) the traditional role of storytellers
g) what makes a good storyteller
h) what makes a good story
i) the universal appeal of stories
j) different types of stories

Helen East is a professional storyteller. She has travelled all over the world, both listening to and telling stories.

3 ▭ 48 Look at the list in 2 again. Listen to the interview and tick the topics which Helen talks about. Does she mention the points you were interested in?

4 Imagine you work for the radio station which broadcast the interview with Helen East. You are going to write a short article about storytellers for your website. Listen again and make notes on what she said about the topics you heard her mention in 2.

5 Compare your notes with a partner. Did you miss anything?

6 Work with a partner and write the article. It should be no longer than 200 words.

Close up

Telling stories

1 Work with a partner. There are five sections which are normally included in a traditional story. Match them to their definitions on the right.

Language reference p100

a) comment

b) background

c) problem

d) resolution

e) introduction

1 A complication or dilemma that affects the main character or characters.

2 The beginning of a story, possibly explaining its origin or giving a general idea of what is to follow.

3 The moral of the story or an explanation of its wider implications.

4 A description of the time and place where the story is set, or its main character/s.

5 The solution to the dilemma or complication that the main character was faced with.

2 What order would you expect the sections to appear in?

3 Put the following story in order according to your answers to 2.

ANDROCLES

Androcles

A As he was wandering about there he found a lion lying down moaning and groaning. At first he turned to run away, but seeing that the lion didn't chase him, he turned back and went up to him. As he approached, the lion put out his paw, which was all swollen and bleeding, and Androcles found that a huge thorn had got into it, and this was causing the lion's pain. He pulled out the thorn and bound up the paw of the lion, who was soon able to get up and lick Androcles' hand like a dog. Then the lion took Androcles to his cave, and brought him meat to eat every day.

B Gratitude is the sign of noble souls.

C Once upon a time a slave called Androcles escaped from his master and fled to the forest.

D But as soon as he came near to Androcles he recognised his friend, and licked his hands like a friendly dog. The Emperor was surprised at this and called Androcles to him, who told him the whole story. When he heard the story the Emperor pardoned and freed the slave, and the lion was let loose into the forest.

E But shortly afterwards both Androcles and the lion were captured, and the slave was sentenced to be thrown to the lion, who hadn't been given any food for several days. The Emperor and all his court came to see the spectacle, and Androcles was led out into the middle of the arena. Soon the lion was let loose from his den, and rushed towards his victim, bounding and roaring.

4 Have you heard this story before? Do you know any other fables like this?

5 〔•• 49〕 Listen to Helen telling a story.

a) Does her story include the five sections in 1?

b) Do you think the story is true?

6 Here is a list of features commonly used by storytellers to add spice to the stories they're telling. Match the features on the left to the extracts from Helen's story on the right.

a) reporting thoughts directly

b) reporting speech directly

c) making the story personal

d) asides to the listener

e) adding detail

f) repetition

1 She was about fourteen, she was dressed in a very short mini-skirt and a tank top.

2 This was a while back, you know, when those big fur coats were in fashion.

3 … and I found this road – Gleneldon Road – and I found number 29 …

4 I couldn't believe it, and then I thought to myself, 'but what about the coat?'

5 … and I said, 'I'm sorry, what is it?', and she said 'My daughter is dead.'

6 … this one actually happened to me …

7 Look at the tapescript on page 155. Can you find any other examples of these features?

8 ▄▄ **50** Here are some examples of how good storytellers use their voices to add to the atmosphere of the story they're telling:

a) changing pace and tone of voice
b) pausing for dramatic effect
c) using stress for dramatic effect

Listen to three short extracts from Helen's story and match them to one of the features above.

9 Look at the tapescript on page 156 and listen again. Prepare to shadow read the extracts in 8 with Helen.

Language reference: telling stories

Staging

Stories are often told in five stages:

Introduction
I was told this story by my grandfather when I was a child.

Background
It was a bright, spring day and the first leaves had begun to show on the trees. My father was in the garden …

Problem
Suddenly I heard a blood-curdling scream …

Resolution
In the end she just breathed a sigh of relief and sank back into her chair, glad that the day was finally over.

Comment
Their lives would never be the same again.

Features

The following are common features of oral story telling:

Reporting thoughts directly
She looked at the wolf and thought, 'That doesn't look like my grandmother!'

Reporting speech directly
The witch stood facing the mirror and said 'Mirror, mirror, on the wall, who's the fairest of them all?'

Repetition
And Pinocchio's nose started to grow, and the more he lied, the more it grew, and the more it grew, the more he lied.

Asides to the listener
And she sat there all day, every day, staring into the fire. Who would have thought that such a pretty child could be so sad?

Adding detail
He was a sad old man. So sad that the puppets cried to see him, so old the wrinkles in his face were deep enough to hide his tears.

Making the story personal
I saw him once, in the distance, a mysterious figure in his black cloak with his silver walking stick in his hand.

Using the voice

Storytellers also use their voices to add dramatic effect in a number of ways, including:

Using stress for dramatic effect
And I'll HUFF and I'll PUFF and I'll BLOW your house down.

Pausing for dramatic effect
And as I pushed open the door … I saw a huge figure standing by the window.

Changing pace and tone of voice
And he walked up to the door v-e-r-y, v-e-r-y s-l-o-w-l-y, and opened it v-e-r-y, v-e-r-y s-o-f-t-l-y.

Urban myths

1 Look at the file card on urban myths. Are there any differences between the definition given here and the story you heard Helen tell?

2 Here are the titles of three classic urban myths. Do you think you've heard any of them?

a) The spider's bite
b) The killer in the back seat
c) The flat tyre

3 Work in three groups. Each group is going to read one of the three urban myths.

Group A turn to page 135.
Group B turn to page 136.
Group C turn to page 138.

4 Work in groups of three with one student from each of the previous groups. Tell your urban myth to the other members of the group. Then discuss these questions:

a) Which story did you enjoy most? Which was the most instructive? The most entertaining? The scariest?
b) Have you heard any similar stories?

5 A new website is being created, dedicated to urban myths. Write an e-mail version of about 200 words of one of the urban myths that your partners told you, to send to the site. Then compare your version to the version at the back of the book. Are there any differences in the content? Did your partner embellish the story or change it in any way?

Telling tales

1 Look at the three passengers in the picture. Where do you think they are going? What's the relationship between them?

2 Read the short story on the next page and check your answers.

At Denver, a great many passengers joined the east-bound Boston and Maine train. In one coach, there sat a very pretty young woman. She was beautifully and richly dressed. Among the new-comers were two men. The
5 younger one was good-looking with a bold, honest face and manner. The other was a large, sad-faced person, roughly-dressed. The two were handcuffed together.

As they passed down the aisle of the coach, the only empty seat was one facing the young woman. Here the linked
10 pair seated themselves. The woman quickly glanced at them with disinterest. Then with a lovely smile, she held out a little grey-gloved hand. When she spoke, her voice showed that she was used to speaking and being heard.

'Well, Mr Easton, if you *will* make me speak first, I
15 suppose I must. Don't you ever say hello to old friends when you meet them in the West?'

The younger man pulled himself up sharply at the sound of her voice. He seemed to struggle with a little embarrassment, which he threw off instantly. Then he held
20 her fingers with his left hand.

'It's Miss Fairchild,' he said, with a smile, 'I'll ask you to excuse the other hand. I'm not able to use it at present.'

He slightly raised his right hand, which was bound at the wrist by the shining bracelet to the left one of his partner. The
25 happy look in the woman's eyes slowly changed to one of puzzled horror. The glow passed from her cheeks. Easton, with a little laugh, as if amused, was about to speak again when the other stopped him. The sad-faced man had been watching the young woman's face with his sharp, searching
30 eyes.

'You'll excuse me for speaking, miss. But I see you know the marshal here. If you'll ask him to speak a word for me when we get to the pen, he'll do it. It'll make things easier for me there. He's taking me to Leavenworth Prison. It's seven
35 years for counterfeiting.'

'Oh!' she said, with a deep breath and returning color. 'So that is what you are doing here. A marshal!'

'My dear Miss Fairchild,' said Easton calmly, 'I had to do something. Money has a way of taking wings. You know it
40 takes money to keep in step with our crowd in Washington. I saw this opening in the West, and … well, a marshal isn't quite as high a position as that of an ambassador, but …'

'The ambassador,' she said warmly, 'doesn't call anymore.

He needn't ever have done so. You ought to know that. So now
45 you are one of those dashing western heroes. And you ride and shoot and go into all kinds of dangers. That's different from the Washington life. You have been missed by the old crowd.'

The woman's eyes, interested, went back, widening a little,
50 to rest upon the shiny handcuffs.

'Don't worry about them, miss,' said the other man. 'All marshals handcuff themselves these days to their prisoners to keep them from getting away. Mr Easton knows his business.'

'Will we see you again soon in Washington?' asked Miss
55 Fairchild.

'Not soon, I think,' said Easton. 'My carefree days are over, I fear.'

'I love the West,' she said. Her eyes were shining softly. She looked away and out the train window. She began to speak
60 truly and simply, forgetting about style and manner. 'Mamma and I spent the summer in Denver. She went home a week ago because Father was ill. I could live and be happy in the West. I think the air here agrees with me. Money isn't everything. But people always misunderstand things and remain stupid.'

65 'Say, Mr Marshal,' growled the sad-faced man. 'This isn't quite fair. I'm needin' a drink of water. Haven't you talked long enough? Take me into the dining car now, won't you?'

The bound travelers rose to their feet. Easton still had the same slow smile on his face.

70 'I can't say no to a need for water,' he said lightly. 'It's the one friend of the unfortunate. Goodbye, Miss Fairchild. Duty calls, you know.' He held out his hand for a farewell.

'It's too bad you're not going East,' she said, remembering again her manner and style. 'But you must go to Leavenworth,
75 I suppose?'

'Yes,' said Easton, 'I must go on to Leavenworth.'

The two men made their way down the aisle into the dining car.

The two passengers in a seat nearby heard most of the
80 conversation. Said one of them, 'That marshal is a good sort of chap. Some of these Westerners are all right.'

'Pretty young to hold an office like that, isn't he?' asked the other.

'Young!' exclaimed the first speaker. 'Why … Oh! …
85 Didn't you catch on? Say, did you ever know an officer to handcuff a prisoner to his *right* hand?'

3 Without looking back at the text, decide if the following statements are true or false.

a) The men chose to sit with the young lady because they knew her.
b) The younger man seemed embarrassed to see the young woman.
c) He tried to hide the handcuffs from her.
d) The men were both on their way to Leavenworth Prison.
e) The young woman and the young man had once been friends.
f) The young man had once been an ambassador.
g) The two men went to the dining car because the prisoner was thirsty.
h) The older man was a prisoner.
i) The younger man was a marshal.
j) The marshal was a kind man.

4 Discuss your answers with a partner. Refer back to the story if necessary.

5 Work with a partner and discuss these questions:

a) Have you ever lied to help someone?
b) When was the last time you did someone a good turn? What did you do for them?
c) When was the last time someone was kind to you? What did they do? Have you been able to repay their kindness?

Compound adjectives

1 Work with a partner. Look at the compound adjectives in the box below and answer the questions that follow.

> newly-arrested   slow-moving   well-informed   good-looking   quick-thinking
> wealthy-looking   record-breaking   roughly-dressed   stress-induced
> well-behaved   softly-spoken   grey-haired   fair-skinned   time-consuming
> smartly-dressed   sad-faced   comfort-loving   grey-gloved

   a) Four of the compound adjectives above were used in the text. What were they used to describe?

   b) Which of the other adjectives can be used to describe the people in the story?

   c) What can the other adjectives be used to describe?

2 What would you call something that
a) has been made carefully? b) will save you time? c) looks tasty? d) dries quickly?

3 What would you call someone who
a) has good manners? b) loses their temper quickly? c) loves having fun? d) works hard?

4 Replace the clauses in *italics* with compound adjectives. Make any other changes that are necessary.

For example:
They've invented a new device *which will save energy*.
They've invented a new energy-saving device.

   a) The building was a real eyesore; *it had been built very cheaply*.

   b) She was wearing a new perfume that *smelt very sweet* and didn't really suit her.

   c) He *had received a good education* and could speak knowledgeably on a range of topics.

   d) He *thinks quickly* and always makes intelligent contributions.

   e) *Her skin is smooth* and she has a beautifully clear complexion.

   f) We bought some gorgeous plates *that were made by hand*.

   g) Peter's parents *have very broad minds* – they let him do whatever he wants.

5 Use each compound adjective in 4 to describe someone or something you know.

The best laid plans ...

1 Here is an article that was published just before the millennium celebrations in London.

   a) What were the main events going to be?   b) What time were they due to take place?

HAVE A BLAST
THE BEST WAYS TO WELCOME THE NEW MILLENNIUM

LONDON: THE MAIN EVENTS
The world's eyes will be on London as the second millennium dawns. Greenwich has been the centre of world time since 1884 and a global television audience of a billion people will
5 be watching the hands of Big Ben as midnight strikes on New Year's Eve, providing the capital with the excuse to have the biggest party of all time. London's official Millennium Eve event is 'Big Time', incorporating a party zone stretching four miles along the River Thames from Tower
10 Bridge in the east to Vauxhall Bridge in the west.

RIVER OF FIRE
At midnight on Big Ben's first chime, 2,000 pyrotechnic candles will be lit creating a 60m high flame that will travel at 1,240kph along the river, firing from 16 barges moored
15 between Tower and Vauxhall Bridges. The 6km river of fire will burn for about 20 seconds and will be visible from both banks of the river and many parts of Greater London.

FIREWORK DISPLAY
A 15-minute pyrotechnic display follows the river of fire,
20 launched from 16 barges on the Thames.

BRITISH AIRWAYS LONDON EYE
Tony Blair will officially open the observation wheel on the South Bank beside County Hall at 8.30pm. He will fire a laser beam to start the wheel turning. It is 135 metres tall and has
25 32 pods, each able to carry 25 people. It will not be open to the public on New Year's Eve, but 250 lucky winners of a British Airways competition will be on the wheel to enjoy the spectacular view of London that can be seen from the top. At 11.50pm the wheel is due to stop turning so those on board
30 can toast the start of the new millennium with champagne.

(Adapted from *The Times*, 11th December 1999)

2 ▭ 51 Listen to a radio programme broadcast on the evening of the 1st of January 2000 and answer these questions:

   a) Which events from the newspaper article are mentioned?
   b) Did all the events go as planned?
   c) What other events do they talk about?
   d) What was expected to happen that didn't?

3 Compare your answers with a partner. Was the night a success? Why/Why not?

4 Work with your partner. Look at the phrases on the left taken from the recording. Match them to the people or the events on the right that they are describing.

a) didn't really *live up to expectations*	1 the people in charge of the London Eye
b) a slight technical *hitch*	
c) the *mix up*	2 the French
d) the *fiasco*	3 the tickets for the Dome
e) it all *fell through*	4 the Millennium Experience Party at the Dome (two phrases)
f) they just didn't *get their act together* in time	
	5 the River of Fire (two phrases)
g) they managed *to pull everything off* without a hitch!	6 the Millennium Bug
	7 a Star Wars type laser show organised for the opening of the London Eye
h) the whole thing was almost *called off* because of a bomb scare …	
i) the show *went on*	8 picking up the tickets at the train stations
j) a bit of *a no-show*	

5 Check your answers with the tapescript on page 156.

6 Match the words and phrases in *italics* in 4 with their definitions below.

1	to succeed in doing something	6	a problem
2	cancelled	7	be as good as anticipated
3	something that was expected to happen but didn't	8	failed to happen
4	confusion	9	get themselves organised
5	something that fails, often causing embarrassment	10	continued

7 Complete the following TV web review using words and phrases from 4.

---

*TV*GUIDE ///

If you missed the last episode of **RUMNEY SQUARE**, *don't despair! Catch up here …*

Well, after the (1) ＿＿ of last week's episode where the wedding of the year had to be (2) ＿＿ after a slight 'technical (3) ＿＿' when Bobby got put on a night train to Glasgow by his drunken mates, will he and Katie manage to (4) ＿＿ and finally do the decent thing in this week's episode?

  Meanwhile, Ted is having problems at work. After the (5) ＿＿ with last month's wages getting lost on the way to the bank it looks like he may well be out of a job. And will we find that Jean's plans for an exotic holiday all (6) ＿＿ when she found out that her estranged husband was back in town?

  All these questions and more will be answered in Rumney Square. Tuesday 8.30pm. Whatever happens, it's bound to (7) ＿＿ !

Close up

The future seen from the past

1 Look at the following extracts taken from the radio programme. Complete the sentences using the phrases in the box.

> *would* go off   *was going to* be one of the centrepieces   *would* be a flood
> *was supposed to* be one of the most spectacular   didn't sound like it *was going to*
> *was due to* begin   *was to* have opened it   *were on the verge of* evacuating

a) It ____ pyrotechnic shows ever seen, measuring 60 metres in height and travelling down the Thames at the incredible speed of 1,240 kph.

b) There was talk at one point of having to call the whole thing off: it ____ happen.

c) … it ____ of the whole evening. Tony Blair ____ with a Star Wars type laser show but it all fell through.

d) … apparently a hoax caller phoned to say that a bomb ____ in the Dome at midnight. The organisers ____ the Dome at 10.45, minutes before the main show ____ – but the Queen stood her ground …

e) Most medical staff had had their leave cancelled to cover what they had imagined ____ of party victims, but it seems that in fact it turned out to be a very quiet night.

2 ◼◼ **52** Listen to the extracts and check your answers.

Language reference p105

3 Work with a partner. Look at the verb phrases in *italics* in the box in 1.

a) Only one of the verb phrases is *not* followed by an infinitive with or without *to*. Which one?

b) These structures all refer to actions or events that were expected to happen in the past. Did they happen?

c) Which phrase suggests that the action or event was imminent?

4 Reorder the words and phrases below to form logical sentences.

a) supposed to / to the seaside / be going / the car / we didn't go / we were / so / broke down / but.

b) I didn't feel / so / but / going to / last night / do my homework / to bed early / I was / very well / I went.

c) due to / heavy fog / we were / by six hours / the plane was / at 8.30 / delayed / leave / but / and / there was.

d) at the last minute / to have met / the minister / at the opening / he was delayed / I was / but.

e) the exam / it was / but actually / we had / pretty easy / would be / imagined that / really difficult.

f) the rescue party / on the verge of / when / giving up hope / we were / arrived.

5 Have you ever found yourself in a similar situation? Tell your partner about it.

Language reference: the future seen from the past

You can use the following phrases to talk about an event or action that was expected to happen in the past, but didn't.

$$
\left.\begin{array}{l}
\textit{going to}\\
\textit{was / were} + \textit{supposed to}\\
\textit{due to}
\end{array}\right\} + \textit{verb}
$$

on the verge of   + *-ing*

We **were going to go** to the cinema last night, but in the end we couldn't be bothered.
They **were supposed to be** going away on holiday this week, but James got the flu.

The phrase *on the verge of* is used to suggest that the action or event was imminent.
They were **on the verge of** cracking the code, but the other team got there first.

You can use *to be to* + infinitive to explain that a formal arrangement had been made.
The Prince **was to visit** the town in mid-May.

You can often use the modal auxiliary verb *would* to talk about the future in the past, especially in conjunction with phrases such as *we had imagined, they had expected, he had thought.*
We **had expected that they would bring** some warm clothes, considering the climate.

A change of plan

1   ▭ 53 Listen to three people describing plans that had to be changed. Answer these questions for each story:

   a)   What was the original plan?
   b)   What went wrong?
   c)   How did they feel about the change of plan?
   d)   Did they do something else instead?

2   Compare your answers with a partner.

Anecdote

1   You are going to tell your partner about a time when you found yourself in one of the situations below. Choose one of the situations to talk about. Before you start to speak, look at the questions and think about what you're going to say and the language you're going to need to say it.

A change in plans
☐   What had you planned? A holiday? A party? A career change? A new home? Something else?
☐   Were you responsible for making the plans or did someone else do the planning?
☐   How far ahead were the plans made? Was there a lot of planning involved?
☐   What exactly was the original plan?
☐   Were you looking forward to it?
☐   What happened to force you to change your plans?
☐   Did the change happen at the very last minute or did you have time to make new plans?
☐   How did you react when your plans fell through?
☐   Did you do something else instead? Do you think it turned out for the best in the end?
☐   Is there anything else you'd like to add?

A time when things didn't live up to expectations
☐   What was the occasion? A holiday? A party? A new job? A date? Something else?
☐   What had you expected to happen?
☐   Why were you looking forward to it?
☐   What actually happened?
☐   In what way did it not live up to your expectations?
☐   Did you feel angry? Upset? Annoyed?
☐   Did you complain?
☐   Was anyone to blame?
☐   Do you think that maybe your expectations were a little unrealistic?
☐   Is there anything else you'd like to add?

A time when things worked out much better than you'd expected
☐   What was the occasion? An exam? A job interview? Meeting someone for the first time? Something else?
☐   Were you really dreading the occasion? Why?
☐   What exactly did you think was going to happen?
☐   How did you feel beforehand?
☐   What actually happened?
☐   What was it that made it much better than you'd expected?
☐   How did you feel after the event?
☐   Did you do anything special to celebrate?
☐   Did you tell lots of people about it?
☐   Is there anything else you'd like to add?

2   Tell your story to your partner. Give as much detail as possible.

3   Did your stories have anything in common?

LANGUAGE TOOLBOX

We reckoned we'd thought of everything but …
We hadn't calculated on …
But then, at the very last minute …
But when it came to …
I had no say in the matter and …
Luckily it all turned out OK in the end.
If it hadn't been for … I'd never have …

LANGUAGE TOOLBOX

I'd thought it would be …
I'd imagined something a little different.
I don't really know exactly what I was expecting.
Things didn't really turn out as I'd expected.
I was really disappointed because …
I suppose I should have known but …

LANGUAGE TOOLBOX

I thought it'd be really …
I was really dreading it because …
When the time came …
I was really pleasantly surprised …
It was totally different from what I'd expected.
In the end it all turned out for the best.

The glass elevator

1   ▶ 54 You are going to write a short story. Before you start, look at the photograph, listen to the recording and imagine the scene that is described to you.

2   Work in groups of four. The four of you are in the lift together. You are going to write about your experience, but first you must decide on the characters. The four characters must all be different from each other in some way (e.g. in age, social status, nationality).

3   When you have decided on the characters for your story, choose one each. Work individually and read the questions below. Think about the answers for your character.

   a)   Why are you in the building? Do you work there? Were you visiting someone? Did you have some business to do there?
   b)   You're in a hurry to go somewhere. Where are you going? Why are you so anxious to get there?

4   Write the first part of the story from the moment you leave wherever you were and walk towards the lift up to the moment when you realise that there is a power cut right across the city. Write in the first person.

5   When you have finished, read your story to your group and discuss the following questions:

   a)   What's going to happen next?
   b)   How are your characters going to react? Will they panic? Will one person take control? Will they start talking to each other?
   c)   How is the story going to end? Will they be rescued by someone from outside? Will the power come back on? How will they get out of the lift?

6   When you have decided on the next part of the story, continue writing your part.

7   When you have finished your story, show it to the other members of your group. Do your four stories coincide? Do you have a favourite version?

12 *Words*

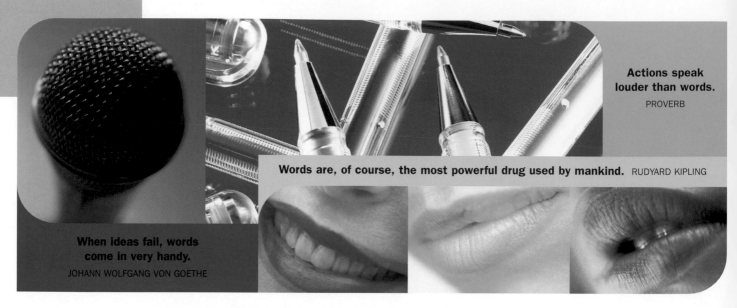

When ideas fail, words come in very handy.
JOHANN WOLFGANG VON GOETHE

Actions speak louder than words.
PROVERB

Words are, of course, the most powerful drug used by mankind. RUDYARD KIPLING

Use the words in the box to answer the questions below.

choice	breakfast	facetious	orange	brunch
smoke	fog	lunch	smog	madam	feedback

a) Which word, read backwards or forwards reads the same?
b) What two words does *smog* originate from? And *brunch*?
c) Which words can you think of a rhyme for?
d) Which word, written in capital letters, reads the same upside down in the mirror?
e) Which word contains all five vowels in alphabetical order?
f) Which word contains the first six letters of the alphabet?

New words

Lexis **1** Work in small groups and answer these questions:

a) What's the longest word you can think of in English?
b) Can you remember what the last new word you learnt in English was?
c) Can you remember what the last new word you learnt in your own language was?
d) Can you think of some English words that are used in your language?
e) Can you think of three English words that people wouldn't have known 50 years ago?
f) What do you think the origin of these new words is?

2 Compare your answers with another group. How many of your words were the same?

3 The words and phrases below have all appeared in the English language in the last twenty years.

a) Which of them have you never heard of before?
b) Work with a partner and discuss what you think they might mean.

clamp (n and v)	decaf (n and adj)	gap year (n)	hacker (n)	quality time (n)
road rage (n)	scratch card (n)	semi-skimmed (adj and n)	spin doctor (n)	
retail therapy (n)	GM food (n)	bad hair day (n)		

4 Read the sentences below containing the words in 3. Did you guess their meanings correctly?

a) I buy a scratch card every time I'm in the newsagent's but of course I never win anything.
b) We both have very demanding jobs, so weekends and holidays are the only time we can get some quality time together.
c) I prefer full fat milk but I'm on a diet so I'd better have semi-skimmed.
d) The party's spin doctors recommended that the Prime Minister flew to the scene of the disaster so that he could appear sympathetic.
e) I just hopped out to get some cash from the cash machine and when I came back my car had been clamped.
f) Retail therapy is cheaper than a session with a therapist – and you get something for your money!
g) I like a nice cup of decaf before I go to bed. Normal coffee keeps me awake.
h) Just ignore her bad temper, she's having a bad hair day.
i) James went to South America in his gap year and then to Oxford University to study archaeology.
j) David is a keen hacker. He spends most of his spare time trying to get into banks' security systems.
k) There's a lot in the news about GM foods because people aren't sure whether it's safe to change the genetic make up of produce or not.
l) I saw a case of road rage on the way home – a man jumped out of his car at the lights and threatened the driver behind him with a knife.

5 Match these definitions with three of the words in 3.

a) A driver's uncontrolled, aggressive behaviour, apparently caused by the stresses of modern driving.
b) A person who is employed by a political party to ensure that information is presented to the public in a positive light for the party.
c) Going shopping in order to cheer yourself up.

6 Write definitions for three of the other words. Read them to your partner and ask them to guess the words.

7 Which of the words in 3 do you think

a) will make a permanent entry into English?
b) will be obsolete in five years' time?
c) you'll remember next lesson?

Listening

1 🔲 55 You are going to hear three conversations. As you listen

a) decide what the relationship between the speakers is.
b) tick the words you hear from the box in 3 on page 108.

2 Check your answers with a partner.

3 Work in small groups. Answer two or three of the questions below.

a) What do you think of GM foods? Do you eat GM foods? Are you prepared to pay more for food which hasn't been modified?
b) Who would you like to spend more quality time with? Why?
c) Spin doctors do more harm than good. Do you agree?
d) Do you like a bit of retail therapy when you're feeling down? What sort of things do you buy? What else do you do to cheer yourself up?

'Well, I can't stand here idly chatting.'

Close up

-ever

1 Match the first half of these sentences from the conversations with the second half.

a) Whichever
b) Whatever you buy,
c) Whenever I hear people getting het up about GM foods
d) So now wherever I am
e) However much they pester you,
f) Whoever calls,

1 don't give them the number.
2 you're having.
3 make sure you put it on his credit card.
4 just say you'll make sure I get their message.
5 you can contact me.
6 it really makes me angry.

2 Use the words in the box to complete these sentences.

Language reference p111

| whichever   whatever   whenever   wherever   whoever   however |

a) ____ he was doing, and ____ he was, he always phoned her on her birthday.
b) ____ decision I make, it's bound to be the wrong one.
c) ____ big or small, all dogs need a lot of care and attention.
d) I'm going to finish this today, ____ happens.
e) ____ many years I live here, I'll never get used to the noise.
f) I can come over ____ suits you. Just let me know.
g) ____ did this terrible thing must be extremely cruel.
h) ____ you need help just give me a call.
i) We've got all afternoon. We can go to the shops or ____ you like.

3 Read these sentences and correct those which are wrong.

a) I'm going to find her, where she is.
b) Whatever you do, don't let the cat out when you open the door.
c) Which dress you choose, make sure it's not too revealing.
d) It doesn't matter whoever takes the letters to the post, as long as they go today.
e) 'Shall we get the 2 o'clock bus or the 3 o'clock?' 'Whichever suits you best.'
f) How much chocolate she eats, she never puts on weight!
g) Who's on the phone, I'll ring them back later.

4 Rewrite these sentences using the words in the box in 2.

a) Even if it takes forever, I'm going to speak English like a native.
b) I don't care what you do, I'll always love you.
c) No matter where I go, I'll never forget you.
d) Every time I go to London I take the train.

5 Look at the sentences below. Are any of them true for you? Discuss your answers with a partner and tell them more.

a) However hard I try, I can never diet for more than three hours.
b) Whatever the weather, I always drink a mug of hot coffee first thing in the morning.
c) Wherever I go, I always take my mobile with me.
d) Whenever I go on holiday, I always send postcards to friends.
e) Whichever size I want, they've always sold out.
f) Whoever wins. it's never me!

Language reference: -ever

The suffix -ever can be combined with question words to create *whichever, whatever, whenever, wherever, whoever* and *however*. They are usually used to mean 'it doesn't matter what / who / how' or 'any thing that / any person who' etc.

*He just does **whatever** he wants, **whenever** he wants to and doesn't care about anybody else.*
***Wherever** you're going on holiday, remember to take enough sun cream.*
***Whoever** it is, I can't talk to them right now.*
***However** you do it, just make sure it's done by this time tomorrow.*

***Whichever** route you choose, it'll take you about three hours to get there.*
*You should always tell the truth, **however** hard it may be.*

Note: Words formed with -ever can also be used to finish an open-ended list:
*I really don't mind what we do. Go to the cinema, go out for a meal, stay in and watch a video, **whatever**. Come round anytime, tomorrow morning, this evening, **whenever**.*

Words

Collocations **1** Match the expressions with *word* in the dialogues below to these meanings:

a) by one person telling another
b) to explain clearly
c) I don't know what to say
d) briefly
e) a quiet person
f) put another way
g) I believe you
h) I promise
i) I didn't say that

1 A: That's a lot of money.
   B: Yes, but *you have my word*, I'll pay you back.
   A: I've heard that before.

2 A: But you said we could go.
   B: No, I didn't. *You're putting words in my mouth.* I said you could go if Peter went with you.

3 A: You, Mrs Arnold, have just won £5,000,000. What do you have to say?
   B: Well, err, *words fail me*. Err, I'm very happy.

4 A: Your grandfather was *a man of few words* but when he did speak everyone listened.
   B: I wish I'd met him.

5 A: It's difficult for me *to put into words* what I feel at this precise moment.
   B: Is there anything I can do to help?
   A: No, I don't think so. Thanks anyway.

6 A: Can I borrow your car?
   B: *In a word?* No.
   A: Oh, go on. I promise I'll be careful.

7 A: How do you get your customers?
   B: *Word of mouth* mostly. If people are happy with my work, they recommend me to their friends.

8 A: I'm afraid there's very little work at the moment.
   B: So, *in other words*, you can't give me a job.
   A: No, I'm afraid not.

9 A: This is the best price you'll get.
   B: Well, *I'll take your word for it* but if I see a cheaper deal elsewhere …
   A: You won't.

2 Do you know any other expressions with *word*?

3 Work with a partner. Write a short dialogue containing at least three of the expressions in 1. Compare your dialogue with others in the class.

The written word

1 Look at the notes below and decide which type of correspondence they are.

> thank you letter   invitation   e-mail   letter of complaint
> love letter   letter of apology

Dear Mr Smith,
I'm writing to say thank you very much for the book which arrived this morning. I'm sure I'll enjoy reading it.
Yours,
Peter

A

Dear Chris
Just a note to see if you can make the meeting on Monday.
T

B

Dear Jo,
Just a line to say that I am so sorry about your vase. You said it was an old one; thank goodness it wasn't an antique!
Much love,
Tracey

C

2 Work with a partner and discuss these questions:

a) Which of the six types of correspondence in 1 have you had to write in your own language?
b) Which of them have you written in English?
c) What other types of correspondence can you think of?

3 Below are six extracts from an article on letter writing. Give each extract one of these titles:

a) Letters of apology
b) Netiquette
c) Signing off
d) Starting a letter
e) Thank you letters
f) Job application letters

1

The universal opening to most letters is 'Dear …' with the exception of those to intimates, which can take the form of 'My dear' or 'Darling' (seriously enamoured). How you address the recipient depends on how well you know him or her. If you are writing to a friend, then the first name is fine. If you don't know them personally, or if they are older, then it is wise to use the formal 'Dear Mr / Mrs Brown'. 'Dear Sir or Madam' is reserved for business correspondence. It is usual to end the salutation with a comma.

2

How you have started a letter dictates how you should sign off. If you began a letter 'Dear First Name', then you sign off with your first name only; if you started with 'Dear Mr Surname' then you sign off with your full name. The adverb you use with 'Yours' depends on the level of formality and familiarity. 'Yours faithfully' is used to end letters which started with 'Dear Sir'. When closing a letter written to a name (i.e. 'Dear Ms Smith', not 'Dear Sir / Madam') 'Yours sincerely' is the most usual and formal. It is ideal in letters to people you don't know.

In addition there are several other sign-offs: 'Much love' and 'Best love', which suggest love of a platonic nature; 'Affectionately' which means just what it says; 'Kind regards', 'Best wishes' and 'Warmest regards' which can be used in conjunction with 'Yours sincerely' to narrow the distance implied by the latter. If in doubt about the familiarity it is always better to err on the side of formality.

3

Although an endangered species, this is one of the most delightful and effective of letters. It is required whenever someone has done you a personal favour or you have received a present or hospitality. Rather like a flower, it becomes less attractive the longer it is left. So remember, the most polite one is a prompt one. A letter of this kind should be short and to the point but personalised, if possible by referring to a particularly good dish, the gift or whatever the reason for writing.

4

These can be immensely important as you will want to make a good impression on a prospective employer. Some companies will ask for a handwritten letter, but otherwise you should type the letter and pay particular attention to the layout and presentation. If you are enclosing a CV try not to duplicate too much information in your letter. Although you are of course selling yourself in the letter, and there is a strong temptation to list all your abilities and achievements, try not to overdo it. It can often be useful to have someone read over the letter and give you their opinion on it once it's finished.

5

These can be difficult to write but certainly a thoughtful letter is always much more effective and sometimes less painful than having to mumble an awkward sorry. Its tone, which should be contrite but not obsequious, is obviously governed by the seriousness of the crime. However, in all cases it should be brief and get straight to the point in the first paragraph. Suggestions for making amends should be mentioned, but attempts to lighten things up with a little humour are risky and best avoided.

6

Just as there are right and wrong ways of writing letters, the sending of messages via the Internet is also governed by certain rules and customs. The essence of electronic mail is speed. The language of the Internet is brief, and makes more use of abbreviations, symbols and acronyms than traditional or snail mail does. E-mail is also less formal, though this should not be achieved at the expense of politeness. Introductory salutations such as 'Dear Siegfried' can often be omitted, and as the sender's e-mail address and the date and time of sending usually appear automatically at the top of the message on the receiving end, these too are omitted. It is, however, important to sign off with your name, as your e-mail address may not be sufficient to inform the recipient of who you are.

When communicating there are two things to avoid: SHOUTING, or the use of upper case letters to make a point; and 'spamming', the sending of junk e-mail to advertise some commercial venture. Spamming is known as the ultimate e-mail faux pas and you'll have people flaming you if you persist. Flaming, incidentally, is when critical comments about you are displayed on the Internet for all to see.

(Adapted from *Debrett's New Guide to Etiquette and Modern Manners*)

4 Read through the extracts again and make a note of any correspondence conventions that you were unaware of.

5 Discuss anything you noted down with a partner.

6 Look at the notes in 1. What mistake has the writer made in each one, according to the extracts?

Lexis 1 Find words or phrases in the extracts which mean the following:

a) call someone by a name or title (extract 1)
b) the person who receives a letter (extract 1)
c) determines (extract 2)
d) write your name at the end of a letter (extract 2)
e) kind behaviour (extract 3)
f) to repeat (extract 4)
g) be clear and direct (extract 5)
h) traditional posted letters (extract 6)

2 Use your answers to 1 to complete the paragraph below about how to write invitations.

An invitation must contain all the information a guest needs to know: who is giving the party, for whom, the occasion, the location, the date, the time and details about how to reply. If you want people to come dressed in a particular way then you must (1) ____ and mention it early in your invitation so people know it's important. Obviously, the type of invitation you're sending (2) ____ the layout and look of the invite. A wedding invitation for example, will look very different to an invite to a birthday party. How you decide to (3) ____ the (4) ____ depends on how well you know them and on how formal the affair is going to be. Hopefully, in return for your (5) ____ you will receive a thank you note shortly after the event.

Writing 1 Choose one of the following to write:

a) An apology for having forgotten a birthday
b) An invitation to a fancy dress party
c) A thank you for an enjoyable dinner party

2 Using the information from the reading extracts, write your correspondence.

3 Work with a partner who chose the same piece of writing. Read your partner's work and make any necessary suggestions for improvements.

Close up

Language reference p115

Patterns with
have

1 Work with a partner and look at the verb phrases in *italics* in the sentences below. Which phrase deals with

a) a result?
b) an arrangement?

1 It can often be useful *to have someone read over* the letter and give you their opinion on it once it's finished.
2 Spamming is known as the ultimate e-mail faux pas and *you'll have people flaming you* if you persist.

2 Do these sentences mention results or arrangements?

a) Don't worry, I'm sure you'll have him smiling and laughing in no time.
b) What's holding you up? You promised me you'd have it working by now.
c) We could have someone come round and do it while we're on holiday.
d) You'll have the neighbours on the phone complaining about the noise.
e) We did most of it ourselves, but we had professionals come in and do the kitchen.
f) You'll have people coming up to you and asking for your autograph.
g) You'll have the police searching the countryside.

3 Look at the sentences in 2. What verb form is used when talking about

a) a result?
b) an arrangement?

4 Think of a situation in which you might hear each of the sentences in 2.

5 Complete the sentences below using the correct form of *have* and the words in brackets.

a) It's been a long time since I ____ (a visitor from abroad/come) to stay at my house.
b) I always ____ (my brother/check) my homework for me before I hand it in.
c) My father's great at telling jokes; he sometimes ____ (us/cry) with laughter.
d) I saw a really exciting film last night; it ____ (me/sit) on the edge of my seat.
e) My mother works such long hours that she ____ (someone/do) the cleaning and cooking for her.

6 Match the first part of the sentence on the left with the best ending for you on the right.

a) Waiting for exam results
b) Poor service in restaurants
c) Watching my parents dancing
d) Sitting in traffic
e) An unexpected present from a friend
f) People talking about politics

1 has me yawning.
2 has me tearing my hair out.
3 has me biting my nails.
4 has me cringing with embarrassment.
5 has me complaining.
6 has me jumping for joy.

7 Work with a partner and discuss your answers to 6.

Language reference: patterns with *have*

You can use *have* to talk about results or arrangements.

Results

You can use *have + someone / something + present participle* to say:

1 that you encouraged someone to do something.
   *In the end I **had them all dancing and singing**.*

2 that you managed to get a machine or an animal to do something.
   *I **had the computer working** five hours after I'd started to work on it.*
   *I **had the parrot talking** in no time.*

3 that something happened as a consequence of an action.
   *The party was a bit noisy; we **had the police knocking** on the front door at one point.*

Arrangements

You use the pattern *have + someone / something + infinitive* to say you have asked someone to do something for you.

*I **had my neighbours look** after the dog last weekend.*
*She **had someone come** round to give her a quote for the decorating work.*

World languages

Discussion 1 Work in small groups and discuss these questions:

a) Is your mother tongue spoken in any other countries?

b) Do you think the majority of languages around the world will eventually die out?

c) Do you think that governments should have programmes to protect minority languages, or should we accept that they will die out?

d) Do you like the way your language is changing?

e) Do you like to adopt new words and expressions?

f) What do you think the future of your own language is?

g) What would the advantages and disadvantages be of having one universal language?

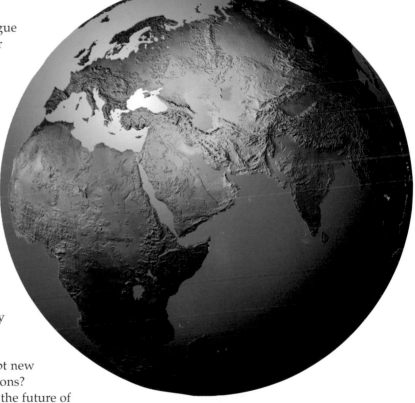

2 Compare your group's answers with another group. Did you have similar ideas and opinions?

Word games

1  56 Listen to people playing three different word games. What are the rules of each game?

2 Work in small groups and play a round of each game.

In their own words

1 Work with a partner. Look at the people in the photographs on the right. What do you know about them?

2 Here are some short extracts from their autobiographies. Read them and decide who is writing.

a) I drank enough just to get tipsy and to feel a little sad.
b) ... I changed my strategy.
c) ... I knew I could survive.
d) ... people turned to look at us hugging each other.
e) And I won't lie; I was scared.
f) When I was among the crowd I raised my right fist, and there was a roar.
g) It was also my way of saying thank you to all those people who had supported and encouraged me.
h) ... I saw a tremendous commotion and a great crowd of people ...

3 Compare your answers with a partner.

4 You are now going to read fuller extracts from the autobiographies. Match each text with its author and answer these questions:

a) What event are they describing?
b) How did they feel?

5 Check your answers to 2 with the texts.

 1

Just before the fight, when the referee was giving us instructions, Liston was giving me that stare. And I won't lie, I was scared. Sonny Liston was one of the greatest fighters of all
5 time. He was one of the most scientific of boxers who ever lived; he hit hard; and he was fixing to kill me. It frightened me, just knowing how hard he hit. But I was there; I didn't have any choice but to go out and fight.
10 The first round, I was dancing, moving back and side-to-side. I hit him with a couple of combinations, and he got me once with a right hand to the stomach. At the end of the round, I went back to my corner, and I felt
15 good because I knew I could survive. Round two, I made a mistake and he caught me against the ropes. I got away from most of the punches, but he hit me good with a left hook that shook me up. Round three, I changed my
20 strategy. I'd planned to fight hard the first two rounds, and then coast while Liston got tired. That way, by round five or six, I'd be rested and he'd be out of energy, and I'd start coming on strong. But at the start of round three, I
25 could see he was frustrated and getting tired already, so I decided to test him then.

 2

It was early evening in Tokyo when the call came through. We were all sitting around in the lounge opposite the hotel reception. The waiter had just delivered a tray of cold drinks.
5 Camilla, our PA, walked in with a smile on her face. 'Simon has a message for you all. He says you should crack open a bottle of bubbly.'
'Why?'
'Because *Wannabe* is number one.'
10 Our hollers and whoops brought the hotel to a standstill as people turned to look at us hugging each other.
'I want to get drunk,' said Mel B, ordering champagne.
15 'We have to be up at eight.'
'So what? We're NUMBER ONE!'
We celebrated at a Chinese restaurant in the hotel. Mel B kept ordering bottles of champagne and we kept coming up with new things to toast.
20 I drank enough just to get tipsy and to feel a little sad. I didn't want to be on the other side of the world. I wanted to be at home.
This was the moment I'd been waiting for – my ultimate revenge on all those people who had
25 dumped, doubted or ridiculed me. It was also my way of saying thank you to all those people who had supported and encouraged me.
I wanted them to see me, so I could say, 'Look at me! I did good! I told you so!'

3

At first I could not really make out what was going on in front of us, but I saw a tremendous commotion and a great crowd of people: hundreds of photographers and television
5 cameras and newspeople as well as several thousand well-wishers. I was astounded and a little alarmed. I had truly not expected such a scene. But this proved to be only the beginning; I realised we had not thoroughly prepared for all
10 that was about to happen.
Within twenty feet or so of the gate, the cameras started clicking, a noise that sounded like some great herd of metallic beasts. Reporters started shouting questions; television crews began
15 crowding in; supporters were yelling and cheering. It was a happy, if slightly disorientating, chaos. When a television crew thrust a long, dark and furry object at me, I recoiled slightly, wondering if it were some newfangled weapon
20 developed while I was in prison. Winnie, my wife, informed me that it was a microphone.
When I was among the crowd I raised my right fist, and there was a roar. I had not been able to do that for twenty-seven years and it gave me a
25 surge of strength and joy. As I finally walked through those gates to enter a car on the other side, I felt – even at the age of seventy-one – that my life was beginning anew. My ten thousand days of imprisonment were at last over.

6 You are going to write a short autobiographical piece. Read the instructions below.

a) Choose an event or moment that was particularly important to you, and that you remember well.
b) Make notes about what actually happened. Remember it's going to be a short piece, so concentrate on one event or moment.
c) Make notes about how you felt at the time. Can you remember any particular sounds, smells or sensations connected with the event?
d) Use your notes to write about your experience in about 200 words.

Spelling simplified

1 Work with a partner and discuss these questions:

 a) Do you think English spelling is difficult?
 b) Which words do you occasionally misspell?
 c) What changes do you think could be made to English to make spelling easier?

2 Look at this article which was written by Mark Twain. Work with a partner and read it aloud.

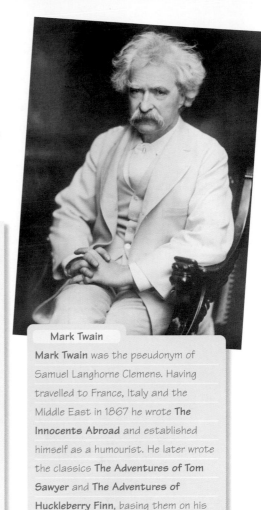

A Plan for the Improvement of English Spelling by Mark Twain

In Year 1 that useless letter 'c' would be dropped to be replased either by 'k' or 's', and likewise 'x' would no longer be part of the alphabet. The only kase in which 'c' would be retained would be the 'ch' formation, which will be dealt with later. Year 2 might reform 'w' spelling, so that 'which' and 'one' would take the same konsonant, wile Year 3 might well abolish 'y' replasing it with 'i' and Iear 4 might fiks the 'g/j' anomali wonse and for all.

Jenerally, then, the improvement would kontinue iear bai iear with Iear 5 doing awai with useless double konsonants, and Iears 6–12 or so modifaiing vowlz and the rimeining voist and unvoist konsonants. Bai Iear 15 or sou, it wud fainali bi posibl tu meik ius ov thi ridandant letez 'c', 'y' and 'x' – bai now jast a memori in the maindz ov ould doderez – tu riplais 'ch', 'sh', and 'th' rispektivli.

Fainali, xen, aafte sam 20 iers ov orxogrefkl riform, wi wud hev a lojikl, kohirnt speling in ius xrewawt xe Ingliy-spiking werld.

Mark Twain

Mark Twain was the pseudonym of Samuel Langhorne Clemens. Having travelled to France, Italy and the Middle East in 1867 he wrote **The Innocents Abroad** and established himself as a humourist. He later wrote the classics **The Adventures of Tom Sawyer** and **The Adventures of Huckleberry Finn**, basing them on his own boyhood experiences.

3 Which of his suggestions do you approve of?

Silent letters

1 Mark Twain recognised that English spelling and pronunciation are often very different. Read these sentences and cross out the silent letters.

 a) Knowing how to pronounce English words correctly is important but there's no doubt that it is one of the hardest things to learn.
 b) Keep your receipt if you want to return a purchase otherwise there's no guarantee you'll get your money back.
 c) I had a really bad case of pneumonia earlier this year. Even watching the TV was tiring so I spent most days just listening to the radio.
 d) Psychiatrists can be very vague. They'll rarely give you a direct answer to a question.
 e) During the flight the plane will climb to 10,000 metres above sea level.

2 The pronunciation of British place names can be difficult too. Look at these place names and cross out the silent letters.

 a) Gloucester
 b) Leicester
 c) Grosvenor Square
 d) Brighton
 e) Greenwich
 f) Guildford

3 🔲 57 Listen and check your answers.

4 Can you think of any more English words which contain silent letters?

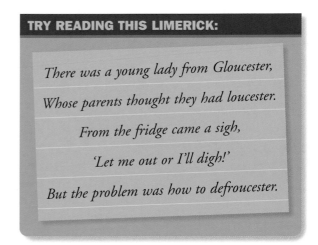

TRY READING THIS LIMERICK:

There was a young lady from Gloucester,

Whose parents thought they had loucester.

From the fridge came a sigh,

'Let me out or I'll digh!'

But the problem was how to defroucester.

13 Conscience

a) Look at the photos above. Which is the odd one out?
b) Which of the people would you give money to?
c) Have you given money to anybody on the street recently? If not, do you ever give money?

Spare change

1   ▭ 58 Listen to six people talking about giving money to people in the street. For each person answer these questions:

a) Do they give money to people in the street?
b) If yes, who do they give money to? If they don't, why not?

Speaker	Give money?	Why/Why not?
1	no	might spend it on alcohol
2		

2   Compare your answers with a partner. Do you agree with any of the speakers' views?

3   Work in small groups and discuss these questions:

a) Is begging prohibited in your country?
b) Do you often see people asking for money on the streets in your town or in other towns in your country?
c) What do you think is the best way to help people who ask for money on the streets?

Close up

Special uses of the past simple

1 Look at these sentences from the recording and answer the questions which follow.

1 I'd rather they actually did something to earn the money.
2 I think it's high time that the government did something about it because it really is annoying.

a) What tense is used after *I'd rather* and *it's high time*?
b) Are the speakers talking about real events which have actually happened or a desired situation?
c) Can you think of other occasions where the past simple is used to talk about unreal events or desired situations?

Language reference p119

2 Add *Jack* to the following sentences where there is an asterisk. What changes do you have to make to the verbs?

a) I'd rather * pay for dinner.
b) I'd rather * not work at the weekends.
c) I'd rather * clean the house.

3 Complete these sentences with an appropriate verb.

a) It's about time people _____ expecting others to look after them.
b) It's high time these young people _____ jobs and started earning a living.
c) It's time we _____ giving more generously to charity.
d) I'd rather the government _____ the responsibility for looking after the poor. I pay enough in taxes.
e) I'd rather people _____ something concrete to help instead of just paying out money to ease their consciences.
f) I'd rather local authorities _____ money on helping local youth clubs or improving leisure facilities for young people than redeveloping old buildings.

4 Complete these sentences with your own opinions.

a) It's about time …
b) It's high time …
c) I'd rather …

5 Compare your opinions with a partner.

Language reference: special uses of the past simple

You have previously seen how the past simple is used to talk about unreal situations:
If we **had** more money, we could improve the facilities for young people in the area.
If only the government **spent** more money on local transport.
I wish there **was** more interest in helping the homeless in this city.

Here are some other ways of talking about unreal, desired situations using the past simple.

It's (about/high) time …
It's **time** you **had** a holiday.
It's **high time** the politicians **stopped** talking and **started** doing something.
It's **about time** you **grew up** and **started** facing up to your responsibilities.

Would rather + subject + past simple
I'd **rather** you **didn't** smoke while I'm eating.
I'd **rather** Kate **didn't** work in the evenings.
I'd **rather** I **didn't** have to work in the evenings.

When *would rather* is not followed by a subject you do not use the past simple. Instead you use an infinitive.
The government **would rather spend** the money on health care than helping the elderly.
I'd **rather not work** in the evenings.

Rather you than me

Lexis: *Rather*

1 Work with a partner. Look at the picture and answer the questions which follow.

In which sentences are the speakers

a) expressing regret?
b) expressing a preference?
c) including a correction?
d) making a comparison/contrast?
e) expressing an opinion?

2 What do you think the expression *Rather you than me* means?

3 Add *rather* to these sentences.

a) It was late when we got home so I didn't return your call.
b) The new art gallery looks like a spaceship.
c) Well, actually, I like the idea of getting some pizzas and just watching TV.
d) I didn't really enjoy it; we walked too far for my liking and I was pretty stiff the next day.

4 Rewrite the following sentences using an expression with *rather*.

a) You mean you had to do five three hour exams! I'm glad it wasn't me!
b) I far prefer to watch a film than read a book for relaxation.
c) They asked us, or actually I mean, forced us to work overtime at weekends.
d) I wish I'd gone to bed early last night instead of having visitors.
e) I would have preferred to stay at home, but I had no choice in the matter.
f) I much prefer doing something cultural on holiday instead of just lying on a beach.

5 Complete these sentences in three different ways that are true for you.

a) I rather like …
b) I'd rather (not) have …

6 Compare your sentences with a partner.

Charity begins at home

1 Work in small groups. Look at the photos above and discuss these questions:

a) How are these people helping charity?
b) What other things do people do to raise money for charity?
c) What kind of events raise the most money?
d) Have you ever done anything to raise money for charity?

2 ▭ 59 Listen to three friends, Sue, Jake and Daniel, a Canadian, talking about doing things to raise money for charity. As you listen, note down answers to these questions:

a) Do they mention any of the ways of raising money you talked about in your discussion?
b) Have any of them ever taken part in a charity event?
c) What other ways of raising money do they mention?
d) Do they agree on what is the best way of raising money?
e) What problems and doubts do they discuss?

3 Compare your notes with a partner and discuss the questions that follow.

Which of the three, Sue, Jake or Daniel (the Canadian):

a) seems to feel passionately about the need to contribute to charity?
b) is the most doubtful about the value of charity events?
c) is the most aggressive in his/her manner of speaking?
d) tries to defend the point of view of one of the other speakers?
e) is often unable to get a word in?
f) seems to be the most well-informed?
g) seems to get a little hesitant and defensive?
h) seems to be the most opinionated?

4 Listen again and read the tapescript on page 158. Find phrases which support your answers to 3.

5 Compare your answers with a partner.

Daniel: So you did a parachute jump for charity?

Sue: Mmm, I must have been mad.

Jake: I can see the fun of a parachute jump but ...

Sentence stress

1 Work with a partner. Look at this question from the conversation. Where would you expect the main stress to fall?

So, you did a parachute jump for charity?

2 Change the position of the stress in the question so that the meaning changes to fit the following replies.

a) No, I did a bungee jump.
b) No, it was my sister.
c) No, I did it for fun.
d) No, but I'm thinking about doing one.

3 Where does the stress fall in the replies?

4 ▄▄ 60 Listen and check the position of the stress.

5 Work with a partner.

Student A: Read out the question, varying the position of the stress each time.
Student B: Listen carefully to the questions and reply by choosing an appropriate response from those given above.

6 Change roles and do the same thing with this question.

So, were you collecting money for Oxfam?

a) No, for the Save the Children fund.
b) No, actually, we were collecting old clothes.
c) No, I was ill that day.
d) Erm, no, for our school actually.

Lexis

1 Complete these extracts from the conversation.

a) ... as far as I know, it seemed to, you know, do the trick ... it seemed to r____ quite a lot of money.
b) ... they get the money that you, you know, you get s____ by people ...
c) But wouldn't it be more sensible to do something you know with a, with a purpose, like c____ money for food or ...
d) ... you can generate more money with a, with a larger e____ than you can with just going d____ t____ d____ ...
e) ... the charity's got to get a p____ , haven't they, so they won't get photos in the paper unless you've got some c____ .
f) The alternative is that maybe a lot of homeless people g____ h____ if somebody doesn't do something ...
g) I mean, this is just to make you f____ g____ a____ yourself.
h) ... you can actually press a button and d____ a cup of rice ...

2 ▄▄ 61 Listen and check your answers.

3 Use your answers to 1 to complete these questions:

a) Have you ever helped ____ money for charity?
b) If you have, was it a ____ event like a parachute jump or a marathon?
c) Were there any ____ present to give the ____ a higher profile?
d) Did you go around ____ money from people's houses ____ ?
e) If you haven't helped a charity like this, is it because you've never had the opportunity? Or do you agree with Jake that people only do these things to ____ themselves?

4 Discuss the questions with your partner.

All in a good cause

1 Work in small groups. You have been asked to organise a fund-raising event. Consider the points below.

WHO THE MONEY IS GOING TO

- Will it be a local charity?
- An international organisation?
- Or maybe a country or group of people which is in particular need at the moment?
- Why have you decided to help this particular cause?

THE KIND OF EVENT YOU'RE GOING TO ORGANISE

- Will it be a sponsored sports event?
- If so, what kind of sport?
- Or will it be some kind of cultural event?
- Maybe a film show or a play or a concert. What will you do exactly?
- Why have you decided on this kind of event?

WHO YOU'RE GOING TO INVITE

- Are you going to invite any celebrities or local dignitaries?
- If yes, who? Why?

THE PRACTICALITIES

- Decide on the date, the time and the venue.

LANGUAGE TOOLBOX

Presenting ideas

I'm here to …

Basically, we believe that …

Our first priority is to …

The main issue here, I'm sure you'll agree, is …

I'm sure you'll agree that …

As you can see, we've given this matter a lot of thought and …

So, to sum up …

I'd like to take this opportunity to …

And to close I'd just like to ask you to …

2 Prepare to present your ideas to the class.

   a) Nominate a spokesperson.

   b) Help the spokesperson to prepare a presentation following the structure given below:

     1 Explain who you are raising the money for and why you chose this cause.

     2 Explain what kind of event you're going to organise and why you chose this kind of event.

     3 Explain the practicalities.

     4 Invite your audience to be generous in their support and answer any questions they may have.

You may want to look back at the tips for giving presentations on page 73.

3 Listen to the other groups' presentations. Which group presented

   a) the most original fund-raising idea?

   b) the most practical fund-raising idea?

Travelling with an easy conscience

1 Work in small groups and discuss these questions:

   a) When did you last go on holiday? Where did you go? Why did you choose to go there?

   b) Was it an all-inclusive holiday or did you fend for yourself?

   c) How did you spend your holiday? Relaxing on the beach? Visiting museums? Getting to know the locals?

   d) Would you go back there again?

2 Read the article on the next page about ethical tourism. Would the writer have approved of your last holiday?

UNEASYVIRTUE

Going on holiday needn't mean leaving ethics at home, says Rosie Burke.

How clear is your conscience? You may eat organic carrots, recycle your newspapers, contribute to charity. But now you're going on holiday so you don't need to think about all that. Do you?

1

'No, it's as important people apply ethical issues to their holidays as to the rest of their lives.' Lara Marsh, campaigns officer at Tourism Concern, doesn't want to spoil your trip but she does think people have an obligation to consider the impact they may be having on their
5 destination. 'Ethical tourism can mean all sorts of things – where you decide to go in the first place, who you travel with and how you behave when you get there. Tourism is the world's largest industry. It can bring benefit but it's not spread evenly.'

2

The World Tourism Organisation predicts that in the next ten years the
10 number of tourists will reach one billion a year with a quarter of those travelling to the Third World. And while some of the developing nations are delighted at the influx of foreign currency, on the whole local people see little benefit from our spending. The World Bank estimates 90 per cent of income from tourism goes straight to the
15 multinational operators with local people seeing as little as 10 pence in every pound. 'Building hotels and resorts can lead to short-term jobs, but they can also lead to the destruction of habitats and so of livelihoods. Precious water supplies are often diverted to the large hotels or swimming pools, fishing grounds are cordoned off for snorkelling
20 and any villages in the way of development are simply mown down,' explains Lara Marsh.

3

'Tour operators are there to make money and there are some who have adopted the buzz words and use them for marketing rather than being genuinely concerned, while others who do good things may be keeping
25 quiet about it,' says Mike Sykes, MD of one operator.

To try and help the 'quiet' ones, Tourism Concern has published a community tourism guide. This shows us how to have holidays in the developing world in ways that benefit poor communities. For example, you needn't book through a large multinational company, you can book
30 directly with a local operator. You need to be careful when deciding your destination. Tourism Concern urges people to react with their feet to hostile regimes. 'If a country has a record of human rights abuses you should simply stay away,' instructs Lara Marsh.

4

But not everyone thinks that absence makes the country stronger.

35 Hilary Bradt, who publishes Bradt guidebooks, believes boycotts are basically detrimental. 'Staying away doesn't do anyone any good while going can make a difference. By depriving an area of tourism it's the locals who are suffering.' The Dalai Lama agrees. He argues that Tibet needs tourists to continue to visit his country so that they can see and
40 report back on the conditions the local people have to cope with.

Tourism Concern would like people on package holidays to widen their horizons and travel beyond the confines of their tourist compounds and luxury hotels. It has produced a film now shown on some flights to Gambia that suggests some steps to ethical behaviour.
45 Tourists are urged to travel further afield, visiting the villages, learning about the country's culture and purchasing local products – as long as they are dressed decently.

5

People in the Gambia have had their modesty offended by tourists' style of dress. But by visiting markets, tourists can inject some money into
50 the local economy by buying home-grown goods, something the large hotels tend not to do. 'I knew of one hotel in the Gambia that imported all their tomatoes from the Canary Islands when they really needn't have done as they had tomatoes growing yards away from their compound,' says Mike Sykes. Hilary Bradt also felt an ethical policy
55 was betrayed on a recent trip cruising poverty stricken areas of Russia. All the food consumed during the cruise had been flown in from Holland.

6

As an industry, tourism is almost impossible to regulate. 'Tourism isn't a single product, there are a whole range of services provided by a
60 whole range of people,' explains Jackie Gibson who works for the Association of British Travel Agents. 'It's up to the airline, to the hotel, to the tour operator and to the local government to limit the damage. In Mauritius they have a local law that no hotel can be higher than the trees which is great, but then they have to justify to the local people why
65 there aren't as many tourists as there might be. It's a question of balance, everything we do has an impact. Tourism can have a beneficial effect, it can also mean that we end up destroying what we're going to see. Most people just think relaxing thoughts on holiday; maybe if they also think about the kind of life the locals are living there and what they
70 can do to help, they'll actually have a better time.'

And you could supplement your suntan with a virtuous glow. ☀

(Adapted from *Voyager*, July/August 2000)

3 Work with a partner. Match the headings below to the numbered spaces in the article.

a) Regulations: is this the answer?
b) Support local industries
c) Don't leave your conscience at home
d) Get to know local cultures
e) Choose your holiday operators with care
f) Tourism: a growing influence

4 Answer these questions:

    a) What factors does the article suggest we need to take into consideration when deciding on a holiday?

    b) Do you consider these things? Is it realistically possible to take all of these things into account?

5 Work in small groups and discuss these questions:

    a) Is your country a popular tourist destination? Are there any areas which are exclusively for tourists?

    b) What kind of tourists visit your country? People on package holidays or independent travellers?

    c) Where do they come from? What do they come to do? Enjoy the sun? Find out about the local culture?

    d) Do you think they contribute to the local economy? If they do, in what way?

    e) Do you think they do any harm? If they do, what kind of damage do they cause?

    f) Do you think tourism needs to be more strictly regulated? If yes, what regulations would you impose? If not, why not?

Lexis

1 Look at the words and phrases in the box which have been taken from the article. Match them to the definitions below. Look back at the article if you need help.

> poverty stricken areas   boycotts   issues   campaigns   impact
> habitats   human rights abuses   livelihoods

    a) geographical areas where particular races or species live

    b) points of interest or discussion

    c) means of making a living

    d) acts which deprive a person or people of their fundamental rights

    e) regions where a large portion of the population live in extremely poor conditions

    f) refusals to trade with other states, or to use or buy a product or service, as a form of protest

    g) a powerful influence

    h) series of activities designed to bring about a result

2 Complete the text below with the words in 1.

Buzz words in your shopping basket?

Ethical (1) _____ are pushing their way into our supermarket trolleys. (2) _____ are not only exercised by governments to put pressure on hostile regimes, they are also used as a powerful tool for change by ordinary consumers. Refusing to buy certain goods or services is often the easiest way for ordinary consumers to make their voices heard. Recent (3) _____ against such things as GM foods, or eggs produced by battery-farmed hens, have had a significant (4) _____ on the buying policies of some of the main high street supermarkets. It is not only by refusing to spend their money that consumers can make a difference, they can also make a difference by spending a little extra on selected goods. Charitable organisations endorse certain trademarks with promises that a percentage of the money paid is going to a good cause, from safe-guarding the (5) _____ of endangered species to fighting against (6) _____ .

Fair World takes it one step further. *Fair World* is a charity that helps producers of staple food products such as coffee, tea and sugar, sell their goods directly to shopkeepers, so ensuring that a high percentage of the profits made from these goods go straight to (7) _____ where they are grown rather than to line the pockets of the middlemen. So when consumers buy these goods they know they are contributing directly to safe-guarding the (8) _____ of those farmers and their families.

3 Work with a partner and discuss these questions:

    a) Do you think consumers can make a difference?

    b) Are there any products you refuse to buy?

    c) Are there any products you make a point of buying?

    d) Is there anything else we can do in our everyday lives to make a difference?

Conscience

Collocations   Look at the collocations with *conscience* in the box. Use them to complete the sentences which follow.

> a guilty conscience   on his conscience   in all conscience   an easy conscience
> eased my conscience   a clear conscience

a) It was a tragic accident. He'll have it ____ for the rest of his life.
b) I was able to leave with ____ , happy that I'd done all I could to help.
c) He suffered with ____ for months after he left his wife and family.
d) I ____ by telling my boss about the mistake I'd made.
e) Can you, ____ , take their money when you know how much they need every penny?
f) You can go on holiday with ____ – I'll look after everything here for you.

Discussion   **1**   Which of these things would make you feel guilty? Add another three things to the list.

a) smoking in an enclosed space
b) throwing litter on the floor
c) not recycling glass, paper or aluminium cans
d) spending money on luxury items
e) eating too much chocolate
f) forgetting someone's birthday
g) not doing your homework
h) letting your mobile phone ring at the cinema
i) losing your temper with someone
j) not keeping a promise
k) keeping people waiting
l) forgetting to water the plants
m) _____
n) _____
o) _____

'No flowers. That means you want me to think you haven't got a guilty conscience.'

2   Compare your answers with a partner. Which three things make you feel the guiltiest? What would you do to ease your conscience in each case?

3   Can you think of a time when you felt guilty about doing any of these things? When was the last time you suffered from a guilty conscience?

14 *Review 2*

Just a coincidence? FASCINATING FACTS!

The world is full of amazing coincidences. You've probably experienced some yourself. (1) ____ are they really that incredible? (2) ____ , bumping into an old school friend in the Australian outback or discovering that your boyfriend or girlfriend bought the same first CD as you is probably not that uncommon. Here are a few coincidences, (3) ____ , that can truly be called 'amazing'.

LIGHTNING STRIKES THRICE

In 1889, a man from Cleveland in the United States was killed in his garden when he was struck by lightning. Thirty years later, his son was also killed in exactly the same spot and incredibly, 20 years after that his grandson was (4) ____ . (5) ____ the grandfather and father had both been struck directly, the grandson was killed by a falling branch – from a tree which had been struck by lightning.

TAXI TERROR

It's not just lightning that strikes – so do taxis. In 1974, Neville Ebbin was killed when he was knocked off his moped by a taxi in Bermuda. Exactly a year later, his brother Erskine was killed in the same place when he was knocked off the same moped. (6) ____ was he killed by the same taxi with the same driver, (7) ____ the very same passenger was in the taxi.

LUCKY HUGH

Have you ever thought about changing your name? Maybe this will make you think again, especially if you're going on a sea voyage. On December 5th, 1664, a ship sailing off the coast of North Wales sank with 81 passengers on board. There was one survivor – a man named Hugh Williams. On the same date in 1785, another ship sank in the same area with 60 passengers on board. There was one survivor – a man named Hugh Williams. On the very same date, in 1860, a ship sank off the coast of Scotland. On this occasion, (8) ____ , there were only 25 passengers on board. (9) ____ , there was once again one survivor – a man named Hugh Williams.

Discourse markers

1 Complete the text with the discourse markers in the box.

> whereas   as well   but also   but incredibly   not only
> however (x2)   but   after all

2 Do you know of any other amazing coincidences or have you experienced any yourself?

Words of wisdom

Rather

1 The word *rather* has been removed from the following quotes. Put it in the correct place in each sentence.

a) We should not grieve, but find strength in what remains behind.
   British poet William Wordsworth
b) Friendship is unnecessary as it has no survival value. It gives value to survival.
   British writer C.S. Lewis
c) I wish I had never read so much. It gives me an inferiority complex.
   British novelist George Orwell
d) The English are a foul-mouthed nation.
   British essayist and journalist William Hazlitt
e) Life is like a tin of sardines. We are all of us looking for the key.
   British playwright Alan Bennett
f) 'When I use a word,' Humpty Dumpty said in a scornful tone, 'it means just what I choose it to mean. Neither more nor less.'
   British writer and mathematician Lewis Carroll in 'Through the Looking Glass'
g) Given the choice, I'd be a failure at something I enjoy as opposed to a success at something I hate.
   American actor and comedian George Burns

2 Which of the words of wisdom do you like the most?

George Orwell

Lewis Carroll

Word games

Compound adjectives

1 Complete the compound adjectives in these sentences. Fill in the crossword with your answers.

a) Because my friend is always very smartly- ____ (9 across) in a three-piece suit and is slightly grey- _____ (4 down), he looks quite distinguished. Everyone thinks he's very good- ____ (12 across)!

b) He recently graduated from university and so is well- ____ (5 down). He's always very well- ____ (1 down) about most subjects and he can talk to you about almost anything. And even though he's got many fixed views and ideas, he is at the same time very broad- ____ (13 across) and willing to listen to most points of view.

c) Everyone's parents love him! In public he's polite and well- ____ (3 across) and he fits into any social situation with ease. If there's a difficult situation he's quick- ____ (6 down) enough to be able to come up with something to say to sort it out. In private though he's not always so well- ____ (2 down)! He loves playing jokes on people and really knows how to be naughty!

d) He's usually calm, and softly- ____ (10 down), but occasionally he can be quick- ____ (6 across) and suddenly get quite angry. You don't ever want to get into an argument with him!

e) In general, he's great company as he's such a fun- ____ (11 across) person. He can at times though look a little sad- ____ (7 across), particularly when he's got something important on his mind.

f) He's very hard- ____ (8 down) and never stops until the job is done, whatever it may be.

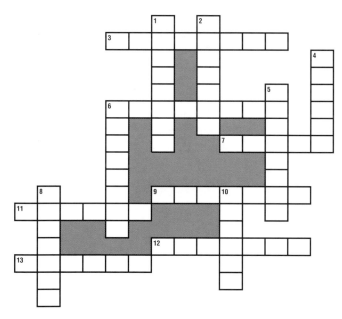

2 Write a description of a friend of yours using at least five compound adjectives.

Internet lexis

1 Find nine more words or phrases connected with the Internet and e-mail in the text on the right. The words may run from one line on to the next.

2 Work with a partner. For each word or phrase, ask and answer questions.

For example:
Which sites are bookmarked on your computer?

> drhtwattachmentgo
> nservermkjhuaeinb
> oxjfderlogonkoowll
> searchengineldpamj
> homepagelokha~~book~~
> ~~mark~~jdonlinejudert
> chatroomakediirkos
> newsgroupgrsedaati

The 21st century

The future seen from the past

1 Complete the article using the phrases in the box.

were supposed to crash	were to last	were on the verge of colonising
would be	were going to be carrying	would be swallowing
were going to be delivering		

In hindsight, it's easy to scoff at past predictions

Not that many years ago, scientists and futurologists predicted that by the beginning of the 21st century we (1) _____ pills for breakfast before strapping on personal jetpacks to fly to work and that we would be living in floating cities and holidaying in cities under the sea.

Even NASA, the American space agency, was laughably wide of the mark. In 1980, it said that we (2) _____ the moon and that by now more than 1,000 people would be permanently living and working there.

Other forecasts, such as the idea that by the year 2000, robots (3) _____ letters to anywhere in the world within one day, seem ridiculously naive in the age of e-mail and the Internet.

The only recurrent theme that emerges from decades of studies looking into the future is that we are much better at creating a future than predicting it.

It was said in the seventies, that by the new millennium computers (4) _____ as intelligent as the human brain and small enough to carry in your pocket, hypersonic aircraft (5) _____ us from London to Sydney in two hours and devices for controlling hurricanes would be used as weapons against enemies. Trains would be replaced by continuous high-speed horizontal escalators, adhesive tape would be strong enough for all structural household repairs and shoes, one pundit proclaimed, (6) _____ a lifetime.

And let us not forget of course that the world's computers (7) _____ in the first few seconds of the new millennium, throwing the world into confusion and mayhem – a bit like the minds of those charged with predicting our future perhaps.

Living on the moon?

(Adapted from *The Daily Telegraph*, 31st August 2000)

2 Think of five more predictions for the future of the world. Work in groups and decide which predictions are

a) the most amusing.
b) the most probable.

Special uses of the past simple

1 How would you like to see the world change in the future? Write five sentences using the prompts

I wish …
If only …
It's high time …
It's time …
I'd rather …

For example:
It's time people stopped being so obsessed with money.

2 Work in small groups and share your ideas. Which are the most common, interesting or unusual ideas?

Greetings from Nepal

Patterns with
have & get

Complete the letter using *have* or *get* with the verbs in brackets in the correct form. The first one has been done for you.

Hi Everyone,

Well, I'm here at last! After spending a few months in Australia with Yuichi, I finally (1) __got him to agree__ (him/agree) to come to Nepal with me. We've been here for over a month now and we're loving every minute!

As you know, I've always wanted to go trekking in the Himalayas and two weeks ago I finally (2) _____ (do) it. The whole experience was absolutely amazing from start to finish. We (3) _____ (a small truck/take) us up into the foothills and when we got out we found ourselves in the middle of nowhere in the middle of the night. Anyway, we finally (4) _____ (go) and then had the most amazing time. We (5) _____ (a local guide/take) us up some routes and we were on top of the world – literally! It was so peaceful. Well, whenever we didn't (6) _____ (people/run) after us offering to carry our bags it was. I have to say it was the best two weeks of my life. I can't wait 'til I (7) _____ (the photos/develop). They'll certainly (8) _____ (you/pack) to come out here!

Anyway, only a few more weeks to go and I'll be back home. It's strange, but even after all this time away, I still feel a bit homesick from time to time. I can't wait to see you all and at last you'll all (9) _____ (meet) Yuichi for yourselves. Be warned though – he'll (10) _____ (you all/teach) him English before you know it!
I'll write again before we head home.
Lots of love,
Marcella xxx

Strange but true

Using modals to talk about the past

1 ⏵ 62 Listen to three true stories. What is the connection between

  a) a large crate and a birthday?
  b) a commuter train and a tidal wave?
  c) a pilot called Jack and armed police?

2 Complete the news stories. For each space, add a modal from the box and put the verb into the correct form. Use each modal at least once.

could	couldn't	can't	would	might	must	should

… And to finish tonight's programme, we said we (1) _____ (bring) you some amusing stories from this week's press from around the world, and here they are:

In the United States, John Franklin, a cleaner from Illinois, decided last month he (2) _____ (post) himself to his best friend as a birthday surprise. He climbed into a large crate and got his wife to post him to his friend's house thirty miles away. He (3) _____ (arrive) the next morning, but unfortunately the crate went missing for six days before finally turning up in Malibu, California. Postal workers (4) _____ (rescue) him earlier, but they mistook his desperate banging for the ticking of a clock. Mr Franklin said he (5) _____ (think) clearly as it seemed like such a good idea at the time. An understatement if ever we've heard one.

Japan now, and Keita Ono's inflatable underpants caused chaos on a rush-hour train in Tokyo last week. Mr Ono, 43, designed the rubber pants so they (6) _____ (inflate) to 30 times their normal size in the event of a tidal wave. He explained that he'd always been afraid of drowning and that he wore them 24 hours a day. Mr Ono thinks that somebody (7) _____ (splash) some water on them, triggering the sensor and accidentally causing them to inflate. He admitted that he (8) _____ (be able) to deflate the pants, but he said he (9) _____ (not/move) at all and was firmly wedged in the middle of the carriage aisle. Things (10) _____ (be) much worse had it not been for a quick-thinking passenger who punctured the pants with a pen.

Finally, Detroit airport was last night put on red-alert when a man boarding a plane greeted the pilot, whom he knew, with the words 'Hi Jack'. Air-traffic controllers, who (11) _____ (pay) too much attention to what was going on, ordered armed police to board the plane, before realising their mistake. A spokesman said that from now on, officials (12) _____ (notify) air-traffic control whenever there was a pilot called Jack on duty.

3 Listen again and check your answers.

Word challenge

1 Play in groups of three.

1 It's ____ far the most interesting place I've visited.

2 Unfortunately, my plans fell ____ .

3 I came ____ against a lot of opposition.

4 ____ a word, the food was terrible.

5 It didn't live ____ to my expectations.

6 I had to weigh it ____ in my mind very carefully.

7 Unfortunately, it was called ____ at the last minute.

8 I have a good chance ____ doing it before the end of the year.

9 I couldn't put it ____ words.

10 I realised it was ____ the law.

11 I'll do it ____ due course.

12 It's been ____ my conscience for a long time.

13 I couldn't do it ____ first.

14 I'll have done it ____ the end of the year.

15 I wondered what the future had in store ____ me.

16 It was a once ____ a lifetime opportunity.

17 She's a woman ____ few words.

18 There was a terrible mix ____ .

19 I did it ____ economic reasons.

20 I needed to pluck ____ courage.

2 Choose five of the sentences and tell the other members of the group about a person or situation in your life which fits the sentence.

Lexis Do this quiz as quickly as you can.

1 Add the missing words.
a I'm sorry, but nothing springs to _____ .
b Don't worry – I'll _____ your word for it.
c She's a law unto _____ .
d I think he's got a guilty _____ .

2 Match the neutral word with its formal equivalent.
a later   1 severe
b very bad   2 prior to
c well-known   3 in due course
d before   4 prominent

3 Which of the following is not a crime?
a arson   c fraud
b libel   d sue

4 Rearrange the last parts of the sentences.
a They managed *off pull to everything*.
b There's been *up mix a terrible*.
c We've had *hitch technical a slight*.
d They need to *act their get together*.

5 Rearrange the mixed-up words.
a The whole evening was one big *caifso*.
b He never actually goes anywhere. He's an *rchamira* traveller.
c Look at all that *fraifgit* on the wall over there.
d He's always been totally *wla-gadibin*.

6 Which one of the following is not possible?
a guilty conscience
b clear conscience
c on his conscience
d dirty conscience

7 Match words from each column.
a scratch   1 year
b bad hair   2 food
c gap   3 card
d GM   4 day

8 Which of the following is not possible?
a first and foremost   c first and finish
b first aid   d first-hand

9 Name someone or something that is …
a time-consuming
b slow-moving
c record-breaking
d stress-induced

10 Which one word completes all the following?
a You have my ____ .
b ____ of mouth.
c In a ____ .
d I'll take your ____ for it!

Additional material

1 Identity

Introduction, 2

Answers

a) Sean Connery
b) Marilyn Monroe
c) Margaret Thatcher
d) Bill Clinton

1 Identity

Mistaken identity, 6

Answers

a) The man has just put his children to bed and is creeping back downstairs so he doesn't wake them up.
b) The man has gone in to buy a surprise birthday present for his wife and has just bumped into a friend of hers.
c) The 'thug' has noticed that something is about to fall from the building site. He's about to push the businessman out of the way so he doesn't get hurt.

1 Identity

The gender gap, 3

Student A

1 Make notes on the following:
  a) What Martians value
  b) How they experience fulfilment
  c) How their clothes reflect their value system
  d) What they are interested in
  e) What they take pride in
  f) What most annoys them

LIFE ON MARS

Martians value power, competency, efficiency, and achievement. They are always doing things to prove themselves and develop their power and skills. Their sense of self is defined through their ability to achieve results. They experience fulfilment primarily through success and accomplishment.

A man's sense of self is defined through his ability to achieve results.

---

5 Everything on Mars is a reflection of these values. Even their dress is designed to reflect their skills and competence. Police officers, soldiers, businessmen, scientists, cab drivers, technicians, and chefs all wear uniforms or at least hats to reflect their competence and power.

They don't read magazines like *Psychology Today*, *Self*, or *People*. They are more
10 concerned with outdoor activities, like hunting, fishing, and racing cars. They are interested in the news, weather, and sports and couldn't care less about romance novels and self-help books.

They are more interested in 'objects' and 'things' rather than people and feelings. Even today on Earth, while women fantasize about romance, men fantasize about
15 powerful cars, faster computers, gadgets, gizmos, and new powerful technology. Men are preoccupied with the 'things' that can help them express power by creating results and achieving their goals.

Achieving goals is very important to a Martian because it is a way for him to prove his competence and thus feel good about himself. And for him to feel good
20 about himself he must achieve these goals by himself. Someone else can't achieve them for him. Martians pride themselves in doing things all by themselves. Autonomy is a symbol of efficiency, power and competence.

Understanding this Martian characteristic can help women understand why men resist so much being corrected or being told what to do. To offer a man unsolicited
25 advice is to presume that he doesn't know what to do or that he can't do it on his own. Men are very touchy about this, because the issue of competence is so very important to them.

Because he is handling his problems on his own, a Martian rarely talks about his problems unless he needs expert advice. He reasons: 'Why involve someone else
30 when I can do it by myself?' He keeps his problems to himself unless he requires help from another to find a solution. Asking for help when you can do it yourself is perceived as a sign of weakness.

(From *Men Are From Mars, Women Are From Venus*, by John Gray, Ph.D.)

2 When you have finished, turn back to page 8.

2 Taste

Introduction, 2

Answers

a) baked beans: Nicholas
b) cauliflower: Melody
c) a bar of chocolate: Zena
d) nuts: David

3 City

Where in the world?, 2

Clue 1

The texts describe five cities from the list below:

Bangkok, Budapest, London, Madrid, Moscow, New York, Paris, Prague, Rome, Tokyo

Look at page 138 if you need another clue.

5 Luck

Winning the big one. Lexis, 2

Answers

(1) c (2) b (3) b (4) a
(5) a (6) b (7) c (8) b

7 Review 1

Relative & participle clauses, 2

Answer

Deeply in love. The tank was full of sharks, not tropical fish!

1 Identity

My girl, 5

Student A

Last night you and your boyfriend decided to go to the cinema tonight to see a film you both really want to see. Tonight is the last night it's showing. He's already cancelled two dates to go. You're not too sure about your relationship at the moment. Your boyfriend seems to be very distant these days. You think there must be something worrying him but he refuses to talk about it. You wish he'd talk to you because you're sure it would help.

You phone your boyfriend to make arrangements to meet. Think about what you're going to say and the language you are going to use.

3 City

One big party, 5

Student A

1 Below are four words from the text. Check their meanings in a dictionary if necessary, and prepare to explain the words to your partner. Do not tell your partner the word you are explaining. Your partner must listen and identify the word from the text.
   a) buskers
   b) check out
   c) eyeball
   d) gorge

2 When you have finished, listen to your partner's description of four more words from the text and identify the words being described.

3 City

Hedging, 9

Most prefer to live in cities if given choice

According to a survey published in the press today, it would appear that most people under the age of thirty would much prefer to live in a large city if given the choice.

By far the most important factor given in their answers would seem to be the fact that it is far easier to find work in larger cities.

However, the results show that there is no doubt that the range of free time facilities on offer is also an important factor in the decision to leave families and homes in rural areas.

6 Mind

Introduction, 2

Answers

a) False: the average male brain weighs 1.4kg and the average female brain weighs 1.3kg.
b) True
c) False: 80% of the average human brain is water.
d) False: the brain is pinkish grey on the surface and white inside.
e) True
f) False: we use 100% of our brains in everyday life.
g) True
h) False: the brain is very active during sleep, but the activity is of a different type to waking activity.
i) False: we yawn more when the brain is being stimulated to allow more oxygen to the brain.
j) True

4 Talk

A tall tale, 3

1 Before telling the story, it's important to identify the main stresses. Before you listen to the story again, look at the tapescript below and decide where the speaker pauses and where the main stresses fall. The first ones have been marked for you.

A rich lady returned home from a <u>ball</u>. // She rang the bell for her butler and when he appeared she said, 'Edward, take off my shoes,' and he did. Then she said, 'Edward, take off my coat,' and he did. 'Take off my dress,' and he did. 'And now take off my underwear,' and he did. 'And now, Edward,' she said, 'if you wish to remain in my service, you are never to wear any of my clothes again.'

2 Compare your answers with a partner.

3 ▪▪ 25 Listen again and check your answers. Make sure you mark any differences.

4 Prepare to 'shadow read' the joke, telling it at the same time as it plays on the tape, mirroring the pauses and intonation. Follow the instructions below:

   a) Listen to the tape again. Read the tapescript quietly to yourself, trying to keep up with the tape as closely as possible.
   b) 'Shadow read' the story. Listen again and tell the joke out loud with the comedian.

1 Identity

The gender gap, 3

Student B

1 Make notes on the following:
  a) What Venusians value
  b) How they experience fulfilment
  c) How their dress reflects their value system
  d) What they are interested in and concerned with
  e) What they take pride in

LIFE ON VENUS

Venusians have different values. They value love, communication, beauty, and relationships. They spend a lot of time supporting, helping, and nurturing one another. Their sense of self is defined through their feelings and the quality of their relationships. They experience fulfilment through sharing and relating.

A woman's sense of self is defined through her feelings and the quality of her relationships.

5 Everything on Venus reflects these values. Rather than building highways and tall buildings, the Venusians are more concerned with living in harmony, community, and loving cooperation. Relationships are more important than work and technology. In most ways their world is the opposite of Mars.

They do not wear uniforms like Martians (to reveal their competence). On the
10 contrary, they enjoy wearing a different outfit every day, according to how they are feeling. Personal expression, especially of feelings, is very important. They may even change outfits several times a day as their mood changes.

Communication is of primary importance. To share their personal feelings is much more important than achieving goals and success. Talking and relating to
15 one another is a source of tremendous fulfilment.

This is hard for a man to comprehend. He can come close to understanding a woman's experience of sharing and relating by comparing it to the satisfaction he feels when he wins a race, achieves a goal, or solves a problem.

Instead of being goal oriented, women are relationship oriented; they are more
20 concerned with expressing their goodness, love, and caring. Two Martians go to lunch to discuss a project or business goal; they have a problem to solve. In addition, Martians view going to a restaurant as an efficient way to approach food: no shopping, no cooking, and no washing dishes. For Venusians, going to lunch is an opportunity to nurture a relationship, for both giving support to and receiving
25 support from a friend. Women's restaurant talk can be very open and intimate, almost like the dialogue that occurs between therapist and patient.

On Venus, everyone studies psychology and has at least a master's degree in counseling. They are very involved in personal growth, spirituality, and everything that can nurture life, healing, and growth. Venus is covered with parks,
30 organic gardens, shopping centers and restaurants.

Venusians are very intuitive. They have developed this ability through centuries of anticipating the needs of others. They pride themselves in being considerate of the needs and feelings of others. A sign of great love is to offer help and assistance to another Venusian without being asked.

(From *Men Are From Mars, Women Are From Venus*, by John Gray, Ph.D.)

2 When you have finished, turn back to page 8.

6 Mind

Mind matters, 3h

The Lost Mariner

The Lost Mariner is about a man suffering from amnesia. He could remember his childhood and the first years of his working life (he worked for the American navy) in great detail but nothing else. His world had stopped in 1945; he believed he was a young man in his twenties, that America had won the war and Truman was the President of the USA. He was unable to remember anything that had happened to him since.

The Phantom Finger

A sailor accidentally cut off his right index finger. For forty years afterwards he was plagued by the phantom of the finger rigidly extended: whenever he scratched his nose or tried to eat he was afraid that the phantom finger would poke his eye out. He knew that it was impossible but the feeling was so strong he couldn't ignore it.

The Dog Beneath The Skin

This case concerns a young man who dreamt he was a dog and could smell like a dog. He then woke up and found he was indeed able to smell like a dog. He could distinguish all his friends by smell; he could smell their emotions – fear, contentment, worry – like a dog. It was a whole new world but then suddenly, after three weeks, this strange transformation ceased.

7 Review 1

Words of wisdom, 2

Answers

Quote 1: Marcus Aurelius Antoninus
Quote 2: Agatha Christie
Quote 3: Franz Kafka
Quote 4: Gordon Hewitt
Quote 5: Franklin D. Roosevelt
Quote 6: J. B. S. Haldane
Quote 7: T. S. Elliot
Quote 8: Anonymous, about Dean Gooderham Acheson

ADDITIONAL MATERIAL

1 Identity

My girl, 5

Student B

> You and your girlfriend had talked about going to see a film tonight but you've had a hard day and you just want to have a quiet night in at home, alone. You're not really bothered about seeing the film anyway and you know your girlfriend's sister would love to see it. Maybe the two of them could go together. You and your girlfriend can go out another time when you're feeling more sociable. You know you wouldn't be good company tonight.

You know your girlfriend will be phoning you soon. Think about what you're going to say to her and the language you're going to use.

3 City

One big party, 5

Student B

1 Below are four words from the text. Check their meanings in a dictionary if necessary, and prepare to explain the words to your partner.
a) rant
b) gawp at
c) handily
d) eateries

2 Your partner will explain four more words from the text. You must listen and identify the words being described. When your partner has finished, explain your four words for your partner to identify.

9 Law

Test yourself, 6

WELSH IN THE WITNESS BOX

During a recent court case held in Wales an English judge learnt a lesson about using Welsh in the courtroom. A Welshman stood in the witness box, accused of shoplifting. Defending him was a Welsh lawyer.

The lawyer asked the judge towards the end of the trial whether he could speak to the jury in Welsh. Not wishing to appear biased towards English, the judge agreed. Shortly afterwards, a verdict of not guilty was returned. What puzzled the judge was the verdict, as the defendant was obviously guilty.

Not being able to speak Welsh, the judge hadn't understood what the lawyer had said, which was 'The prosecutor is English, the prosecution counsel is English, the judge is English. But the prisoner is Welsh, I'm Welsh and you're Welsh. Do your duty.'

11 Stories

Urban myths, 3

Group A

1 Read this urban myth and discuss the questions that follow with your group.

The Spider's Bite

A woman decides to take a trip to a Jamaica. She spends the week lazing on numerous beaches, but on the last day decides to take a tour through a forested area. She comes across a secluded waterfall, where she decides to take a swim and then dry off in the sun. The woman falls asleep in the sun and is woken up by a spider crawling on her cheek. She brushes the spider away and thinks no more of it.

However, after returning home, the woman develops a cyst on her cheek. She goes to her local surgery, where the doctor tells her they will need to burst the cyst to let the fluid escape. As it's a painless procedure, the woman is not anaesthetised. Soon after the doctor makes the first attempt to burst the cyst, the woman hears a gasp and then feels something trickling down her cheek. She assumes it's the fluid. The doctor tells her not to panic. Instinctively, she brings her hand to her cheek to wipe off the fluid. At that point she realises that it's not fluid, but rather something crawling on her cheek.

Spiders … hundreds of tiny spiders are crawling all over her face and on her hand. She lets out a blood-curdling scream. She is so out of control that she needs to be restrained by several members of staff.
To this date, she remains in the psychiatric ward of the same hospital where the procedure took place.

a) Is the story credible?
b) What makes it a good story?
c) What information needs to be delayed until the end?

2 Imagine a friend of a friend told you this story and swore that it was true. You are going to tell it to some other students in your class. Before you do, think about how you could adapt the story to make it sound as if it could have happened to someone you know. Think about what you know about storytelling. Remember that urban myths grow and change each time they're told.

3 When you have finished, turn back to page 101.

4 Talk

Conversation piece, 2

Definition 1

conversation /ˌkɒnvəˈseɪʃ(ə)n/ *n*. **1** the informal exchange of ideas, information, etc. by spoken words. **2** an instance of this. [Middle English via Old French from Latin *conversatio -onis* (as CONVERSE¹)]
conversational /ˌkɒnvəˈseɪʃ(ə)n(ə)l/ *adj*. **1** of or in conversation. **2** fond of or good at conversation. **3** colloquial. □**conversationally** *adv*.
conversationalist /ˌkɒnvəˈseɪʃ(ə)n(ə)lɪst/ *n*. a person who is good at or fond of conversing.
conversation piece *n*. **1** a small genre painting of a group of figures. **2** a thing that serves as a topic of conversation because of its unusualness etc.

Definition 2

conversation /ˌkɒnvəˈseɪʃn/ noun ★★★
❶ [C] a talk between two or more people, usually a private and informal one: *Later in the evening, the conversation turned to politics.* ✦ **+ with/between** *a conversation with my neighbour/between two friends* ✦ **have a conversation** *She had a long telephone conversation with her mother.*
❷ [U] informal talk between people: *With so much loud music, conversation was almost impossible.* ✦ **topic of conversation** *He's so boring – his only topic of conversation is football.* ✦ **(deep) in conversation** *I found her deep in conversation with one of the tutors* ✦ **snatches of conversation** (=short parts of a conversation) *From snatches of conversation I overheard, I realized they were in financial difficulties.*
get into conversation to start talking to someone you have never met before: *She met Harry at the airport and they got into conversation.*
make conversation to talk to someone that you do not know well, just in order to be polite, not because you really want to talk to them. This type of conversation is also called **small talk**: *'It's a nice party, isn't it?', I said, trying to make conversation.*
conversational /ˌkɒnvəˈseɪʃənl/ adj ❶ a conversational style of writing or speaking is informal, like a private conversation: *She spoke in a quiet conversational tone.*
❷ relating to conversations: *conversational skills*
-conversationally adj: *'Have you been here before?' he enquired, conversationally.*
conversationalist /ˌkɒnvəˈseɪʃənəlɪst/ noun [C] someone who enjoys conversations and always has interesting or funny things to say: *a delightful conversationalist*
ˌconverˈsation piece noun [C] an interesting or unusual object that attracts attention and makes people start talking about it.

11 Stories

Urban myths, 3

Group B

1 Read this urban myth and discuss the questions that follow with your group.

THE KILLER IN THE BACK SEAT

One night a woman went out for drinks with her friends. At the end of the night she got in her car and drove onto the deserted motorway. She noticed a pair of headlights in her rear view mirror, approaching at a pace just slightly quicker than hers. As the car pulled up behind her she saw that it had its indicator on – it was going to pass – then suddenly it swerved back behind her, pulled up dangerously close and flashed its headlights.

She began to feel nervous. The lights dimmed for a moment and then they flashed again. The frightened woman struggled to keep her eyes on the road and didn't dare look at the car behind her. Finally, she reached her turning but the car continued to follow, flashing its lights periodically.

Through every red light and turn it followed her until she arrived home. She decided that her only hope was to make a mad dash into the house and call the police. As she jumped from the car so did the driver in the car behind her – and he shouted, 'Lock the door and call the police!'

When the police arrived the horrible truth was finally revealed to the woman. The man in the car behind her had been trying to save her. As he pulled up behind her and his headlights illuminated her car, he saw the silhouette of a man with a butcher's knife rising up from the back seat to stab her, so he flashed his headlights and the figure crouched back down.

---

a) Is the story credible?
b) What makes it a good story?
c) What information needs to be delayed until the end?

2 Imagine your neighbour told you this story about a friend of hers. You are going to tell it to some other students in your class. Before you do, think about how you could adapt and embellish the story to make it sound as if it could really have happened in your home town. Think about what you know about storytelling. Remember that urban myths grow and change each time they're told.

3 When you have finished, turn back to page 101.

2 Taste

The demise of a great little restaurant, 4

Student A

1 Read the text and make notes about the changes that
have taken place:
   a) in the area surrounding the bar.
   b) in the bar on the jetty.
   c) to the boat and the journey to the island.

2 Compare your answers with another Student A.

3 Work with your original partner who read part B.
Close your book and use your notes to tell your
partner about the changes to the bar and the journey.
Your partner will give you information about the
changes to the restaurant.

4 Discuss whether your predictions about the changes
were correct.

My wife had heard all about Le Palmier and was looking
forward to our visit as much as I was. Driving to the jetty,
we were surprised to find that what had once been a tiny
village was now a thriving tourist town. As I parked the
5 car I looked across the water to the island, where I saw a
brand new sign with the restaurant's name in lights. We set
off for Dominique's bar in the hope of finding her still
serving exquisite wine from a barrel.

It was not to be. At the edge of the water stood a large
10 bar with tables inside and out. As I pushed open the door,
pop music blared out at me. I made my way to the bar to
find out about the possibility of getting a table that
evening. The woman I spoke to looked familiar and I
realised I was speaking to Dominique. As she looked at her
15 list of bookings, I noticed that a number of coach parties
were booked in. It all looked terribly efficient.

We were in luck – there had been a late cancellation. We
ordered a drink and settled down to wait for our turn on
the launch. But while the wait was the same – about an
20 hour – the surroundings were not. As we sat sipping our
pricey beers people came and went all around us. The bar
clearly catered for more than the restaurant clientele, but
the number of people who were looking expectantly out
across the water worried me slightly. Eventually our names
25 were called along with around twenty others. I wondered
how we were all going to fit into the five-seater launch that
I remembered from my earlier visit.

But there was no small launch any more. Instead,
bobbing up and down at the end of the walkway, I saw a
30 sleek boat with plenty of seating and an enormous motor
at the back. We were helped aboard by a smartly-dressed
crew member. As the boat sped off towards the island I
glanced back towards our rented car, and saw a crowd of
teenagers gathered around it. I wondered whether the
35 stereo would still be there when we returned.

The journey across the water was speedy and efficient.
Gone was the opportunity to chat with Marianne and find
out what Didier had caught that day. Instead we listened to
more music.

1 Identity

Mistaken identity, 2

Answers

a) True
b) Unknown: the text doesn't tell us if he parked it or
   not.
c) True
d) Unknown: we don't know if the driver and the
   owner are the same person.
e) Unknown: we don't know who drove it away or
   why.
f) Unknown: we don't know if the police officer came
   because s/he was called, just happened to be passing
   or maybe saw what was happening on a security
   camera.
g) Unknown: we don't know whether the police officer
   was a man or a woman.
h) Unknown: in addition to the man who appeared and
   the police officer, we don't know if the driver and the
   owner are two different people or the same person.

2 Taste

A taste for travel, 3

Answers

Anne: Thailand   Bill: Hungary
Kim: Southern India   Steve: Spain

10 Firsts

Great firsts. Word stress, 3

Student A

1 Read these words to Student B, who will underline
the main stress.

   a) summit   b) pioneer   c) expedition
   d) dangerous   e) communication

2 Listen to Student B reading these five words.
Underline the main stress.

   a) conquer   b) marathon   c) impossible
   d) international e) attention

3 Check your answers with your partner.

3 City

Where in the world?, 2

Clue 2

Here are photos of the five cities, but not in the correct order.

---

11 Stories

Urban myths, 3

Group C

1 Read this urban myth and discuss the questions that follow with your group.

> ### THE FLAT TYRE
>
> Two university students decided to go skiing for the weekend but planned to be back on campus in time to revise for an important exam on the Monday morning. However, they were having such a good time on the slopes that they decided to forget about studying for the exam in order to get some final runs in before heading back to university. They knew that they would have to come up with a good excuse for not being prepared for the exam so they decided to tell their lecturer that they had set off with plenty of time to get back and do some studying but that they had got a flat tyre on the way back and therefore deserved to take the exam at a rescheduled time.
>
> When he heard the story, the lecturer agreed that it really was just bad luck, and suggested that they took a few days to study and do the exam at the end of the week. The students, of course, were delighted. At the appointed time, the lecturer greeted them and placed them in two separate rooms to take the exam.
>
> The few questions on the first page were worth a minor 10% of the overall mark, and were quite easy. Each student grew progressively more confident as they worked their way through the questions, sure that they had got away with fooling their lecturer. However, when they turned to the second page they discovered that really they hadn't.
>
> The only question on the page, worth 90% of the exam, read: 'Which tyre?'

  a) Is the story credible?
  b) What makes it a good story?
  c) What information needs to be delayed until the end?
  d) What's the moral of the story?

2 Imagine your hairdresser told you this story about a friend of theirs. You are going to tell it to some other students in your class. Before you do, think about how you could adapt and embellish the story to make it sound as if it could really have happened in your home town. Think about what you know about storytelling. Remember that urban myths grow and change each time they're told.

3 When you have finished, turn back to page 101.

---

14 Review 2

Word challenge, 1

Student A

You are the referee for the game. Students B and C take it in turns to ask each other to fill in the missing words in the grid on page 131. You must check their answers.

(1) by	(5) up	(9) into	(13) at	(17) of
(2) through/apart	(6) up	(10) against	(14) by	(18) up
(3) up	(7) off	(11) in	(15) for	(19) for
(4) In	(8) of	(12) on	(16) in	(20) up

2 Taste

The demise of a great little restaurant, 4

Student B

1 Read the text and make notes about the changes that had taken place:
a) in the seating area and the kitchen.
b) to the menu.
c) to the vegetable gardens.

2 Compare your answers with another Student B.

3 Work with your original partner who read part A. Close your book and use your notes to tell your partner about the changes to the restaurant. Your partner will give you information about the changes to the bar and the journey.

4 Discuss whether your predictions about the changes were correct.

Arriving on the island that second time was a totally different experience. There was now a mass of tables on a huge concrete terrace exposed to the sun. Between the tables ran waiters, carrying trays of drinks and food. Our
5 waiter spoke to us in English and thrust menus into our hands as soon as we sat down.

I looked through the windows into what had been a small and homely kitchen, and saw four chefs sweating over huge stoves. There was no sign of Marianne or Didier
10 and I didn't recognise their son amongst the army of waiters. On the paper tablecloth was a basket, but the bread in it was not home-made. It was what you could buy in any supermarket on the mainland.

Looking at the menu I realised that the motor boat was
15 picking up more than just passengers: the greatly expanded menu offered dishes which could not have been created using ingredients just from the island. Worst of all, the squid was now served in batter and accompanied by chips.
20 I asked the waiter what had become of Didier and Marianne. They had retired about five years earlier and

sold the business to an entrepreneur from the capital. Only Dominique remained. She had married a local boy and was managing the bar on the jetty. The restaurant was
25 obviously profitable. As we sat and ate an unremarkable meal the boat came and went two or three times, bringing new customers and taking away those who had already eaten.

After dinner we wandered unnoticed around the back of
30 the main building and looked out over what had been the gardens. There were now a number of small concrete buildings, some with lights shining from the windows. The new owner had obviously decided that there was money to be made from offering tourists more than just dinner. They
35 could now come and spend the night, have breakfast in the morning and then return to the mainland.

As we climbed aboard the boat, considerably poorer, I found myself thinking about Marianne and what she would think if she could see the place now. My reverie was
40 broken as we chugged to a halt at the end of the jetty. I looked over to the car and wondered whether the stereo was still there.

8 Cyberspace

Future perfect, 2

STEPHEN HAWKING

Stephen Hawking is popularly considered to be one of the great geniuses of our time. A physicist whose research into cosmology and black holes has earned him many honours, he has also written the worldwide bestselling book, *A Brief History of Time*. Diagnosed with motor neurone disease when he was 21, he continues his research at Cambridge University. Over time the disease has caused him to lose his voice and most movement in his body, but has not affected his brain. He is confined to a wheelchair and communicates using a voice synthesiser and a computer.

He raises his eyebrows for 'yes', winks his left eye for 'no', but generally communicates via a voice synthesiser at a rate of fifteen to twenty words a minute. To use the voice synthesiser he first types what he wants to say onto a computer screen. To do this he applies pressure to two pads, one in each hand, to select letters, words and phrases from an index on his computer monitor. He scrolls up and down the screen constantly, at great speed. But, inevitably, the writing process is extremely slow. Only when he has constructed the whole sentence or paragraph on screen does he activate his robotic voice to speak it.

10 Firsts

Great firsts. Word stress, 3

Student B

1 Listen to Student A reading these five words. Underline the main stress.

a) summit
b) pioneer
c) expedition
d) dangerous
e) communication

2 Read these words to Student A, who will underline the main stress.

a) conquer
b) marathon
c) impossible
d) international
e) attention

3 Check your answers with your partner.

Verb structures

Basic structures

| ASPECT | VOICE | TENSES | | MODALS |
		Present	Past	will (would, must ...)
simple	active	He **writes** letters.	He **wrote** letters.	He **will write** letters.
	passive	Letters **are written**.	Letters **were written**.	Letters **will be written**.
continuous	active	He **is writing** letters.	He **was writing** letters.	He **will be writing** letters.
	passive	Letters **are being written**.	Letters **were being written**.	Letters **will be being written**.*
perfect	active	He **has written** letters.	He **had written** letters.	He **will have written** letters.
	passive	Letters **have been written**.	Letters **had been written**.	Letters **will have been** written.
perfect continuous	active	He **has been writing** letters.	He **had been writing** letters.	He **will have been writing** letters.

*Note: You usually avoid saying *be being* or *been being*. Therefore, the future continuous passive and the present/past continuous passives are rare. For the same reason, the perfect continuous passive is almost never used.

Phrasal verbs

See unit 1.

Type 1: not separable
She quickly **looked over** her notes before starting her speech.
He **got over** his divorce remarkably quickly.
Can you **look after** the kids while I go to the shops?

Type 2: separable
He **finished** the sandwich **off** in a single mouthful.
He **finished off** the sandwich in a single mouthful.
He **finished** it **off** in a single mouthful.

Type 3: two particles
I couldn't **put up with** it any longer.
She finally managed to **stand up to** her boss in the meeting.
I'm really **looking forward to** the party.

Inversion

See units 3, 5 and 9.

Not only **do we need** food and drink to stay alive, we also need love and affection.
Little **did I suspect** that I would come to love his strange ways.
Barely **had I opened** the door when I heard a loud noise upstairs.
We cannot rely on him to be there on time, **nor can we depend** on his discretion.
So surprised **were we** by his extreme reaction that we said nothing in reply.
Had I known you were going to be so late I'd have left without you.

Unreal conditionals

See unit 5.

	If clause	Main clause
Present reference	If I **was** on holiday	I **wouldn't feel** so stressed.
	If I **wasn't working**	I'**d be feeling** a lot more relaxed.
Future reference	If I **wasn't going** away next week	I'**d be** happy to come to the party on Saturday.
	If I **was staying** at home	I'**d be coming** to the party on Saturday.
Past reference	If I **had had** a little more free time	I'**d have been** happy to come to the party.
	If I **hadn't been working**	I'**d have been doing** something else.

Notes:
Any of the *if* clauses can be used in combination with any of the main clauses.
In formal language the structure *If I **were** you* is frequently used to give advice.

Patterns with *wish*

See unit 5.

1

Fact	Wish
I **don't have** much chance to speak English.	I wish I **had** more chance to speak English.
Pete'**s travelling** a lot for work at the moment.	I wish Pete **wasn't travelling** so much.
I **didn't know** what I was doing.	I wish I'**d known** what I was doing.
I **was wasting** my time.	I wish I **hadn't been wasting** my time.
We'**re going to be working** hard next week.	I wish we **weren't going to be working** so hard.
I **can't come** to the party.	I wish I **could come** to the party.
The sun **isn't shining**.	I wish the sun **would shine**.

2
We wish **to inform** you that the building will be closed until five o'clock today.

Participle clauses

See unit 6.

Present participle clause	**Eating a plum**, I came across a maggot. **Having some time to myself**, I drove to the coast for a couple of days.
Past participle clause	**Built in 1998**, this is probably one of the best examples of modern architecture in the city centre. The police, **trained in crowd control**, had trouble holding back the angry mob.
Perfect participle clause	**Not having seen the news**, she hadn't heard about the earthquake. **Having finished the book**, he breathed a sigh of relief.

Verbs of the senses

See unit 6.

Ability / sensation (stative verbs)	Voluntary action (dynamic verbs)
I **can see** for miles and miles.	**Look at** that ship on the horizon.
I **could feel** the wind in my hair as I walked along the cliff.	We **were just feeling** the material when the shop assistant accused us of stealing.
I **can hear** the church bells ringing from my house.	**Are you going to listen** to the news?
Can you smell something burning?	**Smell** this! I think it's gone off.
He **could taste** the nuts as soon as he took the first bite.	**Would you taste** this for me? Does it need more salt?

Modals

See units 8 and 9.

Modal verbs are always followed by an infinitive form. (See Basic structures table)

You**'ll be coming** to the party, won't you?
He **must have been** really angry when he found out.
I **should know** better I suppose.
You promised you**'d take** me out for dinner tonight.
Could you phone me when the order arrives, please?
You really **ought to have told** someone about the missing money.
He **may have taken** the bus, but he's probably gone by car.
You **can't be seeing** Mary tonight – she's going out with Pete.
They **might have been shouting** for help, but I thought they were just enjoying themselves.

Patterns with *get*

See unit 10.

He **gets really impatient** if he has to wait too long in a queue.
I **got first prize** in the poetry competition.
We hardly **get to see** you at all these days, you're so busy.
She **got her boyfriend to book** the flight for her.
Hurry up! We'll never **get going** at this rate!
I'll **get the car working** for you by tomorrow.
They **got their photos developed** overnight.
The cat **got run over** by a bus.

The future seen from the past

See unit 11.

They **were going to go** by car, but in the end they decided that it was cheaper by bus.
I **was supposed to be going** on holiday next week but I've had to postpone it because of work.
The baby **was due to be born** last week, so they're going to induce it.
They **were on the verge of calling** the whole thing off when she showed up.
The Prime Minister **was to open** the new hospital but he was held up in traffic.
He had thought that the show **would be** spectacular, but he was sadly disappointed.

Patterns with *have*

See unit 12.

You'll **have them queueing up** for more, believe me.
You'll **have people coming up to you** on the street asking for your autograph.
It's a good idea to **have a mechanic look** at the car before you buy it.
You should always **have the dentist check** your teeth every six months or so.

Special uses of the past simple

See unit 13.

It's time you **stopped** wasting time and got down to a bit of work.
It's about time we **headed** for home.
It's high time the government **did** something about the situation.
I'd rather you **didn't mention** it, if you don't mind.

Other structures

-ever

See unit 12.

Whichever queue I stand in, it's always the slowest.
However angry he gets, I just can't take him seriously.
Whoever came in last, please shut the door.
The dog barks like mad **whenever** he sees the postman.
I always take a photo of my family, **wherever** I travel to.
Whatever Joe says to Donna, he always upsets her.
Come round before dinner, after we've eaten, or even later. **Whenever**.
Give the letter to the secretary or the receptionist. **Whoever**.

Grammar glossary

                                  modal
                                auxiliary

verb   adjective conjunction verb   adverb   article   pronoun   main verb

Learn these useful words and you can understand more about the language you are studying.

       determiner   noun pronoun   main   preposition noun   auxiliary
                                verb   verb

Adverbials can be words or phrases. They are used to give additional information about a verb or an adjective or to comment on a statement.
For example: *I **usually** try to go swimming **twice a week**. **Frankly**, I think that was a **really** awful thing he did.*

Backshift is when a verb moves 'one tense back' in a conditional clause or reported statement.
For example: *'I **can't** come.'* → *He said he **couldn't** come.*

Clauses are groups of words containing a verb.
For example: ***He said*** *that he'd be late.*
      main clause   subordinate clause

Collocations refer to words that frequently occur together.
For example: *Common sense Get on well Merry Christmas*

Discourse markers are words or phrases that indicate the relationship between ideas.
For example: *Frank is a really good manager of people, **whereas** Tom is better with figures.*

Dynamic/stative. Verbs can have dynamic or stative meanings. Verbs with dynamic meanings refer to action or change.
For example: *I **walked** to the shops. I **read** the book. I **got** very excited.*
Verbs with stative meanings refer to a state or condition. They are not usually used in continuous forms or imperatives.
For example: *I **know** her very well. I **believe** in miracles.*

Expressions are groups of words that belong together where the words and word order never or rarely change.
For example: ***black and white** **That reminds me**, I must buy some toothpaste. **How do you do?***

Fronting is when a word or phrase which is not usually used in the initial position of a sentence is placed at the beginning to create emphasis.
For example: ***Gone** are the long summer evenings when we could sit outside until late.*

Hedging is a tactic used to avoid stating a fact too categorically.
For example: ***It seems that** the President may have made a mistake.*

Inversion is when the auxiliary verb is placed in front of the subject.
For example: ***Do you come** here often? **Are you** sure? Never **have I heard** such nonsense. So shocked **was I** by the news that I let out a cry.*

Noun phrases in their simplest form can be a pronoun or a noun. Complex noun phrases can also include determiners, some description before the noun and some description after the noun. The description after the noun is often a reduced clause or a prepositional phrase.
For example: ***A strong cup of tea with a couple of biscuits** always goes down well after work.*

Objects usually come after the verb and show who or what is affected by the verb.
For example: *She closed **the window**. My neighbour hates **me**. I've made **a cup of tea**.*
NB: some verbs take a direct object (DO) and an indirect object (IO).
For example: *She gave **him** (IO) **a kiss** (DO). He sent **her** (IO) **some flowers** (DO). I teach **students** (IO) **English** (DO).*

Particles are the prepositions or adverbs that form part of a phrasal verb.
For example: *give **away** give **up on***

Participle clauses do not include a subject or linking words and are often used to avoid repetition and to shorten complex sentences.
For example: ***Sweating from his long run**, he collapsed on the chair. The new bridge, **built in 2001**, was the pride of the community.*

Phrasal verb is the term which commonly refers to all multi-word verbs which consist of a verb + particle(s).
For example: *to pick up to look through to run over to put up with*

Prepositional phrases are phrases which consist of a preposition followed by a noun phrase or clause.
For example: *in my opinion through the window since I left school*

Relative clauses can be either defining or non-defining. A defining relative clause is necessary to identify the person or thing being talked about in the main clause.
For example: *The people **who live next door** have got three kids.*
A non-defining relative clause is not necessary for identification and just gives extra information.
For example: *The Smiths, **who have got three children**, live next door.*
NB: relative clauses are usually introduced by relative pronouns *who, that* or *which* or by relative adverbs *whose, when, where, why*.

Stative. See **Dynamic**.

Subjects usually come before the verb and refer to the main person or thing you are talking about.
For example: ***Money** doesn't grow on trees. **My tailor** is rich. **The biggest rock and roll group in the world** have started their world tour.*

Phonetic symbols

VOWELS AND DIPHTHONGS

/ɪ/	big fish	/bɪg fɪʃ/
/iː/	green beans	/griːn biːnz/
/ʊ/	should look	/ʃʊd lʊk/
/uː/	blue moon	/bluː muːn/
/e/	ten eggs	/ten egz/
/ə/	about mother	/əbaʊt mʌðə/
/ɜː/	learn words	/lɜːn wɜːdz/
/ɔː/	short talk	/ʃɔːt tɔːk/
/æ/	fat cat	/fæt kæt/
/ʌ/	must come	/mʌst kʌm/
/ɑː/	calm start	/kɑːm stɑːt/
/ɒ/	hot spot	/hɒt spɒt/
/ɪə/	ear	/ɪə/
/eɪ/	face	/feɪs/
/ʊə/	pure	/pjʊə/
/ɔɪ/	boy	/bɔɪ/
/əʊ/	nose	/nəʊz/
/eə/	hair	/heə/
/aɪ/	eye	/aɪ/
/aʊ/	mouth	/maʊθ/

CONSONANTS

/p/	pen	/pen/
/b/	bad	/bæd/
/t/	tea	/tiː/
/d/	dog	/dɒg/
/tʃ/	church	/tʃɜːtʃ/
/dʒ/	jazz	/dʒæz/
/k/	cost	/kɒst/
/g/	girl	/gɜːl/
/f/	far	/fɑː/
/v/	voice	/vɔɪs/
/θ/	thin	/θɪn/
/ð/	then	/ðen/
/s/	snake	/sneɪk/
/z/	noise	/nɔɪz/
/ʃ/	shop	/ʃɒp/
/ʒ/	measure	/meʒə/
/m/	make	/meɪk/
/n/	nine	/naɪn/
/ŋ/	sing	/sɪŋ/
/h/	house	/haʊs/
/l/	leg	/leg/
/r/	red	/red/
/w/	wet	/wet/
/j/	yes	/jes/

STRESS

In this book, word stress is shown by underlining the stressed syllable.
For example: <u>wa</u>ter; re<u>sult</u>; disa<u>ppoint</u>ing

LETTERS OF THE ALPHABET

/eɪ/	/iː/	/e/	/aɪ/	/əʊ/	/uː/	/ɑː/
Aa	Bb	Ff	Ii	Oo	Qq	Rr
Hh	Cc	Ll	Yy		Uu	
Jj	Dd	Mm			Ww	
Kk	Ee	Nn				
	Gg	Ss				
	Pp	Xx				
	Tt	Zz				
	Vv					

Tapescripts

1 Identity

 01

Steve
(I = Interviewer; S = Steve)
I: Steve, what would you say was your home town?
S: Um, ah, that's a difficult one because I've travelled around so much. Still, um, Toronto, I suppose. I mean, I've lived there for more than twenty years and that's where I was born.
I: Your parents weren't born there, though, were they?
S: Oh no, my parents were born in England, in Manchester.
I: Both of them?
S: Yeah, both of them.
I: And what would they say was their home town?
S: Well, my Dad's really proud to be English and proud to be from Manchester, but he's also proud to be Canadian – a naturalised Canadian. He's just become Canadian after thirty-five years of living there and he's really proud of that, but I guess it would be difficult for them to answer too.
I: And when someone asks you where you're from, what do you say?
S: Canada.
I: That's because you live abroad?
S: Yes, but when I'm back home at my parents' house, they've moved since I left Canada, and someone asks me where I'm from, I say Toronto.
I: And what would you say was maybe the most important thing for you in defining yourself, you know, your personal identity?
S: Wow! Well that's a big one.
I: You know, like is it your town, your country, your language, your job?
S: Well, it isn't my home town I don't think. Or my country. Maybe it's language, because Canada has got the two languages and people tend to define themselves according to language so I'd say I was English speaking Canadian, I suppose, you know, as opposed to French speaking Canadian. But it's not really that at all. I mean it's more to do with my attitude. Yeah, you know, my attitude, my opinions about things. I guess that's who I am.

David
(I = Interviewer; D = David)
I: If someone asks you where you come from, what do you say?
D: I usually say I'm Welsh. Or it depends I suppose depending on who's asking or where I am at the time. Obviously if I'm back home in Wales, then I give the name of my home town – Aberystwyth. Even though I haven't lived there in years.
I: Were you born there?
D: Yes I was, and spent most of my childhood there as well, until I was eighteen.

I: And, if you're not back home, I mean, what if you're on holiday or whatever?
D: Yes, sometimes, when I'm abroad people take it for granted that I'm English, or maybe they're just using the word English to mean British. That can be quite annoying, or not that exactly. It's when I explain that I'm from Wales and they say, 'Isn't that in England?' Now that, that's annoying.
I: Is it really that important to you?
D: Oh, that's a big question. Um, yeah, I suppose it is. I suppose it's kind of a central part of my identity. Part of how I see myself, define who I am.
I: Do you speak Welsh?
D: Yes, I do. Maybe that's part of the reason why it's so important. I mean, I think the language you speak really defines the way you think sometimes. Or at least I feel like it's another side to me. Like there's my English side and there's my Welsh side. I haven't lived in Wales for years and sometimes I really miss speaking the language like I'm missing a part of myself.
I: Do you speak Welsh at all these days?
D: Yeah, on the phone to my Mum, or my brother. Once or twice a week. But that's about all.
I: So, what would you say is your mother tongue, then? Welsh or English?
D: Both I suppose. I mean I was brought up speaking both as a kid. It's impossible not to be an English speaker in Wales. You're just surrounded by the language everywhere. On the TV, in films. There is a Welsh TV channel and weekly papers and stuff, but it's just not such a strong presence I suppose. I mean, it is possible to ignore it. It is totally possible to live in Wales and not be a Welsh speaker – well most people aren't.

Valeria
(I = Interviewer; V = Valeria)
I: So if I asked you to say who you are, I mean like, how you define yourself, what would you say was the most important factor? Your home town? Your job?
V: Difficult to say. Both I suppose. I mean, I've lived here all my life, and so have my family. My family have actually lived in the same house for seven generations. Well, OK, that's a bit of an exaggeration. But we do still have a house in a village nearby that we use in the summer, and my grandmother was born there, and her grandparents before her … I love that house, its big thick stone walls and vaulted ceilings …
I: So maybe the house is what you identify with?
V: Oh no, not only the house, the village, the town, the whole region really.
I: And what about your job?
V: Mmm, yes, well being a notary is kind of a family trade. I mean, again we go back generations and generations … my father, my grandfather … I'm

actually the first woman in our family to become a notary and I really like the idea that I'm the seventh generation of notaries in the family and that a woman can carry on what was basically a male tradition until very recently.
I: And did you always know you were going to follow in your father's footsteps? Or did you resist it at all at any time?
V: No, no, there was no question of resisting at all. I'm really happy with my choice. I really love my job. You know, it's such an old tradition, such a, I know this is going to sound a bit pompous, a bit clichéd, but it's such a respected profession and I feel really proud about carrying on the family tradition.

 02

a) He's just become Canadian after thirty-five years of living there and he's really proud of that …
b) … sometimes, when I'm abroad people take it for granted that I'm English, or maybe they're just using the word English to mean British.
c) There is a Welsh TV channel and weekly papers and stuff, but it's just not such a strong presence I suppose. I mean, it is possible to ignore it. It is totally possible to live in Wales and not be a Welsh speaker …
d) … I've lived here all my life, and so have my family. My family have actually lived in the same house for seven generations.
e) … I really like the idea that I'm the seventh generation of notaries in the family and that a woman can carry on what was basically a male tradition until very recently.

 03

(M = Martha; L = Liz)
M: Oh, you've got *Men Are From Mars, Women Are From Venus*. I saw it.
L: Yeah, Trish lent it to me. Have you read it?
M: No, well not properly. I just saw it in a bookshop and I flicked through it just briefly. I read the first few pages though, the bit … oh, what was it? The bit about men and women being from different planets. You know. It sounded really funny. I think, um, it's quite a nice idea but maybe just a little bit contrived. A bit obvious, you know. Have you read it?
L: Yeah, I've just finished it. I know what you mean about it seeming a bit contrived, but I do think it's actually quite a neat way of putting the idea across. You know, it's very clear. And it's very original and I didn't find it at all patronising.
M: That's good. I got the impression that it's very politically correct. What did you think of it? Do you think that men and women are from different planets?

L: Well, sort of. I quite liked what it had to say actually. For example, how men and women cope with stress and problems. How we cope differently. How men like to sort things out on their own.

M: Oh, that's true.

L: Take time to think things through quietly, all on their own.

M: Well, actually, that really means just bottling things up, doesn't it?

L: Well, it's interesting you should say that because that's exactly what the book predicted that that's how a woman would interpret it.

M: Really?

L: Because women actually differ from men in that they prefer to talk about problems and vent their feelings, whereas, as I say, men think it's far more efficient to sort things out on their own.

M: When I was flicking through, I caught a glimpse, a bit about how men really take pride in being able to do things and achieve things actually without help, totally on their own.

L: I think they do. I think they do actually and I think that's the root of some of the problems really because women like to talk things through and express themselves and it really gets them down if they've got a partner who won't join in, won't tell them anything.

M: Yeah. So what solution did the book come up with?

L: Well, tolerance really. You know, the best thing to do is be aware that we're different. Realise that men and women have a different style of approaching things and then learn to put up with it. Makes sense.

M: Yeah.

04

***My Girl* by Madness**

My girl's mad at me, I didn't want to see the film tonight,
I found it hard to say, she thought I'd had enough of her.
Why can't she see,
She's lovely to me,
But I like to stay in and watch TV on my own every now and then.

My girl's mad at me, been on the telephone for an hour,
We hardly said a word. I tried and tried, but I could not be heard.
Why can't I explain,
Why do I feel this pain?
'Cos everything I say she doesn't understand, she doesn't realise,
She takes it all the wrong way.

My girl's mad at me, we argued just the other night,
I thought we'd got it straight, we talked and talked until it was light.
I thought we'd agreed,
I thought we'd talked it out,
Now when I try to speak she says that I don't care.
She says I'm unaware and now she says I'm weak.

05

(B = Brian; S = Suzi)

B: Hello?

S: Hi, it's me!

B: Hiya! How are you doing?

S: Fine, a bit stressed out, had a hard day at work, you know, the usual.

B: Yeah, me too.

S: So, what about the film then? I just phoned the cinema to check the times and it's on at 7 o'clock and 9.30. Which do you reckon?

B: Listen, love, do you mind if we go another night? I'm tired, I just fancy a quiet night in, you know, bit of a veg on the sofa, watch some footie on TV.

S: But it's the last night. You said you really wanted to go!

B: Why don't you go with your sister? You said she wanted to see the film …

S: This is the third time you've pulled out. What's going on?

B: Nothing. I just don't fancy it tonight, that's all.

S: Come on, if there's something wrong you can tell me. I'm not going to fly off the handle.

B: There's nothing wrong …

S: Yes, there is. You've been off for days. You don't talk to me, you don't want to see me.

B: That's not true.

S: Are you bored with me? Is there someone else? Have I done something wrong?

B: No, no, of course not.

S: You never used to shut yourself away like this, you used to want to spend time with me. What's changed?

B: Nothing's changed. Of course I want to see you.

S: But not tonight, eh? The football's more interesting I suppose.

B: Oh, you know that's not true. It's just that I'm tired, that's all. It's been a hard day. I just need a quiet night in …

S: Alone!

B: Look, if it's that important to you, I'll come. What time did you say?

S: No, forget it! I wouldn't want you to go out of your way or anything!

B: Don't be like that. Come on, shall I come and pick you up?

S: No, forget it. I've gone off the idea. Let's just drop it.

B: Look, I'd love to do something tomorrow, yeah?

S: Whatever. Just please yourself. You always do!

B: Suzi, don't … Suzi. Suzi?

06

1 But not tonight, eh? The football's more interesting I suppose.

2 But not tonight, eh? The football's more interesting I suppose.

3 No, forget it! I wouldn't want you to go out of your way or anything.

4 No, forget it! I wouldn't want you to go out of your way or anything!

2 Taste

07

1
Erm, bitter coffee in a plastic cup and milk in plastic containers. Yeah, either that or a greasy burger on a plastic tray. Looks great in the picture but tastes disgusting and is definitely over-priced.

2
Erm … watermelon maybe, or strawberries … no, I know, big bowls of fresh salad with home-made dressing, served with cheese, bread and a glass of chilled white wine.

3
Roast dinners, you know, huge plates of roast lamb served with mashed potatoes and tiny, sweet green peas, and on top of it all, swimming in it, the best gravy you have ever tasted.

4
Crunchy milk chocolate biscuits dipped in coffee, curled up on the sofa watching your favourite film.

5
No food really, I mean, I associate it more with not being able to eat anything, well, at first at least … and later … maybe chocolate or fruit for some reason … I don't know, something like strawberries, yes, succulent sweet strawberries with fresh cream.

6
I don't know, hot chocolate? Erm, no, fish 'n' chips or a Chinese takeaway – or some kind of microwaveable convenience food that doesn't need any cooking.

08

Anne
The food? Mmm, it's superb, really hot and spicy, but quite delicate too. Kind of like a cross between Indian and Chinese food but with its own special flavours too. They use a lot of lemon grass and coconut and a lot of fish. I really liked the soups. You can buy them from stalls on the corner of the street. You choose the meat you want in your soup and the kind of noodles – long thin white rice noodles, or big fat, thick yellowish ones, and there are these tubs of spices too and you choose as much or as little of whatever you want. Then you sit there on the street, or in the market or wherever you are and eat it. I had some for breakfast one day – it was great! Really great!

Kim
The food? Well, it took a bit of getting used to actually. I like hot, spicy food, but this was too much for me at the beginning. I reckon I built up a kind of immunity to it as time went by though and I got to like it by the end. It's nothing like the kind of food we get in restaurants back home. I loved the ritual of it, going to the small street cafés where they serve your food on a banana leaf. They wash the leaf and then serve a huge helping of rice right in the middle and give you generous helpings of all the various different sauces on offer that day. You don't get a knife and a fork. You eat with your right hand, making little balls of rice and then soaking up the sauce with these little balls – it takes quite a long time to get good at it. When you've finished they bundle the banana leaf up with any leftovers and throw it out on the street where the goats and cows eat them. I love that side of it too, nothing goes to waste!

Bill
The food? Well, to tell you the truth I didn't really like it that much. It isn't the healthiest of diets. Everything is either fried or cooked in pig's fat and mmm, I don't really like cabbage that much and that's a staple part of their diet, like a lot of places in Central Europe. It's usually pickled and served with sour cream – so, no, it isn't really my favourite. Having said that, there were

some things I loved – the bread for example, it's really soft and tasty, and so many different kinds, and the scones and pastries too are really good. And some of the soups, the various kinds of goulash – that's their national dish – and the bean soups are really delicious and the paprika makes them quite spicy – great on a cold day.

Steve
The food? It isn't particularly elaborate, but it's good. The seafood is especially good, and there's just such a variety, so many different kinds of shellfish, I wouldn't know the names for half of them in English. Another favourite of mine is the grilled green chilli peppers. They serve them up by the plateful to be shared between friends over a beer or two. There's always one that's so spicy it almost blows your head off. More than anything else I love the eating out culture. It's quite informal, you go to a bar and order huge platefuls of various different specialities and share them, everybody eating off the same plates. It's very sociable – a really nice social eating ritual.

▰▱ 09

a) Mmm, it's superb, really hot and spicy …
b) Well, it took a bit of getting used to actually.
c) Well, to tell you the truth, I didn't really like it that much.
d) … and mmm, I don't really like cabbage that much …
e) … no, it isn't really my favourite.
f) It isn't particularly elaborate, but it's good.

▰▱ 10

(S = Sarah; A = Angela; D = David)
S: … I can't believe he bought her plastic flowers for her birthday. I mean, that is so tacky. That is such bad taste.
A: I don't know. It's the thought that counts.
D: No! Come on! Plastic flowers don't count!
A: Well, no, it might not be your cup of tea but you know, one man's wine is another man's poison.
D: Eh?
S: What?
A: Well, I mean I know people who like plastic flowers and they don't necessarily have bad taste.
D: It depends what you consider bad taste.
S: Yes, I mean, taste is a very personal thing.
A: Yes. Beauty is in the eye of the beholder and that sort of thing.
S: Exactly. Everyone's different and so I suppose everyone has a different idea of what good taste is.
D: Yes, so it really depends on your own taste, doesn't it?
S: Well, yeah, but having said that, no-one thinks plastic flowers are in good taste, do they?
D: No. Good taste is …
A: It's really hard to say what good taste is. Bad taste is like being flash, you know what I mean, like wearing a big gold medallion, or something.
D: Oh yes, definitely! Things like that are awful, aren't they?

A: Socks!
D: Socks and sandals, and white socks and black shoes, definitely!
S: Not necessarily, some people like them.
A: Good taste is really then, I suppose, it might be an ability to judge the beauty or the elegance of things.
D: Yes, possibly.
S: No. I don't think beauty's got anything to do with it. I think it's knowing what's right for the moment. It's knowing what's appropriate that's good taste.
D: Yes, I think you've got a point there. It's also about being able to judge the quality of things. Good quality stuff is usually quite tasteful. And yes, Sarah, you're right – it's about choosing the right thing at the right time too.
A: That reminds me of Rebecca the other day at Jo's wedding. Talk about the wrong clothes at the wrong time!
S: What, wearing that blue dress thing?
A: Yeah, it was obviously expensive, but talk about bad taste.
D: Absolutely. She looked completely out of place.
S: Well, yes, I suppose you're right. But Rebecca, you know, Rebecca has class, which isn't the same as taste. It's not the same.
D: No, but class doesn't excuse her bad taste.
S: But it does in a way, because having class means being confident in yourself. You don't worry what other people think, you just do what you want to do and people accept you for what you are.
A: But class is about knowing how to behave, not how to dress.
S: I don't totally agree there, not these days. Class means being yourself and not caring what other people think.
D: Yes, but I think there's more to it than that. I think it's that you know how to behave in every circumstance, no matter how difficult the situation might be and how to deal with it. That's class.
A: Yes, yes, I guess it is. That feeling you can take everything in your stride … you're not fazed by any situation or any group of people, you just carry on being yourself regardless.
D: You're cool; you don't get upset, you don't get het up, you know. Yeah.

▰▱ 11

(S = Sarah; A = Angela; D = David)
a
S: … I can't believe he bought her plastic flowers for her birthday. I mean, that is so tacky. That is such bad taste.
A: I don't know. It's the thought that counts.
D: No! Come on! Plastic flowers don't count!

b
S: Yes, I mean, taste is a very personal thing.
A: Yes. Beauty is in the eye of the beholder and that sort of thing.
S: Exactly. Everyone's different and so I suppose …

c
A: … wearing a big gold medallion, or something.
D: Oh yes, definitely! Things like that are

awful, aren't they?
A: Socks!
D: Socks and sandals, and white socks and black shoes, definitely!
S: Not necessarily, some people like them.

d
S: It's knowing what's appropriate that's good taste.
D: Yes, I think you've got a point there. It's also about being able to judge the quality of things. Good quality stuff is usually quite tasteful. And yes, Sarah, you're right – it's about choosing the right thing at the right time too.
A: That reminds me of Rebecca the other day at Jo's wedding. Talk about the wrong clothes at the wrong time!
S: What, wearing that blue dress thing?
A: Yeah, it was obviously expensive, but talk about bad taste.
D: Absolutely. She looked completely out of place.
S: Well, yes, I suppose you're right. But Rebecca, you know, Rebecca has class …

e
A: But class is about knowing how to behave, not how to dress.
S: I don't totally agree there, not these days. Class means being yourself and not caring what other people think.
D: Yes, but I think there's more to it than that. I think it's that you know how to behave in every circumstance, no matter how difficult the situation might be and how to deal with it. That's class.
A: Yes, yes, I guess it is. That feeling you can take everything in your stride …

▰▱ 12

1 No
2 Yes
3 Yes
4 Yes
5 No
6 No

▰▱ 13

a) The best way to eat fish is raw.
b) French cuisine is the best in the world.
c) People who smoke in restaurants are inconsiderate.
d) If you want to get to the top, you have to start at the bottom.
e) Life is too short to waste time worrying about what other people think.
f) Travel is the best way of broadening the mind.

3 City

▰▱ 14

(M = Mike; S = Sue)
M: … Thank you John, and now it's back to the studio for the answers to last week's quiz. Sue?
S: Thanks Mike. Hello, yes, and there are a few surprises in the answers this week. So let's start with the first question, which I think held the biggest surprise for our contestants. According to data collected by the UN, 53% of the world's population lives in cities, whilst 47% live in rural areas. In

the EU the percentage of people living in urban centres rises to a staggering 74% and an even higher 76% in the USA. It would appear that there is a steady movement towards urban areas and that the proportion of city dwellers will continue to rise.

Although it may seem a fairly straightforward question to answer, there is still some discussion as to which is the world's largest capital. This is mainly due to the difficulty in deciding where the world's largest cities actually end as they all tend to be surrounded by a mass of satellite towns which all merge into one large agglomeration. If we take 'city' to mean the population which lives within the city limits, then Mexico City, with a population of more than 20,000,000, is the world's largest capital, closely followed by Seoul at 12,000,000 and Tokyo at 8,000,000. Likewise, it is very difficult to tell which is Europe's noisiest capital, mainly as there don't seem to be any standardised noise pollution measurements across the countries of the EU, and very few exhaustive studies have been carried out. However, it is widely recognised that Athens is the European capital which suffers from the worst noise pollution levels. It's not known whether this information is based on popular opinion or on statistical data from Greek authorities however. Judging from the entries we've received, this will come as quite a surprise to some of our listeners.

On to the fourth question. There is still some debate over this one. The Syrians claim that their capital city, Damascus, is the world's oldest city, though other Middle Eastern inhabitants would claim that their capitals are just as old. Sources seem to suggest that the Syrians are right and that their capital is indeed the oldest in the world, having been continuously inhabited since 5000 BC.

Question five was pretty straightforward. There is no doubt whatsoever about which of the world's capital cities is the highest. La Paz, in the Bolivian Andes, stands four kilometres above sea level.

And finally, the last question, again a fairly straightforward question. The first city to have reached a population of 1,000,000 was Rome which had a population of over a million during the heyday of the Roman Empire in 133 BC. London reached the mark in 1810 and New York in 1875. Today there are over 300 cities in the world that boast a population in excess of one million. So, the winners this week are, Jane Turbot from Whitstable in Kent, Carol Jackson from St Andrews …

📼 15

a) It would appear that there is a steady movement towards urban areas …
b) … there is still some discussion as to which is the world's largest capital.
c) … it is widely recognised that Athens is the European capital which suffers from the worst noise pollution levels.
d) It's not known whether this

information is based on popular opinion or on statistical data from Greek authorities however.
e) Sources seem to suggest that the Syrians are right …
f) There is no doubt whatsoever about which of the world's capital cities is the highest.

📼 16

(A = Alison; B = Bart)
A: Have you seen this? The article about that new survey …
B: Yes, I was reading it earlier. No surprises there I don't think … seems pretty obvious to me. You don't need a survey to tell you that, do you?
A: Yeah, well, I don't know, I mean it's not that simple is it? I mean, some people like living in the country …
B: Yeah, and you can see why; less stress, less traffic, less smog … but I don't think it's just a simple question of what you like, you know …
A: No, it's more like … it seems like it's a question of work and money more than anything else, I mean …
B: Yeah, it said that, didn't it? The main reason was that they couldn't find a job in the country …
A: Well, it doesn't say that exactly, but yes, it says it's er, it's, you know, easier to find work in large cities and I reckon that's true, don't you?
B: Yeah, but I don't think that's the main reason. I mean, it might be the main reason for older people … you know, no jobs, rural unemployment, whatever …
A: Yeah, there's a lot of that …
B: But it seems to be talking more about young people … I mean, the statistics here are referring to people under thirty and you know, I reckon that even if, even if there were plenty of jobs in the rural areas, well, they'd still go to the cities, wouldn't they?
A: Do you think so? Maybe you're right. Maybe it's more a kind of lure of the bright lights thing …
B: Yeah, you know, nightlife, music, youth culture in general …
A: Yeah, it says something about that, doesn't it? That bit where it talks about, what is it … 'leisure time activities' or something like that?
B: 'Free time facilities'.
A: Yeah, that was it.
B: … pubs and clubs more like!
A: Yeah, and cinemas and exhibitions and stuff as well …
B: Nah, discos and the chance to meet other young people more like …
A: Yeah, OK, the social side of things, but it's important, isn't it?
B: Yeah, this survey seems to reckon it's the second most important factor in fact after getting a job. You know, if young people decide to leave their homes in the country, then they reckon the social side of things is the second most important thing they consider. What other things do you think they mentioned?
A: Oh, I don't know. Maybe they said there were more opportunities for continuing their education, like going to colleges and stuff. They might be thinking about facilities for their families in the future, like being near

good schools and stuff. Um, what about better living conditions … more modern houses which need less work doing to them and stuff?
B: Yeah, I suppose they're all things you'd have to think about, aren't they?
A: Yeah, the survey makes quite a lot of sense.
B: Mmm.

📼 17

(H = Helen; R = Robert)
H: Well, I don't really think it's particularly dangerous. Not any more than any other large city. You have to be sensible, take the normal precautions. I mean I wouldn't walk down a street and stare at somebody and I certainly wouldn't walk home alone, and I wouldn't go down unlit alleys, you know, dark alleys at night, and obviously there are certain areas that you just know you wouldn't go into, but I think on the whole it's not a particularly dangerous city.
R: Yeah, I think I agree, but, um, actually there have been a couple of stories in the papers recently about this spate of muggings that's been going on.
H: Oh yeah, I read about that. Yeah, because they say things are changing and things are getting worse in the city. I did have a friend, actually, she was on the underground, and her wallet was snatched from her bag just as the train was coming into the station, and of course they got off straight away and there was absolutely nothing she could do about it.
R: Well, I sympathise with her. I mean I've seen that happen too, and, er, you've just got to watch it in a place like that, or like the street market. You've got to be really careful there because there is a big crowd and a lot of pickpockets and they can steal something and run away.
H: But I don't think it's really dangerous. They're not violent people, you just have to be sensible and keep your eyes open, and …
R: Well, I don't know. This article I read they said that a lot of the thieves were carrying knives, which means if you resist then, er, you could get badly hurt, so that really makes you think, doesn't it?
H: Mmm, I said it wasn't violent, maybe it is. I heard about a group of tourists the other day who were mugged. What do you do if you see something like that? You don't really know what's going on and you don't really want to get involved in case you get hurt.
R: Yes. I think it's stupid to try and be a hero. I mean you could get very badly hurt and all they want is just money. I mean I know that is a terrible thing to say, but it's just money. It's not worth losing your life for.
H: I suppose so. Apparently these guys had a knife and they cut one of the women's handbags from her shoulder. I think she thought they were going to stab her husband actually.
R: Did you hear if anybody was hurt at all?
H: No, no-one was hurt. Apparently the woman had had her passport stolen, and her travellers cheques taken but

the sad thing was that they had only just arrived and they didn't want to leave all their stuff in the hotel. They thought it was safer with them.

R: Yeah, well that's a problem with tourists though, isn't it? They're easy targets. They stand out in a crowd, thieves know they're probably carrying money and documents around and they don't speak the language, and they're vulnerable, aren't they?

H: Well …

R: I mean it happens to locals as well. There is a friend of mine who was jumped from behind, you know, and they got her bag and they ran away, and she tried to run after them but the thieves were too quick obviously.

H: Was she hurt at all?

R: No, no, but she was really angry.

H: Of course.

R: She didn't lose anything really valuable so, um, she didn't report it to the police in the end actually.

H: I think she should have done that actually. I think it's quite important when something like that happens because it might be mild at the moment but they could get worse. I think they need to know if a crime's happened actually.

R: Yeah. Well, I mean, there should be more police around anyway, shouldn't there? There should be more police on the streets at night.

H: I think you're right.

R: You can be on main streets and there's nobody, just a police car driving up and down every now and again, would …

H: You would feel better protected I think.

R: Yeah, and it would put the muggers and thieves off, wouldn't it?

📼 18

a) … there are certain areas that you just know you wouldn't go into …
b) … actually there have been a couple of stories in the papers recently about this spate of muggings that's been going on.
c) … and her wallet was snatched from her bag just as the train was coming into the station …
d) You've got to be really careful there because there is a big crowd and a lot of pickpockets …
e) You don't really know what's going on …
f) … I know that is a terrible thing to say, but it's just money.
g) I think she thought they were going to stab her husband actually.
h) … but the sad thing was that they had only just arrived …
i) She didn't lose anything really valuable …
j) I think they need to know if a crime's happened actually.

📼 19

An urban poem

The most unusual thing I ever stole? A snowman.
Midnight. He looked magnificent; a tall, white mute
beneath the winter moon. I wanted him, a mate
with a mind as cold as the slice of ice

within my own brain. I started with the head.

Better off dead than giving in, not taking what you want. He weighed a ton; his torso,
frozen stiff, hugged to my chest, a fierce chill
piercing my gut. Part of the thrill was knowing
that children would cry in the morning. Life's tough.

Sometimes I steal things I don't need. I joy-ride cars
to nowhere, break into houses just to have a look.
I'm a mucky ghost, leave a mess, maybe pinch a camera.
I watch my gloved hand twisting the doorknob.
A stranger's bedroom. Mirrors. I sigh like this – *Aah.*

It took some time. Reassembled in the yard, he didn't look the same. I took a run
and booted him. Again. Again. My breath ripped out
in rags. It seems daft now. Then I was standing
alone amongst lumps of snow, sick of the world.

Boredom. Mostly I'm so bored I could eat myself.
One time, I stole a guitar and thought I might
learn to play. I nicked a bust of Shakespeare once,
flogged it, but the snowman was strangest. You don't understand a word I'm saying, do you?

4 Talk

📼 20

1
Well, I like to be able to take an active part, so it helps if there aren't some people who hog the conversation all the time and also people need to have a sense of humour about things, I think, not to take things too seriously and you need a conversation that flows, so that you can … well, you don't get stuck on one point.

2
Um, a good conversationalist. I'd say it's someone who's got a point that they want to put across during the conversation. Someone with something to say as opposed to someone who just talks endlessly about various subjects and doesn't engage in one particular subject and I'd say it was someone who listens to other people as well, um, that's what I'd say.

3
When people aren't really interested in what you're saying, um, that's very annoying indeed. Also people who interrupt you continually with grunts or opinions of their own or whatever, and also some people don't care about whose turn it is to talk, so they just, you know, butt in when you're in the middle of a thought and obviously, you know, when the topic's boring. That's very irritating. And sometimes, you know, the conversation goes nowhere, it's going nowhere, and that is also extremely irritating.

4
I really hate it when I'm with someone who just drones on and on in a conversation, and who doesn't give you a chance to speak at all. Oh, and I also really hate it when they just carry on and they don't care whether or not you are interested at all in what they're saying. They seem oblivious to how you are reacting to them. I hate that.

5
It's good when you're talking about things which you've got in common with the person you are talking to, like you're on the same wavelength and you can share the same tastes or experiences so you know where the other person's coming from. It's also nice if you can share a joke or a personal story or an anecdote or something like that.

6
I can't stand it when you have to do all the talking yourself, when the other person's not responding, or when they are responding but it's with monosyllabic answers, you know, just going yeah, er, um, and that's all you're getting back, and when you have to work to keep the conversation going, that's really bad, when you're having to hunt around for things to say, because you're just not getting anything back.

📼 21

1
(H = Helen; K = Kate)
H: He can be a bit difficult at times. You know sometimes he'll just get really angry about something really trivial like, I don't know, not collecting the dirty glasses quickly enough or something like that, but he'll shout and rant for a while and then half an hour later he'll have forgotten all about it. And then he'll be all sweetness and light after that.

K: The woman I used to work for, she was exactly the same. Do you know, she'd complain about everything, and no matter how clean the bar top was, she'd make us clean it over and over again, like three or four times. She'd complain if we were milliseconds late for work, she'd complain if we didn't look smart enough and no matter how late it got she would make us stay until all the cleaning up was finished.

H: Oh, no, no, he's not that bad actually. No, really not, and sometimes he can be really nice, really generous. Like sometimes after we've shut, he'll buy everybody a drink at the end of the night, um, and he'll order in some pizza for everybody and then we'll all sit round and have a nice drink and a chat, and a bite to eat.

K: Oh, that sounds really nice.

H: Mmm, it is, yeah.

2
(B = Bob; J = Jack)
B: I know, I know exactly what you mean. I mean, sometimes, you know, what I do is, I'll, I'll sit down, you know, I'll get myself all sorted out, get everything ready, and then something catches my eye in the room, like, I mean, I've got the telly on, you know, in the corner, you know, I have the sound turned down, but I just notice

the picture – and I'm like, well, I've got to see what that, I mean I've got to see that programme, you know, it'll only take twenty minutes, and then of course, then I'm off and I'm away and I'm here. Oh! It's terrible!

J: I know, just before I start, I'll go and make a cup of coffee and then I'll just have a sit down with my cup of coffee rather than work …

B: And you've got to make yourself, you know, a jam sandwich or something to go with it …

J: Absolutely.

B: To go with the coffee. Yeah, yeah, you can look around and think 'Well, actually it's more important that I tidy the flat.'

J: Yeah, and you've got to wash up your cup of coffee.

3

(A = Adam; F = Fiona; N = Nick)

A: … Apparently it's doubled in the last two years. It's absolutely extraordinary.

F: Really? That's amazing. Oh, hang on, hang on, er, I'd like you to meet Nick, actually. He … Nick, hi, I'd like you to meet Adam. Adam … Nick.

A: Nick! Nick Watkins! How are you?

N: I don't believe it!

A: We were at school together.

F: No. Really?

N: Gosh! What, twenty years ago?

F: That's a long time.

N: Oh my goodness me!

A: Gosh! Yeah, we used to live next door to each other.

N: That's right. That's right. And you always used to be late to the bus stop.

A: That's right, every morning!

F: I can believe that.

A: Yes, the bus would wait for me because he knew I'd always be a minute late.

N: And we would sit at the back of the bus.

A: We would.

N: We had our little club for two.

A: That's right. And you, you'd always forget to do your homework and you'd have to crib off mine.

N: Yes. Got me where I am today! And do you remember you started me off smoking? Remember we'd go down by the river and smoke at lunchtimes?

A: No, you smoked long before then.

N: I didn't.

A: You did.

▭ 22

a) … he'll shout and rant for a while and then half an hour later he'll have forgotten all about it. And then he'll be all sweetness and light after that.

b) … he'll buy everybody a drink at the end of the night, um, and he'll order in some pizza for everybody and then we'll all sit round and have a nice drink and a chat, and a bite to eat.

c) … I'll go and make a cup of coffee and then I'll just have a sit down with my cup of coffee rather than work …

▭ 23

(A = Adam; N = Nick)

A: Yes, the bus would wait for me because he knew I'd always be a minute late.

N: And we would sit at the back of the bus.

A: We would.

N: We had our little club for two.

A: That's right. And you, you'd always forget to do your homework and you'd have to crib off mine.

N: Yes. Got me where I am today! And do you remember you started me off smoking? Remember we'd go down by the river and smoke at lunchtimes?

▭ 24

The children? All grown up and left the nest. Timothy, my eldest, got married fifteen years ago to a girl he met outside an ice-cream kiosk. Her name's Kate, she was, and still is, a very docile sort of person and was just right for Timothy. Timothy's very highly-strung and always has been. When I think back to his childhood the picture that always springs to mind is that of him sitting at the piano playing brilliantly and being so involved. But that's what he's like. Whatever he's doing he'll do it with total commitment and concentration. I suppose you could say he's a perfectionist, which must be tiring for Kate sometimes. He's been looking particularly run-down of late but that's because he will work all hours. I tell him it's ruining his health but will he listen to me? Of course not! Anyway, they have just the one child, David. He's twelve now and absolutely wild. Though I don't like to criticise my own son, the fault nevertheless lies with him. He appears indifferent to David's behaviour and though I've heard Kate talk to him about it he won't listen to her. They really should have been stricter with him from the beginning. They wouldn't listen to me when I told them that a little discipline would go a long way and now they're paying the price.

My second, Rebecca, got married the same year as Timothy and is now in the middle of extremely bitter divorce proceedings. I knew it would end up this way but there's no use trying to change the minds of two people in love. Fortunately there were no children. Poor Rebecca, she was never very good at making the right decisions but her eternal optimism will get her through this period, I'm sure.

Now Sam, ahhh Sam, my youngest daughter and without a doubt my favourite, though of course I never let it show. A real rascal when she was young, who would charm everyone. She had us all wound round her little finger – real bundle of joy. A little on the lazy side, but good at heart with her head screwed on properly. She married Anthony – a real marriage of hearts and they're still as much in love now as they were twelve years ago. They have three adorable children, Nicholas, Peter and Sarah, who are well-mannered and not too noisy.

▭ 25

A rich lady returned home from a ball. She rang the bell for her butler and when he appeared she said, 'Edward, take off my shoes,' and he did. Then she said, 'Edward, take off my coat,' and he did. 'Take off my dress,' and he did. 'And now take off my underwear,' and he did. 'And now, Edward,' she said, 'if you wish to remain in my service, you are never to wear any of my clothes again.'

5 Luck

▭ 26

(M = Mary; S = Sarah; D = Dave; B = Bob)

M: … here are your keys back, thanks. What's that horn on your keyring for?

S: It's a souvenir from Italy. I got it last year when we were there on holiday. It's supposed to bring good luck but it doesn't seem to be working so far! I suppose I did win a tenner on the lottery a couple of weeks ago, but that's about it!

D: Gullible tourists! It's all a racket to make money! You make your own luck in this world.

S: Well, how come people have been carrying round lucky charms with them for so long then? I mean, the Egyptians have been carrying scarabs around and wearing them as jewellery for thousands of years. I think the ancient Egyptians believed that they'd protect them from death and people who died were buried with them.

D: How come you know so much?

S: I'm interested in things like that. Did you know that people in India wear peacock feathers on their clothes to keep evil away?

M: That's interesting because here peacock feathers are supposed to bring bad luck and you shouldn't have any in your house. The eye pattern on them is supposed to be the evil eye. I remember my brother picking one up once and bringing it home and my mum wouldn't let him keep it because it was unlucky.

B: Hmm. I've never heard about that but I know that the eye thing is quite popular in Turkey. You see them all over the place there. People hang them in their houses and in their cars and they're supposed to protect you from the evil eye and bad luck.

S: I've seen them – they're really pretty, aren't they?

D: It's all a load of mumbo jumbo. My mate went out with a Japanese girl when we were at university and she had this little cat statue which went everywhere with her. It had one arm up in the air which was supposed to attract good luck but she dropped it one day and the arm came off. You should have seen the state she got into over it! Just a silly little thing like that! What's the point?

S: Well, everyone's allowed to have their own beliefs, aren't they? I bet you've got a lucky pair of socks or something you wear if you've got a special date or an interview or something!

D: I haven't!

M: I've got a little dragon brooch that I wear sometimes. A Chinese friend of mine gave it to me years ago and told me it would protect me against unhappiness and the loss of love. I should have been wearing it the night Phil told me he didn't want to see me any more!

D: There you are, you see – not a very lucky charm, is it?

M: I wasn't wearing it though. If I had been things might have worked out differently.

D: Rubbish! You believe what you like, but I'm sticking to my theory that life's what you make it, and having lucky rabbits' feet, plastic pigs or Egyptian beetles isn't going to make the slightest bit of difference to whether I get married, make a million or get the job of my dreams.

S: You do that!

 27

(A = Angela; S = Sarah)

A: Have you read this article about the lottery in the *Tatler*?
S: Yeah, it's fun isn't it?
A: Do you think it's true?
S: I don't know, it might be … but even if it isn't, it's a good story.
A: Yeah, and all that stuff about what she'd have done if she'd actually won 'the Big One'.
S: Yeah, I really like that bit about how it would have changed her dog's life, like he'd be wearing a diamond-encrusted collar right now …
A: Nah, I think it's more likely that she'd be driving a snazzy little red sports car!
S: And I like that bit about how she usually picks her numbers …
A: Yeah, that bit about the birthdays and stuff.
S: And the ideal partner …
A: And the bra! I think I should try that!
S: Do you think she'd have got the jackpot if she'd been playing her usual numbers?
A: I don't know, I don't think it actually says anything about that …
S: I got really close to winning once. If I'd played my brother's birthday instead of mine I'd have won.
A: How much would you have won if you had?
S: Oh, millions no doubt! I would have bought a new house, a car, a luxury yacht and I wouldn't be working as a secretary any more, I can tell you! I still got fifty quid mind you, but I wish I'd chosen a 17 instead of a 19 … I certainly wouldn't be sitting here having this conversation if I had!
A: I never even buy a ticket – it's just a waste of money.
S: How boring! If you're not in it, you can't win it!

 28

Did I tell you about what happened to us last week? No? Well, we were out in a bar in town, quite a crowd of us, and of course Kelly had her mobile phone with her. Anyway, while we were in the bar Kelly left her mobile in her coat pocket and we were chatting and laughing and having a good time. It was some time later when Kelly noticed this couple rummaging around in the pile of coats and then getting ready to leave. Well, Kelly was a bit suspicious, so she went over to check if her phone was still there and of course it wasn't! So she went to follow the couple outside to ask them if they'd taken her phone and a couple of the others went with her. They were just approaching the couple when Hannah had a brainwave. She had her mobile on her too, so she phoned Kelly's number and just as Kelly was asking the couple whether or not they'd got her phone, it started ringing in one of their pockets! They couldn't very well deny having it and handed it over very sheepishly! Lucky, eh?

 29

The way I came to miss the end of the world – well, the end of the world I had known for close on thirty years – was sheer accident: like a lot of survival, when you come to think of it. In the nature of things a good many somebodies are always in hospital, and the law of averages had picked on me to be one of them a week or so before … my eyes and indeed my whole head was wreathed in bandages.

Customarily the west-bound buses thundered along trying to beat the lights at the corner; as often as not a pig-squeal of brakes and a salvo of shots from the silencer would tell that they hadn't.

But this morning was different. Disturbingly because mysteriously different. No wheels rumbled, no buses roared, no sound of a car of any kind, in fact, was to be heard. No brakes, no horns, not even the clopping of the few rare horses that still occasionally passed. Nor, as there should be at such an hour, the composite tramp of work-bound feet.

… 'Hey!' I shouted. 'I want some breakfast. Room forty-eight!'

For a moment nothing happened. Then came voices all shouting together. It sounded like hundreds of them, and not a word coming through clearly. It was as though I'd put on a record of crowd noises – and an ill-disposed crowd at that. I had a nightmarish flash wondering whether I had been transferred to a mental home while I was sleeping, and that this was not St Merryn's Hospital at all. Those voices simply didn't sound normal to me. At that moment bed seemed to be the one safe, comforting thing in my whole baffling environment. As if to underline that there came a sound which checked me in the act of pulling up the sheets. From the street below rose a scream, wildly distraught and contagiously terrifying. It came three times, and when it had died away it seemed still to tingle in the air.

You'll find it in the records that on Tuesday, 7 May, the Earth's orbit passed through a cloud of comet debris. All that I actually know of the occasion is that I had to spend the evening in my bed listening to eye-witness accounts of what was constantly claimed to be the most remarkable celestial spectacle on record.

… The nurse who brought me my supper had to tell me all about it.
'The sky's simply full of shooting stars,' she said. 'All bright green. They make people's faces look frightfully ghastly. Everybody's out watching them, and sometimes it's almost as light as day – only all the wrong colour. Every now and then there's a big one so bright that it hurts to look at it. It's a marvellous sight. They say there's never been anything like it before. It is such a pity you can't see it, isn't it?'
'It is,' I agreed somewhat shortly.
'Oooh!'
'Why "oooh"?' I inquired.
'That was such a brilliant one then – it made the whole room look green. What a pity you couldn't see it.'
'Isn't it. Now do go away, there's a good girl.'

Was I more scared of endangering my sight by taking off the bandages, or of staying in the dark? … I had the sense and the self-control to get out of bed and pull the blind down before I started on the safety-pins. Once I had the coverings off, and had found out that I could see in the dimness, I felt a relief that I'd never known before. … I discovered a pair of dark glasses thoughtfully put ready. … Cautiously I put them on before I went right close to the window.

… At the far end of the wide corridor were the doors of a ward. … I opened the door. It was pretty dark in there. The curtains had evidently been drawn after the previous night's display was over – and they were still drawn.
'Sister?' I inquired.
'She ain't 'ere,' a man's voice said. 'What's more,' it went on, 'she ain't been 'ere for ruddy hours, neither. Can't you pull them ruddy curtains, mate, and let's 'ave some flippin' light? Don't know what's come over the bloody place this morning.'
'Okay,' I agreed.
Even if the whole place were disorganised, there didn't seem to be any good reason why the unfortunate patients should have to lie in the dark.
I pulled back the curtains on the nearest window, and let in a shaft of bright sunlight. It was a surgical ward with about twenty patients, all bedridden. Leg injuries mostly, several amputations, by the look of it.
'Stop fooling about with 'em, mate, and pull 'em back,' said the same voice.
I turned and looked at the man who spoke. He was a dark, burly fellow with a weather-beaten skin. He was sitting up in bed, facing directly at me – and at the light. His eyes seemed to be gazing into my own, so did his neighbour's, and the next man's …
For a few moments I stared back at them. It took that long to register. Then:
'I – they – they seem to be stuck,' I said. 'I'll find someone to see to them.'
And with that I fled the ward.

… A Triffid is certainly distinctive … a height of seven feet or more, here was a plant that had learned to walk. … People were surprised and a little disgusted to learn that the species was carnivorous … but actually alarming was the discovery that the whorl topping a Triffid's stem could lash out as a slender stinging weapon ten feet long, capable of discharging enough poison to kill a man if it struck squarely on his unprotected skin.

6 Mind

 30

Mike

Mmm … sight I suppose. Yes, the most important one is sight I suppose … I mean, if you're blind, if you can't see, then although you can lead a full life and all that, I think it does make you more vulnerable, more dependent on other people, I don't know, for silly little things like, for example, like shopping in a supermarket or whatever and I would really hate it if I couldn't see what things or people looked like … or the expression on a person's face when they're talking to you. I mean, you wouldn't even know if they were looking at you or whether they looked interested in what you were saying.

Maria
No, I haven't, but I read this article about a man who'd gone deaf and then his hearing was restored to him, and he spoke about how isolating it can be if you can't hear. He said that you miss out on a lot of things, that although you can communicate fine when you need to, you miss out on the subtleties of a conversation, and the thing he missed most was humour … the humour in spontaneous conversation … because it all gets slowed down when you're signing. And he really missed listening to music, that was the worst part he said. That and not being able to hear his wife's voice. And he said that it was really strange to start with when he regained his hearing. Everything sounded much louder. He said he actually misses total silence sometimes, just not hearing anything, and that it can be really relaxing.

Helen
Umm, I don't know … but maybe smell I suppose … like someone can just walk past you on the street and you catch the smell of their perfume and it reminds you really strongly of someone … or food … I can't remember where I was the other day, but I suddenly smelt the most wonderful cooking smells; coconut oil and eastern spices and it reminded me so strongly of my holidays in Thailand … I could see the palm trees, taste the food, feel the sun on my skin … yes, I think smell triggers the strongest, most vivid memories.

Nick
This may seem like a strange answer, but maybe touch … you know, the sense of touch … I think it's probably the one we take most for granted, being able to feel things and it's not, it's not, you know, a sense that's limited to one part of your body either – it's everything, every single pore, every single bit of your skin. I remember seeing a documentary about a man who'd been born deaf and mute and had later lost his sight in an accident – he lived a full life – he was eighty something and he still worked and even travelled. He just lived his life totally through his sense of touch. In this programme they showed him visiting other people like him in Japan. It was amazing – they used an international signing language which was based on touch – they would touch each other and sign on each other's palms, and they could feel each other talking – and it showed them going to a drum concert too – like a traditional Japanese drum concert – and they could feel the music, I mean they could feel the vibrations of the drums, even though they couldn't hear them. It was just totally amazing.

Petra
Well, usually I'm renowned for my sense of smell! Sometimes I can smell things that no-one else notices. That can be good because I'm really sensitive to things like gas leaks and anything that smells bad … things like food that's gone off. My mum often asks me to smell meat or fish or milk or whatever to see if it's OK … but recently I've had quite a heavy cold and it's really affected my sense of smell. I mean, I can smell really strong things, like coffee or if something's burning in the kitchen, but I can't smell other things like perfume so I don't know how much to put on. And I really miss the subtler smells in the kitchen. It affects my taste too. Everything tastes so bland.

31

a) Yes, the most important one is sight I suppose … I mean, if you're blind, if you can't see, then although you can lead a full life and all that, I think it does make you more vulnerable, more dependent on other people …

b) … I would really hate it if I couldn't see what things or people looked like … or the expression on a person's face when they're talking to you. I mean, you wouldn't even know if they were looking at you or whether they looked interested in what you were saying.

c) … I read this article about a man who'd gone deaf and then his hearing was restored to him, and he spoke about how isolating it can be if you can't hear.

d) … he really missed listening to music, that was the worst part he said. That and not being able to hear his wife's voice.

e) … I could see the palm trees, taste the food, feel the sun on my skin …

f) … they used an international signing language which was based on touch – they would touch each other and sign on each other's palms, and they could feel each other talking – and it showed them going to a drum concert too – like a traditional Japanese drum concert – and they could feel the music, I mean they could feel the vibrations of the drums, even though they couldn't hear them.

g) … I'm really sensitive to things like gas leaks and anything that smells bad …

h) … I can smell really strong things, like coffee or if something's burning in the kitchen, but I can't smell other things like perfume so I don't know how much to put on. And I really miss the subtler smells in the kitchen. It affects my taste too. Everything tastes so bland.

32

(S = Sue; J = John; P = Pete)
S: Look John, would you mind leaving the room for a minute? There's something I need to discuss with Pete here.
J: No, of course not. I'm feeling a bit peckish anyway. Would you mind if I popped out for something to eat?
S: No, go ahead.
P: Well, what is it, Sue?
S: I've got some bad news I'm afraid.
P: Oh, dear. I think I know what you're going to say. Do you mind if I smoke?
S: If you must.
P: So what is it?
S: We've lost the contract.
P: Hmm. I thought as much. Mind you, it doesn't come as much of a surprise. Not after last year's fiasco.
S: Yes, I suppose so …

33

I'm Going Slightly Mad by Queen
When the outside temperature rises
And the meaning is oh so clear,
One thousand and one yellow daffodils
Begin to dance in front of you, oh dear.
Are they trying to tell you something?
You're missing that one final screw,
You're simply not in the pink my dear,
To be honest you haven't got a clue.
I'm going slightly mad,
I'm going slightly mad,
It finally happened, happened,
It finally happened, ooh oh,
It finally happened.
I'm slightly mad. (Oh dear!)
I'm one card short of a full deck,
I'm not quite the shilling,
One wave short of a shipwreck,
I'm not my usual top billing,
I'm coming down with a fever,
I'm really out to sea,
This kettle is boiling over
I think I'm a banana tree.
Oh dear, I'm going slightly mad
I'm going slightly mad
It finally happened, happened
It finally happened uh huh
It finally happened.
I'm slightly mad (Oh dear!)
I'm knitting with only one needle,
Unravelling fast it's true,
I'm driving only three wheels these days,
But my dear how about you?
I'm going slightly mad,
I'm going slightly mad,
It finally happened,
It finally happened, oh yes,
It finally happened.
I'm slightly mad!
Just very slightly mad!
And there you have it!

7 Review 1

34

(I = Ian; H = Helena; J = John; A = Angela; T = Tom)

a
I: You haven't forgotten it's Sara's party this evening, have you Helena? You are coming, aren't you?
H: Well, I'm a bit tired actually and I'm not that bothered to be honest Ian … I think I might just stay here if you don't mind and … er, … OK, if that's what everyone's doing, why not? Yeah, yeah, I'll come along, but just for a while.

b
I: I'll give Tom a ring to see if he fancies coming along to the party. We haven't seen him for ages, have we? Have you got his new phone number?
H: Er, no, er, I haven't I'm afraid. I don't know if anyone's got it actually. Oh, hang on, I think John might have. I think he's got it. Give him a ring and ask him.

c
H: Do you know if Angela's going to be at the party tonight? I need to, er, speak to her about something.
I: Well, I think she is. I think I overheard her saying she was going, but I could be wrong.

d
H: This isn't like you John! Jeans and a T-shirt!
J: Yeah, I know – work took longer than I

expected, so, as you can see, I had to get ready in a bit of a hurry.

e
J: Hi Ian, haven't seen you for ages. How's it going?
I: Fine, really good. Hey, I love the T-shirt. Snazzy!

f
J: Sorry, … what? … Oh, this T-shirt? Yeah, I bought it in Ibiza a few years ago.
I: You've been to Ibiza? I didn't know that! How was it?

g
H: Hi Angela. Hey, how are things with you and Tom? Has he said sorry yet for the other night? Do you know who he was with?
A: No, and I don't think he will apologise. He doesn't seem to think he's done anything wrong. Can you believe it?

h
H: You'd have thought he'd offer some explanation! I mean, he must have some excuse or something.
A: He's certainly tried, but I didn't believe a single word of it. Wait 'til I find out what he was up to! And I don't know where he is tonight. Aaaargh!

i
A: You're going home? OK, see you soon Helena. What about Ian? Is he going with you?
H: No, I'm going on my own. I'm a bit tired. He'll be dancing all night. I think you'll find he'll be here for breakfast. See ya!

j
T: Hello?
J: Hi Tom. I didn't see you at the party last night. Where were you?
T: Oh, hi John. Well, I didn't quite make it actually. I was all set to go … my flatmate Sam and I were on our way to the party and we stopped in a bar for a quick drink. We ended up staying there for something to eat and by the time we'd finished it was a bit late to go to the party so we just went home. How was it anyway?

8 Cyberspace

🔲 35

(I = Interviewer; S = Steven Poole)
I: How popular are video games, and why are they so popular?
S: Video games these days are extremely popular. One in four households in Britain has a Playstation and in 1999 the video game industry made nearly a billion pounds, which was 60 percent more than cinema box office takings. So why are video games so popular? Well, they combine very fast moving, well-designed graphical images with very interesting sound design and music. But crucially they're interactive, so they change according to what you do from moment to moment, so the computer system concentrates on what you are saying to it, and poses you very interesting challenges and difficulties at very high speeds. So, in this sense the video game is a much

more challenging and involving art form than older things such as cinema or television.
I: What was the first video game, and who played it?
S: The first commercial video game came along in 1971. It was called *Computer Space*. Unfortunately it wasn't very successful because it was a very complicated game involving space ships and torpedoes and black holes and so forth. The same man who had invented that invented a game called *Pong* in 1972 and that's when the video game explosion really took off. It was a very very simple tennis game. You had two white bats and a ball travelling across the screen making little blippy noises, and er, it was put in bars next to pinball machines and so on, and it became a very popular activity, more popular than the pinball.
I: So, how have games changed and developed since those early days?
S: The very early video games like *Pong* just took place on one screen and the boundaries of the screen were the boundaries of the playing area. But then the space in video games started to get larger. The games started to scroll from side to side or up and down, so that the playing area became larger than the total size of one screen. The graphics in games slowly became more colourful and more detailed and then the big innovation took place in the 90s, which was the invention of full 3D. This meant that you started to control characters who explored fully realised, solid 3D environments. You could wander round landscapes and buildings and look at them from any angle.
I: There's a common criticism that video games are very violent. What's your view on that?
S: A lot of people think that playing violent video games might be bad for children; it might make them into violent people themselves. But I don't think that's true. After all, millions of people around the world play these games and the vast majority of them are very peaceful people and never pick up a gun in real life. The violence in video games after all is very crude, cartoon violence. It's very exaggerated. It bears no relation to real life and people who play video games know this. They aren't stupid. Now, it's certainly true that if a slightly disturbed child plays these video games too much, then he might become more violent, but then it's true that that sort of child would become more violent if he watched a film or listened to a heavy metal record, or did any one of a number of other things. Video games themselves can't be blamed for causing people to act violently in real life.
I: What's the profile of a typical games player?
S: A lot of people still think the typical video game player is a teenage boy locked in his smelly bedroom, not having any kind of social life, just playing games all day. But that's not true. The average age of a Playstation owner nowadays is 26 and although video gamers in this country are still

mostly male, because the games are largely designed by men and marketed to men, that's not the case in Japan or America where many more women have become interested in video games. Also, the idea that video gaming is an anti-social activity is no longer true at all. It's a very sociable one. Not only can you invite your friends round to your home to play a four-player game of *Micro Machines*, you can go to a bar and play games on networked PCs there. And these days of course, many many people over the world play video games on the Internet. Hundreds of thousands of people can be playing a game at the same time and they can be making friends on different continents through video games.
I: Do you think that video games could be considered an art form?
S: I think video games are close to becoming an art form in themselves. Certainly, when cinema was only around 30 years old, as video games are today, a lot of people thought films were mindless entertainment and rotted people's brains and were no good. But now we know that cinema is an art form and we have film critics who can analyse films and enhance our enjoyment of them, and I think in the future this will be true of video games as well.
I: What will the next developments be?
S: Well, the current research in video games is concentrating on artificial intelligence. People want to play video games that give a greater illusion of interacting with real characters. A game like *Black And White* is brilliant at doing this, where you teach creatures who actually learn from you and then they go off and do their own thing and they seem to have their own brains and their own wills.

🔲 36

a) So why are video games so popular? Well, they combine very fast moving, well-designed graphical images with very interesting sound design and music. But crucially they're interactive so the computer system poses you very interesting challenges and difficulties at very high speeds. So, in this sense the video game is a much more challenging and involving art form …
b) The very early video games like *Pong* just took place on one screen. But then the space in video games started to get larger. And then the big innovation took place in the 90s, which was the invention of full 3D. This meant that you started to control characters who explored fully realised, solid 3D environments.
c) A lot of people think that playing violent video games might be bad for children but I don't think that's true. After all, millions of people around the world play these games and the vast majority of them are very peaceful people and never pick up a gun in real life. The violence in video games after all is very crude, cartoon violence. Now, it's certainly true that if a slightly disturbed child plays these video games too much, then he might

become more violent, but then it's true that that sort of child would become more violent if he watched a film or listened to a heavy metal record …

d) … that's not the case in Japan or America where many more women have become interested in video games. Also, the idea that video gaming is an anti-social activity is no longer true at all. Not only can you invite your friends round to your home to play a four-player game of *Micro Machines*, you can go to a bar and play games on networked PCs there …

e) … a lot of people thought films were mindless entertainment but now we know that cinema is an art form and we have film critics who can analyse films and enhance our enjoyment of them, and I think in the future this will be true of video games as well.

📼 37

1

I'm terrible on the Net, I'm really, really bad at it, but I really enjoy it. I kind of start off surfing, looking for something specific. I might want some information on a particular, on a particular subject, but I get carried away, I get diverted, I end up looking at something completely unrelated, and inevitably, um, actually I have to confess I end up shopping, or window shopping anyway, which is, um, well, it's, it's, it's quite seductive on the Net because there's some really, really, really, funky shopping sites. You can pick up all sorts of different things and you can go through it and normally the graphics are like really good and, um, I've downloaded I think nearly all the, all the kind of sound software that you need, so I end up watching film bites on different products, and getting kind of, well, getting completely carried away. But I never get my credit card out, so that's quite good but on the other hand, I do tend to do it in the middle of the day which makes it a bit expensive, but, um, I really enjoy it.

2

I work as a doctor in a very busy medical practice, um, and I never thought I'd have time to use the Internet, but I discovered of course, how useful it is for e-mailing and sending messages, um, particularly work related messages, and also I've, I've discovered that I can find information out much quicker than by looking up the telephone book for instance, or, or the newspaper to find out train times or maybe what's on at my local cinema, and if I have a problem, um, a professional problem, I can also get in touch with colleagues and find out their opinions. I don't use it socially though – I hardly ever use it to talk to friends. Frankly I still like the old-fashioned telephone.

3

Er, I'm fairly new to the whole kind of computer thing, but I have started to use the e-mail, um, mainly for personal use and, um, I find it very handy if I forget someone's birthday, I can just sort of quickly send an e-mail, send a card which is quite nice, um, but I rarely use the Net, um, I have yet to work out how to do that, but I'm sure in the next couple of weeks I'm going to give it a go.

4

I use the Net for a couple of reasons, one because I have family that are scattered all over the world and I find that's a quite a good way to keep in touch with them and again it's quite cheap, but I primarily use it because I'm doing a degree part-time and I find it really helpful for various reasons and probably the best thing is that I can get in touch with the lecturers and the professors without actually having to speak to them in person which I find to be a plus. They are very hard to track down and they seem to be, it seems to be easier for them to communicate with me or with students in that way so, so that's one advantage and I suppose the other advantage is that on the Net you have access to various different libraries and so it is very easy to track down materials and books and reserve them or find out where they are anyway and, and find out if you have, you can gain access to them, so that's primarily why I use the Net.

📼 38

a) I kind of start off surfing, looking for something specific. I might want some information on a particular, on a particular subject, but I get carried away, I get diverted, I end up looking at something completely unrelated …

b) … there's some really, really, really, funky shopping sites. You can pick up all sorts of different things …

c) … I've downloaded I think nearly all the, all the kind of sound software that you need, so I end up watching film bites on different products, and getting kind of, well, getting completely carried away.

9 Law

📼 39

1

(D = David; M = Margaret)
D: So, have you spoken to Mike?
M: Yes.
D: And does he reckon you have a case?
M: Well, he says I certainly have a case but it'll probably cost me more than it's worth to take them to court. So I'm not sure what to do.
D: Well, I think you should sue them, even if you only get minimal compensation. It's the principle that counts. People can't just go round spreading lies and rumours like that. What I mean is you have to stand up for yourself, you know, show that it's important to you.
M: Yes, I agree. The only reason I'm hesitating is because I don't want any more bad publicity.
D: Well it might not all be bad, and you know what they say, there's no such thing as bad publicity. But if you want a second opinion, the best person to ask is Fred MacIntyre.
M: But surely it's too late now anyway? I mean it's been almost three weeks since they published the article …

2

(R = Rani; D = Daniel)
R: … And then?
D: Well, I suppose what I should have said is 'Yes, officer. I'm sorry, but I was

in a terrible hurry.'
R: But you didn't.
D: No, I tried to deny it, you know, make out that I couldn't possibly have been doing 100 miles per hour.
R: And?
D: And, he gave me an on-the-spot fine and said that if it happened again I'd lose my licence.
R: Ooh, how much?
D: Fifty pounds.
R: Oooh!
D: That's a lesson I won't forget in a hurry!
R: What, don't lie to a policeman?
D: No, it's better to be late than fifty pounds worse off!

3

(F = Fiona; D = Doug)
F: Yeah, being on the jury was a really weird experience.
D: How long did it last?
F: Um, a couple of weeks. It was fascinating, seeing how a court works, you know, how formal it all is and everything. We had to stay in a hotel overnight because we couldn't come to a verdict in one day. That was quite exciting.
D: Really? What was it for then? Murder?
F: No, nothing that drastic! It was your usual story of a guy setting up a company, borrowing money from banks, getting things on credit and then using the company money to buy himself and his girlfriend some nice treats, you know, a Ferrari, a Rolex …
D: A couple of diamond rings!
F: Exactly. But the main issue was that the accused used to be a local politician! Didn't you read about it in the papers? It was quite big news at the time.
D: Yeah, now you come to mention it, I do remember something … John Limes or something like that?
F: Yes, John Limey.
D: And what did you decide?
F: Well, in the end the verdict we returned was unanimous – guilty!

📼 40

1

Well, I think if you do something like go into somebody's garden without asking them first, then, then I think that it's not too bad so you shouldn't, you shouldn't be punished for it, but I really think that you should go and say sorry.

2

Well, I suppose it's not really an offence is it, not, not a serious offence? I just think people do it without thinking. Um, they see other people do it so they do it themselves and then you end up with a really filthy street. People should think more about the environment, about their surroundings and perhaps rather than punishing them they should, they should have a deterrent fine or, or, you know, enough of a fine to make them think twice about doing it again, frankly.

3

Well, let's be honest, it's the most serious thing you can ever do, isn't it? I mean it's the most brutal thing you can ever do and I personally think it should be an eye for an eye, a tooth for a tooth, a life for a life. If you're going to do this kind of thing, you know, you deserve what you get.

4
Well, my mother always said that when she was a little girl, she had her mouth washed out with soap and water and I think that is still the best way. I really do.

5
Um, I'm not really sure to be honest. Er, I think, ban, a ban I think. Er, six months, a year, depending on how much you've had I suppose, but I don't really have a strong opinion about it.

6
I think give the person a bucket and a cloth and make them scrape the stuff off the walls themselves. I think it's really important. You have to see the consequences of your actions and be made to fix up your own mess. Other than that, maybe give them art classes, so they do it properly.

7
Well, I think this is, you know, a really violent theft. You know, it's a dreadful crime and I think you should be quite heavily punished for it really. Um, I think you should get at least fifteen years. I mean, this might act as a deterrent, especially for younger people thinking that it's just a bit of fun and, um, it's maybe an easy way of getting money.

8
Well, first of all I think the damage these things do should not be underestimated. This is in no way a nuisance crime. It is extremely, extremely serious. It can have worldwide effects. It can lose businesses and individuals millions of pounds and I think the punishment should reflect this. It's a difficult one because I think perhaps prison is too harsh but perhaps we should consider community service. I mean, a lot of these people that commit this kind of crime are obviously extremely talented and have a lot of knowledge and maybe that could be put to better use. Or perhaps a large fine. Er, gosh, how much I don't know, but that would be decided by the courts, but I think that would certainly make these criminals, because that's what they are, think twice about doing it again.

9
Well, I think it should be imprisonment for quite a long time because this is a crime that can also involve torture and can also involve murder as well, so it is a very serious crime and it can do an enormous amount of damage to the victim if they survive and to the victim's family, so I think it's quite a serious offence.

📼 41

(T = Tim; A = Anne)
T: Have you ever had anything stolen?
A: Er, yes I have, a brand new car! I'd had it for just under a month.
T: You're kidding!
A: No!
T: You were insured of course?
A: Of course, but the insurance company wouldn't pay up.
T: What do you mean, wouldn't pay up? I mean, a brand new car and you didn't insure it against theft?
A: Of course I did, and I was insured

against theft … but they just didn't want to pay up. It was a bit of a complicated case … Fortunately my boyfriend at the time was a lawyer so in the end we managed to sort it out.
T: So, what happened then?
A: Well, you see, these three teenagers stole my car … they'd broken out of this special school for young offenders and well, it seems they wanted to run away, so they decided to pinch a car – my car! Anyway, while they were driving away they started arguing and drove the car straight into a tree.
T: Oh no!
A: The car was a write-off, a total write-off. I couldn't believe it when I saw it!
T: What about the kids?
A: Well, they weren't seriously hurt or anything, miraculous really, considering … but they got arrested of course and sent back to the school. I was just relieved I'd taken out insurance and I was already thinking I'd get another car with the insurance money … maybe buy a second hand one this time and make a bit of money on the deal!
T: Sounds like a good idea … but they wouldn't pay up you said?
A: Yeah, when I explained to the insurance company what had happened, they told me they would need to see my insurance documents. So, I went down to the garage where my car had been towed, only to find that all my documents had mysteriously disappeared from the glove compartment.
T: So what did you do?
A: Well, I went back to the insurance people and explained the situation and they said it didn't matter because they had their own copy of the original contract and that anyway, I wasn't covered.
T: But didn't you say …
A: Well, I thought I was covered but they said I was insured against theft, but that the car had been found, so technically it was no longer stolen. The problem was that I wasn't covered for any damage incurred in the event of theft.
T: Surely they can't include such a ridiculous clause?
A: Well, apparently they can and they did. The box with this condition had been ticked. I hadn't read all the small print in the contract.
T: But why not? You really should have read it before signing it you know. You were almost asking for trouble.
A: Thanks! Yeah, I suppose with hindsight I ought to have done, but I couldn't be bothered at the time.
T: But couldn't you have asked your boyfriend to check it over for you? He was a lawyer, wasn't he? Or you could have asked a friend.
A: Well, I suppose I could have done, but you know how these things are, they're standard forms so I thought I'd be all right. Anyway, I have no idea if I had actually ticked the box or not. I might have done but I didn't have my copy and so they might have simply ticked the box themselves to save them having to pay out the equivalent of £8,000.
T: They wouldn't have done that, surely?

That's quite a serious accusation …
A: I don't know. They certainly could have done it if they'd wanted to.
T: It would have been far too risky, I mean, you might have found your copy of the contract.
A: Not if they had it.
T: What do you mean?
A: Well, the man who ran the insurance company office was the brother of the man who owned the garage where my car was towed. I reckon they must have taken it from the car, along with all the other documents.
T: That sounds too far-fetched, they wouldn't have dared do something like that, surely? I mean, I know you must have been upset at the time, and of course, you may be right … but they can't have just stolen the documents like that!
A: I know it all sounds very improbable, but it all looked terribly suspicious at the time.
T: So what happened in the end then?
A: Well, my boyfriend decided the best way to get the money back would be to sue the boys' school, which he did, and four years later we got the money back. Not that I saw much of it.
T: What, all swallowed up by the lawyers?
A: Yeah, my husband.
T: Oh, you married your boyfriend!
A: Yeah, to avoid the legal fees!

📼 42

a) a brand new car
b) they just didn't want to pay up
c) second hand
d) What did you do?
e) I went back
f) they said it didn't matter
g) I was insured against theft
h) I ought to have done
i) I couldn't be bothered
j) you could have asked a friend

📼 43

Love in the First Degree by Bananarama
Last night I was dreaming I was locked in a prison cell
When I woke up I was screaming, calling out your name
Whoa, and the judge and the jury
They all put the blame on me
They wouldn't go for my story
They wouldn't hear my plea

Only you can set me free
'Cos I'm guilty
Guilty as a girl can be
Come on baby can't you see
I stand accused of love in the first degree
Guilty
Of love in the first degree

Someday I believe it, you will come to my rescue
Unchain my heart you're keeping and let me start anew
The hours pass so slowly
Since they've thrown away the key
Can't you see that I'm lonely
Won't you help me please

Only you can set me free
'Cos I'm guilty
Guilty as a girl can be
Come on baby can't you see

I stand accused of love in the first degree
Guilty
Of love in the first degree

Guilty of love, guilty of love in
Guilty of love, guilty of love in
Guilty, of love in the first degree
And the judge and the jury
They all put the blame on me
They wouldn't go for my story
They wouldn't hear my plea

10 Firsts

44

(D = David; S = Sue)
D: Have you seen this article about why men want to climb Everest?
S: Well, because it's there, surely?
D: That's not what the article reckons. It reckons that they do it for the attention.
S: What? Well, I suppose that could be true but I can think of a lot of easier ways of getting attention!
D: Yeah, but this article says that psychologists reckon their desire to climb high mountains can be traced back to the fact that they just weren't shown enough love by their mothers.
S: Oh, give over!
D: No really, there's an article here on the Internet. It says they're making up for this lack of motherly love and attention by doing daring, dangerous feats.
S: Whatever next!
D: And it has some pretty harsh things to say about the kind of people who are attracted to mountaineering.
S: Yeah?
D: Yeah. Listen to this, 'Mountain men are "overdependent on external admiration … intensely envious, exploitative in relations with others."'
S: Wow! That's a bit harsh, they have after all been neglected by their mothers. Did they canvass any mountaineers on this finding?
D: Yeah, there are a couple of good quotes actually. What about this one; 'Maybe mountaineers should do a study of narcissism, competition and the desire for fame among academics,' Alan Hinkes.
S: Who?
D: Alan Hinkes, you know, that English climber …
S: Oh yeah, he's trying to be the first Englishman to climb all the highest peaks, isn't he?
D: Yeah, that's the one.
S: So, does he have anything to say in his defence?
D: Well, his answer's pretty straightforward really, he just says he does it for fun; 'You are out exercising in the middle of fantastic scenery with some good mates. It is a very simple pleasure … that's all.'
S: Mmm, a nice leisurely hike in the summer I can understand. Hiking up an enormous mountain, no.
D: Mmm, and then there's the danger element too. I can kind of understand the challenge of seeing how far you can push your body, you know, test yourself to the limits and all that, but not to the point of putting your life in danger.
S: Yeah, I reckon they must be really

driven by something, a need to prove themselves, a need to achieve something really special. I don't think that's necessarily negative, I mean we wouldn't make any progress at all, would we, if we didn't try to do the impossible … that's how progress happens.
D: Yeah, good point, but at what cost? I mean it's one thing to put your own life in danger, but what about the effects on other people? I mean, some of these people have families, and what about the sherpas and the local guides?

45

D: Mmm, and then there's the danger element too. I can kind of understand the challenge of seeing how far you can push your body, you know, test yourself to the limits and all that, but not to the point of putting your life in danger.
S: Yeah, I reckon they must be really driven by something, a need to prove themselves, a need to achieve something really special. I don't think that's necessarily negative, I mean we wouldn't make any progress at all, would we, if we didn't try to do the impossible …

46

a) altitude
b) coordination
c) exciting
d) challenge
e) emergency
f) achievement
g) apparatus
h) mountaineers
i) circumnavigate
j) ascent

47

1
(M = Martin; K = Kate)
M: Well, I never win anything. Did you ever win anything?
K: Well, yes I did, actually. Yes, I came in first in this little competition in the local newspaper, and it was this competition where you had to, um, finish the phrase 'School is …'
M: Right.
K: And design a poster and so I said, because I was quite a good student at the time, I said 'School is the key to a new and better world'. And I had a little rocket ship blasting off and everything …
M: So you were how old then?
K: I was eleven.
M: Oh, eleven, right, right. So what did you win then?
K: Well, I won a twenty dollar gift certificate to Hathaway House Bookshop, and I spent the whole summer kind of eking it out because twenty dollars was quite a lot back then, so I still have the books that I bought and I still have the *Wuthering Heights* and … yes, so …
M: So how do you feel when you look at those books?
K: It was a proud moment for me and my mother.
M: Lucky you.

2
(J = Jenny; H = Howard)
J: … I got my fifty pence back. Have you ever won anything?
H: Oh, do you know, I've won a couple of things actually. The thing that springs to mind is, um, I was quite young and away on holiday with my family and extended family, um, at a holiday camp.
J: Oh, right.
H: Lots of organised games and things like that and I think my sister and the older kids were off doing something else and, er, my mother entered me into the Tarzan Call competition.
J: I'm sorry, the what?
H: The Tarzan Call competition. Don't you remember? Oooooh, oooooh, ooooh. I used to be much better at it than that. So, anyway, there I was in this big draughty hall with loads of other kids who were all up on stage. I remember we were extremely late for this thing and, er, I was fully clothed and my mother undressed me. I was quite young, about five, down to my pants.
J: Why?
H: My underpants. Well, because Tarzan always ran around in a loin cloth.
J: Oh, I see. All the other kids were …
H: They were all there in their trunks or something like that, so there I was, on stage doing the Tarzan Call competition and extremely nervous – first time in front of an audience, but I won. I can't quite remember what I did win, I just remember the feeling of coming first. It was great.
J: Exciting.
H: Yeah.

3
(E = Emma; R = Rob)
E: Well, I suppose you've had lots of girlfriends, but I mean, can you even remember the first one?
R: The first one? Oh, oh yes, I can. OK. Thirteen years old, a girl called Lucy Dunkerly who I fancied for ages. I was thirteen.
E: Oh, how old was she?
R: Twelve. I had fancied her for ages. I eventually plucked up the courage to ask her out and she said yes and I was so shocked it was ridiculous. And, I sort of, I used to live in this village really far away from sort of the town where we sort of used to live near and I had to get my dad to drive me out so that we could pick her up and I took her to see this terrible film, I can't even remember the title of it, but it had Michael J. Fox in it and it was really bad. I remember always sort of people giving advice to you saying, 'Oh, don't sit on the back row,' and all this kind of thing because it will make … and everyone will poke fun and everything and it was so embarrassing and eventually we sort of sat in the middle of the cinema and watched this film and it was really nice. And at the end of the night got picked up and sort of taken home, and that's when I sort of got my first kiss as well, which was very, very frightening. I probably did really badly as well, but, um, …
E: Well, it's not a competition. How did you feel, sort of, did you see her again?

R: Yeah, we did. We continued going out for about three weeks.
E: That long!
R: Which is nothing, really, is it? But …
E: It's quite a lot when you're eleven or thirteen.

11 Stories

48

(I = Interviewer; H = Helen)

I: Helen, let me first ask you a bit about your background. We're here in London but you weren't born here, were you?

H: No, I was born in Sri Lanka and after that I lived for a while in Norway and in Nigeria and my father moved on to Iceland – I've spent a lot of time there and I've also lived for some time in India so, I've spent a lot of time in many different cultures that have a very strong oral tradition, but I decided to come to England and settle in England when I was about twenty-one, twenty-two and I moved to London.

I: What exactly does a professional storyteller do?

H: Everything. A professional storyteller has to work with all ages, and in all situations and they have to be able to tell all different kinds of stories. I think traditionally professional storytellers were the people who were genealogists and historians and everything else was domestic storytelling – whether it be the passing of news and information by people travelling from village to village or whether it be the stories that mothers, fathers and grandparents told to their children, or the stories that friends told each other, they were all happening domestically, but what has happened now is that domestic storytelling has all but died out and so the job of a professional storyteller is to cover everything. So you must work with history and information about the past. You also have to work with the whole area of belief – myth, which goes into religion. You have to work in education, so you have to use teaching stories that are teaching all ages about simple behaviour and about complex moral and social issues and you also have to tell as a mother does to a child to create that intimacy, that close connection between teller and listener. Stories are told inside, outside, in bizarre as well as very normal situations, so really a professional storyteller has to be able to do all different kinds of storytelling.

I: And how did you first get into storytelling?

H: Well, I've always been into storytelling as long as I can remember – I was listening to stories, reading stories, and telling anybody who'd listen and luckily I had a younger sister who would listen and in fact wouldn't go to bed unless I told her stories, and then my friends, they like stories, but actually professionally it was accidental. When I arrived in London I saw an advert for a storyteller wanted to work in Brixton, to work in the streets and the adventure playgrounds and on the housing estates and the idea, it was for the libraries, the idea was to encourage people by hearing stories to come into the library and read them.

I: And what do you think is the universal appeal of stories?

H: I think primarily it's human contact. What stories do is they connect people to each other, to the listener, put all the listeners together, listener to teller, listeners to each other, they connect you with your inner world, your private dreams. They connect you with the natural world, with the environment all around you, and at the same time they entertain you, they amuse you, and they are put in a form that are memorable, so you can carry them away with you. So I think that's the universal appeal of stories and of course they're free! Now stories, when I say stories, I mean everything – could be a joke, could be an anecdote, could be a family story, a little bit of family history, could be a personal event that did happen, could be a wildly exaggerated tall tale that might have a grain of truth. It could be a folk tale, a wonder tale, it could be a ghost story, a myth, something to do with that great scale of human belief or it could be what we call an urban myth. An urban myth is set in an urban rather than a rural situation and it deals with primarily urban considerations and one of the most important urban considerations is living all together – it's people, it's society, so an urban myth is a rumour often with an element of humour and it's a rumour that's rooted in possibility and it has a contemporary ring but yet these stories that people think happened here and now, they are very, very often hundreds and hundreds and hundreds of years old. One of the most common urban myths is the story of the vanishing hitch-hiker. Everybody knows somebody who knows somebody who knows somebody that this happened to and yet this story actually has its antecedents in ancient Rome and perhaps even before that, only naturally the girl wasn't picked up in a car, she was picked up in a coach or a chariot or lifted onto the back of a horse, but the story remains the same.

49

(I = Interviewer; H = Helen)

I: Do you have an urban myth you could tell us?

H: Well, I know lots of urban myths but this one actually happened to me, so it wasn't so much an urban myth as a really disturbing experience.
You see, what happened was, it was when I first moved to London and I was driving up from the North and I was rather nervous because I had only just passed my driving test and I had a very old car and it was also very bad weather. So I was driving along and rather anxiously leaning over the wheel and peering out and then all of a sudden somebody stepped out right in front of me and I only just managed to jam the brakes on and I zipped into the slip road and I thought I'd hit whoever it was, so I jumped out of the car, shaking all over, and there was a girl. She was about fourteen, she was dressed in a very short mini-skirt and a tank top. She was soaking wet and she was still standing in the middle of the motorway. So I yelled and screamed at her because I had been so scared and then I noticed that she was crying, so of course I calmed down and I got her out of the road and I asked her if she needed some help and she said 'I want a lift.' So I let her get into the car and we started driving along and it turned out that she was going to London as well, and she was going to Streatham. She had been out at a party and she lived actually at 29 Gleneldon Road. I remember it was really impressed in my mind. So we were driving along and then I noticed that she was shivering and this being an old car I didn't have any heating or anything so I told her that I had a coat in the back that she could borrow. This was a while back, you know, when those big fur coats were in fashion.
So, she wrapped herself up in that and we drove, and I must say I forgot about her because she stopped talking. I suppose she must have fallen asleep, and I just concentrated on the road. It must have been quite late when we got to London, and as we drove in off the ring road, there was a little bit of a problem, and I had to brake very suddenly and automatic reflex, I just flung my arm out in front of my passenger, forgetting that you know, she had a seat belt, and when I looked round to make sure she was all right, she wasn't there.
So then I had to stop and pinch myself and I was sure I hadn't been dreaming but she definitely wasn't there and I got out the car and I looked at the car and I got back in the car, and then I looked in the back, and my coat wasn't there either. I couldn't believe that it was just a dream, I couldn't explain the disappearance of the coat, so in the end I drove all the way to Streatham, and I found this road – Gleneldon Road – and I found number 29 and I stopped outside it and of course it was about one o'clock in the morning by then, but there was a light on, so I went and I knocked and the door was opened by a woman who was probably late 30's, 40's perhaps, but she looked just like this girl. So I just stared at her, and after a while she said, 'Yes?', 'Yes?' and she made as if to shut the door.
Well, I suppose it was late at night, and I said, 'Excuse me, it's just that I've just, I just gave a lift to your daughter,' and she looked at me and her face crumpled up and she said, 'How could you, how could you?' I didn't know what was going on, and I said, 'I'm sorry, what is it?' and she said 'My daughter is dead.' I said, 'I'm so sorry, I'm so sorry, it must have been somebody else. It's just such a coincidence. She said this was her address and I picked her up, oh, it must have been about seven or eight hours ago, I picked her up just outside York on the M1.'
She stared at me then, and she said,

'My daughter died on the M1, outside York exactly a year ago.' My legs started to give way underneath me. I couldn't believe it, and then I thought to myself, 'But what about the coat?', and I said, 'But how can it be, because she got in the car and I talked to her and she was there, and she even put my coat on, and a ghost wouldn't put on a coat.' And the woman said, 'Well, if you don't believe me, go and look at her grave.' And there and then she came out, and she was still in her slippers but she took me up the road and left and right and there was a big church. She stopped at the gate of the churchyard and she said, 'My daughter, she's in there, the third grave to the right of the church. You'll excuse me if I don't go any further.'

So of course I understood and I went in and it was very dark, but there was a light outside the church and I could just make out the third grave. Sure enough, it was fairly new, grass just growing, flowers on it, and I looked – date, the girl had died exactly that day a year before. Fourteen years old. But folded up on the grave was my fur coat.

It's hard to believe, isn't it? If it hadn't happened to me, well I wouldn't be telling you now.

📼 50

1

So I yelled and screamed at her because I had been so scared and then I noticed that she was crying, so of course I calmed down and I got her out of the road and I asked her if she needed some help and she said 'I want a lift.'

2

… and she even put my coat on, and a ghost wouldn't put on a coat.

3

Sure enough, it was fairly new, grass just growing, flowers on it, and I looked – date, the girl had died exactly that day a year before. Fourteen years old. But folded up on the grave was my fur coat.

📼 51

(B = Becky; J = John)

B: Good evening and welcome to the first show of the year 2000! Today we have John Ruskin in the studio with us. John's been following the events of the Millennium, and I must say John, you're looking remarkably wide awake.

J: If only! You don't look so bad yourself! Were you one of the hordes lining the river last night, waiting to see the river of fire?

B: No, I took up a last minute invitation from some friends to whizz down to the coast for a house party!

J: You did well. Most Londoners were not impressed by the party laid on by the capital. The river of fire didn't really live up to expectations. It was supposed to be one of the most spectacular pyrotechnic shows ever seen, measuring 60 metres in height and travelling down the Thames at the incredible speed of 1,240 kph … but a slight technical hitch meant that 99% of the population didn't actually see it.

B: So there was a river of fire then?

J: Yes, but it was only visible by helicopter!

B: Fantastic! So the crowds lining the banks of the Thames must have been pretty disappointed.

J: Yes, I think we all were really. The organisers are blaming the weather conditions but I think they miscalculated how much, or should I say, how little, people would have been able to see from the ground. The helicopter crews flying over the city to cover the events claim to have had superb views. I must admit I thought the fireworks display in Paris was much better.

B: Yes, it was spectacular wasn't it? The whole of the Eiffel Tower lit up like that. Amazing!

J: Yes, especially considering the terrible weather and the flooding that France has been suffering over the last week. There was talk at one point of having to call the whole thing off: it didn't sound like it was going to happen.

B: Really?

J: Yes, but they pulled it off – and in superb fashion, really put us to shame in fact what with the, well, you know, the mix up with the tickets for the Dome, the fiasco with the trains, the London Eye …

B: Oh yes!

J: I mean, it was going to be one of the centrepieces of the whole evening. Tony Blair was to have opened it with a Star Wars type laser show but it all fell through. Thanks to bad organisation and bad time management it just didn't happen … they just didn't get their act together in time. The Ferris wheel failed some fairly routine safety check at the last minute. I mean, that's pretty bad, isn't it? France had to contend with a major hurricane and they managed to pull everything off without a hitch!

B: Typical!

J: And then of course there was the Millennium Experience party at the Dome. Up to a third of the tickets hadn't been distributed by yesterday so the guests had to pick them up at the train stations on the way, and that was a fiasco. The train service was slow and irregular and some of the guests actually never made it to the Dome. In fact the whole thing was almost called off because of a bomb scare …

B: A bomb scare?

J: Yes, apparently a hoax caller phoned to say that a bomb would go off in the Dome at midnight. The organisers were on the verge of evacuating the Dome at 10.45, minutes before the main show was due to begin – but the Queen stood her ground – and, as we know, the show went on.

B: Sounds like a bit of a disaster all round really …

J: Well, it wasn't all bad news. On a happy note, there were no rushes at the hospitals and everything seemed to pass off very peacefully. Most medical staff had had their leave cancelled to cover what they had imagined would be a flood of party victims, but it seems that in fact it turned out to be a very quiet night. And of course the Millennium Bug was a bit of a no-show. To date, the only failures reported here in the UK were a weather vane in Portsmouth and a set of traffic lights in Inverness.

B: Could it all have been an elaborate hoax on the part of the IT technicians to get a bit of extra cash over the holidays?

J: Well, yes it might well have been …

📼 52

a) It was supposed to be one of the most spectacular pyrotechnic shows ever seen, measuring 60 metres in height and travelling down the Thames at the incredible speed of 1,240 kph.

b) There was talk at one point of having to call the whole thing off: it didn't sound like it was going to happen.

c) … it was going to be one of the centrepieces of the whole evening. Tony Blair was to have opened it with a Star Wars type laser show but it all fell through.

d) … apparently a hoax caller phoned to say that a bomb would go off in the Dome at midnight. The organisers were on the verge of evacuating the Dome at 10.45, minutes before the main show was due to begin – but the Queen stood her ground …

e) Most medical staff had had their leave cancelled to cover what they had imagined would be a flood of party victims, but it seems that in fact it turned out to be a very quiet night.

📼 53

1

I had planned to go on holiday to South America. I was supposed to go visit friends and travel around for six weeks. It was my dream to visit Machu Picchu in Peru. I'd been thinking about it for years and so I had booked time off of work and I had my itinerary all worked out and I had bought all my hiking gear and everything, but luckily I hadn't paid for the ticket yet because you see, what happened was this big problem came up at work. A client had moved the deadline forward and so I actually had to cancel the whole trip and I … I couldn't believe it actually, I really could not believe it. I was so disappointed because I had been hoping and thinking and dreaming about this for years and, um, so this friend of mine suggested that we should just go to Egypt, after the project deadline, um, just sort of a last minute thing, and I, you know, I was very stressed by that point and I definitely was in need of a holiday so, so we went and in fact I ended up doing a scuba diving course in the Red Sea and now I am a convert to diving. I can't, you know, can't get enough of it, so I am really glad that things turned out the way they did in the end.

2

Ah, well, there's a, there's a funny story there actually. You see, this job wasn't actually the job that I'd applied for. I, um, I had been offered the post of a lecturer in a university in Kuala Lumpur, and you know I quite fancied, I was up for the travel and everything. I was very excited, and er, so I'd made all sorts of plans. You know and

I'd, I'd done all the boring medical stuff. I had the jabs, bought the guide books and, er, and of course I had completely axed the winter wardrobe, which was a little foolish as it turned out, but as I was going to be there for two years, you know, what did one need you know, the winter woollies for? And I was really looking forward to living in a tropical climate. I thought, 'Well this will be a nice change', and er, there I was, my bags practically packed and their economy crashed and they cut back on their budgets and there was no job and, er, that was a month before I was due to leave. So there I was, I practically didn't have a home to live in because, of course, I'd given up the tenancy on my flat and, er, so I mean I was frantic. I was looking in the journals, you know, 'Oooh, where do I find another job?', and it was a terrible time of year to job hunt believe me, and then I couldn't believe it. I mean, suddenly here was this job in Madrid. Well, I mean, it was a total change of plan because actually it does get very cold in Madrid in the winter. I don't know whether people have been there, but believe me it does, so of course it was a complete new winter wardrobe and, er, there I was. But, erm, ah, no, I'm glad it worked out like that really because I mean I, I love Madrid and I've been there for three years now, and I may stay for longer, you know.

3

Well, I'd organised a surprise party for my friend's 30th birthday and it was at my home and oh, it was great. We, a couple of friends and myself, we'd decorated the house out with streamers and balloons and it looked fantastic and this big banner saying 'Happy Birthday' and we'd prepared loads of food and the, the house was going to be just bursting because we'd invited close to fifty people. And the guests were supposed to arrive half an hour before my friend was due to turn up, so it could all be a surprise. And we, I told her to come and meet me at my house because she thought we were going to go out for dinner. Um, I sort of, all this pretext had been made up and everything, so all of our friends arrived and then all of a sudden, twenty minutes before she was supposed to turn up, I get this phone call from my friend saying that her dad was ill and she had to go and see him, and she wouldn't turn up until much later. So, there was nothing I could do. I had all these people at the house so we just decided to start the party. Um, and she did, you know, my friend turned up and she was still surprised and it was lovely, um, I was a bit upset that the surprise got ruined because we had gone to so much trouble but the party was brilliant. It all went you know, really well, but, um, it taught me never to plan a surprise again because you never know what's going to happen.

▭ 54

It's twilight on a cold winter's evening. You are in a tall building in the middle of a large city. You are on one of the top floors. You are getting ready to leave. You walk towards the lift. It's a glass elevator on the outside of the building. The lift arrives. You get in. The view is beautiful with all the lights of the city coming on against the backdrop of the turquoise twilight sky. The

lift starts to go down. You look out at the view. Suddenly the lift stops and the lights go out. You realise that the lights have gone out throughout the city.

12 Words

▭ 55

1
(C = Claire; K = Karen)
C: Do you want tea or coffee?
K: Whichever you're having.
C: Coffee. Decaf or normal?
K: Normal. I need some caffeine.
C: Milk?
K: Yeah. Full fat.
C: I've only got semi-skimmed.
K: That's fine.
C: There you are.
K: Thanks.
C: So what are you going to do this afternoon?
K: I thought I might go off and get some retail therapy in.
C: Good idea … but whatever you buy, make sure you put it on his credit card!
K: Yes, I will. When are you picking Mum up from the station?
C: Twenty past five.
K: OK, so let's meet up at about eight then?
C: Yeah, fine.

2
(D = DJ; R = Robin Jones)
D: This afternoon we've got Robin Jones in the studio, talking about GM food. Robin, where do you stand on the GM food argument then?
R: Whenever I hear people getting het up about GM foods it really makes me angry. I mean, we've been genetically modifying things for centuries and nobody says a word, but the idea of doing it with a bit more sophistication and everyone starts flapping and fussing.
D: But that's only right. I mean, we don't know what the effects of altering a plant's DNA are going to be.
R: Effects, effects! What are you worried about? Is eating too many genetically modified peas or whatever going to turn you into a monster?
D: Ah, but what happens if eating too many genetically modified peas gives you cancer?
R: How can peas give you cancer?
D: Well you never know. It depends what they put into the pea's DNA.
R: Well, it's not going to be something carcinogenic is it? More likely something to make them frost resistant to keep the farmers happy and greener and bigger to keep the customers happy.

3
(M = minister; S = secretary)
M: … 705
S: 0338 1945705.
M: That's it. So now wherever I am you can contact me, but only in real emergencies.
S: OK.
M: And on no account whatsoever must you give my number out. Whoever calls, just say you'll make sure I get their message.
S: But what about other ministers?

M: Especially the other ministers. However much they pester you, don't give them the number.
S: OK. Where are you off to now?
M: To get some quality time in with my kids.
S: OK. And when will you be back in?
M: Not until tomorrow morning.
S: Don't forget you have an appointment with Reginald Clarke at ten.
M: Who?
S: The spin doctor.
M: Oh yes, Reg. Fine. Thanks for reminding me. I think I'd like the meeting in the Blue Room.
S: No problem, Sir.

▭ 56

1
(A = Andy; E = Emma; B = Beryl; C = Chris; D = Donna)
A: OK, Emma, you choose the topic …
E: Er, films.
B: That's too difficult!
C: No it's not!
B: OK.
D: I'll start! *American Beauty*.
A: OK. It goes clockwise, so Chris, you're next!
C: *Black Beauty*.
E: *Charlie's Angels*.
A: *Dracula*.
B: *Elephant Man*.
D: Er, *Forrest Gump* …

2
(A = Ann; K = Katy; P = Pete; M = Mike; S = Sue)
A: I'll start and Katy and Pete can go next as they know the game. Let's start with 'umbrella'. Your turn Katy.
K: Avocado.
P: OK, operation.
A: Your turn Mike. Have you got it?
M: Yes, I think so. November?
A: Yes! Your turn, Sue.
S: Er – banana?
All: No! Try again.
S: Garlic.
All: No!
S: I give up.
A: OK. My go again. What was the last word? November? Um, rubbish.
K: Helicopter.
P: Radio.
M: Orange.
S: I think I've got it – elephant!
A: Well done! Let's play something else …

3
(H = Helen; K = Kiki; J = John)
H: Right Kiki, your topic is libraries. I'm timing you. Your minute starts … now!
K: Oh no! Right, libraries are really interesting places. They're full of books and they're somewhere you can go when you want to find out all sorts of information, especially if you haven't got access to a computer. Um, …
J: Ha! You said 'um'. My turn …

▭ 57

a)   Doctor Foster went to Gloucester in a shower of rain.
b)   Have you been to Leicester Square? You see people from every country under the sun there.
c)   I'd love to live in Grosvenor Square – it's a very desirable part of London.
d)   My cousins live in Brighton.

e) Greenwich has a fantastic market on Sundays.

f) Guildford's about an hour's drive out of London.

13 Conscience

▭ 58

1

Well, I don't think it's such a good idea to give money because, er, well, I'd be really worried that somebody would spend it on alcohol rather than something nourishing or, you know, because they always say, like, 'penny for a cup of tea' or whatever. Um, so what I think I might do is, um, buy a sandwich or hot drink or something in winter or … and give it to them there, or maybe find some old clothes.

2

Yes, I usually put a couple of coins in a donation box, um, I mean, obviously if it's, if I'm not in a hurry and if it's easy to get at the change. Um, the thing I don't do is I don't believe in giving money to beggars.

3

Well, I never give any money to anybody. As far as I'm concerned it just encourages them. You know, I pay my taxes so the state will look after these people. I mean that's what we're paying all these high taxes for and you know what, quite frankly, I just think it's sheer laziness. I mean, I think they could get up off their bums and get a job if they really wanted to. It's just that they don't want to work.

4

Well, I don't mind giving money to people who are doing something to earn it, I mean, you know I'd rather they actually did something to earn the money, you know like, like street artists or, or buskers. I mean, I think someone who is actually playing music, it puts people in a good mood on the way to work, so you know, I usually give those people something. A few pennies.

5

Yeah, I never give money on the street any more. Um, I, um, I do give money through my bank, um, to charities that, um, I'm particularly concerned about. Once a month they get money from my bank. And that way I find I know where it's going and it also means that you're giving extra money because of tax relief.

6

It really annoys me. These people with their squeegies. I don't see why I should give money for cleaning my windscreen. I haven't, I haven't asked them. I think it's high time that the government did something about it because it really is annoying. No, I never give them anything.

▭ 59

(D = Daniel; S = Sue; J = Jake)

D: So, you did a parachute jump for charity?

S: Uh, huh, I must have been mad because it was the most frightening thing I ever did, but as far as I know, it seemed to, you know, do the trick … it seemed to raise quite a lot of money.

D: I've always wanted to do a parachute jump but I, I've never really had the kind of guts to do it.

J: I can see the fun of a parachute jump but what does the charity get out of it?

S: Well, they get the money that you, you know, you get sponsored by people or they …

J: What? You ring people up and say, give me so much money and I'll jump out of an aeroplane?

S: Yeah, yeah, because I think people are more willing to do that because the, you know because it's something that kind of is right at the edge of the sort of comfort zone, so people are going, 'Oh I wouldn't do that, I'll, I'll give … '

D: Did you raise a lot?

S: I don't really know, you know, that's one thing that does bother me that you know, you never really know how much these charities …

J: That bothers me too, I mean, what does it cost to take an aeroplane up? You know, and presumably they have to insure you, um …

S: Yeah, I suppose so, but then, you know, people wouldn't do it, would they? I mean they wouldn't be organised if you didn't, if they didn't raise money, if the …

D: Well, that's right. I mean you, you, you have to have some sort of … I mean, before we had any kind of a welfare system, um, charities were the only, the only way that we could possibly er, er, support people who were less fortunate than we were.

J: But wouldn't it be more sensible to do something you know with a, with a purpose, like collect money for food or …

D: Well, there is something to an event. OK, if you have a big event it focuses people's attention on things and you can generate more money with a, with a larger event than you can with just going door to door …

S: Yeah, you can have celebrities along and you know they can all …

J: Yeah, well, they're doing it for publicity. What are they getting out of it?

S: I think they want to give as well, you know, they want to give something. It's like these sort of champagne receptions, you know, you've got to get, the charity's got to get a profile, haven't they, so they won't get photos in the paper unless you've got some celebrities.

J: Yes, but what worries me is how much they spend setting up the event. You know, it's really expensive now and you, you know, I get letters from people saying, come to this black tie ball to raise money for a particular charity, tickets are 150 quid each.

D: But on the other hand what's the alternative? The alternative is that maybe a lot of homeless people go hungry if somebody doesn't do something, and it takes an awful lot to get people off their butts to go and do stuff.

J: But it's such a contradiction that, you know, people will revel in something luxurious in order to help people who have got nothing. I mean …

S: Yeah, but, you know, the thing is that it must, it absolutely must make money for the charities because they wouldn't bother doing it …

J: I reckon if you saw the figures at the end of that. I mean I know that these big fund-raising things … I know for instance that whoever organised it, is on a percentage of what money is raised …

S: Oh, you're just being cynical.

J: I'm being realistic. I'm being realistic because I think that by the time you've paid for the event, you know, probably that champagne's cost a lot of money, the food's cost a lot of money, hiring a hotel …

S: Maybe people donate it though, you never know, do you?

D: And also, it's, there's got to be a bottom line level of help for people and at least if something is going through it's got to be better than nothing …

S: I tell you what does bother me though …

J: It's just to make you feel good though, isn't it? I mean, this is just to make you feel good about yourself.

S: No, I think …

D: I think that's a bit simplistic …

S: Yeah.

D: And not necessarily accurate at all. I think we are moving from a time of extreme selfishness to a time of a bit more benevolence. I think people have got to a point now where we, we do feel a bit guilty about things and so we should. And so we should. There's a huge inequality in the world now and it's about time we did start doing things and …

S: There's one thing that does bother me though, and like these big organisations. You sometimes hear in the newspapers or whatever that the money you actually give doesn't actually get through to places like Africa or …

J: Quite, because of the administration is absolutely enormous.

D: That's why I like …

J: People jetting around the world, you know, um, staying in smart hotels, um, distributing money. I mean how much of your, of your money to a, to a famine charity actually buys food?

D: Well, that's what makes … there's a lot of great things now … of course if you go out and look on the web and things like there's all these great erm, sites where people …

S: Oh yeah, you can press a button and erm …

D: … where you can actually press a button and donate, and donate a cup of rice, er, there's, they have a row of sponsors and by pressing the button … oh, the World Hunger site is a really good example of that …

S: Mmm, yeah, I do that …

D: … where you, where you press a button and er, they donate a cup of rice to …

J: I can see the sense of that. That seems much more sensible to me than jumping out of an aeroplane, frankly, for a few bob.

S: Well, thanks very much!

▭ 60

a) A: So, you did a parachute jump for charity?

B: No, I did a bungee jump.
b)   A: So, you did a parachute jump for charity?
     B: No, it was my sister.
c)   A: So, you did a parachute jump for charity?
     B: No, I did it for fun.
d)   A: So, you did a parachute jump for charity?
     B: No, but I'm thinking about doing one.

61

a)   … as far as I know, it seemed to, you know, do the trick … it seemed to raise quite a lot of money.
b)   … they get the money that you, you know, you get sponsored by people …
c)   But wouldn't it be more sensible to do something you know with a, with a purpose, like collect money for food or …
d)   … you can generate more money with a, with a larger event than you can with just going door to door …
e)   … the charity's got to get a profile, haven't they, so they won't get photos in the paper unless you've got some celebrities.
f)   The alternative is that maybe a lot of homeless people go hungry if somebody doesn't do something …
g)   I mean, this is just to make you feel good about yourself.
h)   … you can actually press a button and donate a cup of rice …

14 Review 2

62

… And to finish tonight's programme, we said we'd bring you some amusing stories from this week's press from around the world, and here they are:

In the United States, John Franklin, a cleaner from Illinois, decided last month he would post himself to his best friend as a birthday surprise. He climbed into a large crate and got his wife to post him to his friend's house thirty miles away. He should have arrived the next morning, but unfortunately the crate went missing for six days before finally turning up in Malibu, California. Postal workers might have rescued him earlier, but they mistook his desperate banging for the ticking of a clock. Mr Franklin said he can't have been thinking clearly as it seemed like such a good idea at the time. An understatement if ever we've heard one.

Japan now, and Keita Ono's inflatable underpants caused chaos on a rush-hour train in Tokyo last week. Mr Ono, 43, designed the rubber pants so they would inflate to 30 times their normal size in the event of a tidal wave. He explained that he'd always been afraid of drowning and that he wore them 24 hours a day. Mr Ono thinks that somebody must have splashed some water on them, triggering the sensor and accidentally causing them to inflate. He admitted that he should have been able to deflate the pants, but he said he couldn't move at all and was firmly wedged in the middle of the carriage aisle. Things could have been much worse had it not been for a quick-thinking passenger who punctured the pants with a pen.

Finally, Detroit airport was last night put on red-alert when a man boarding a plane greeted the pilot, whom he knew, with the words 'Hi Jack'. Air-traffic controllers, who can't have been paying too much attention to what was going on, ordered armed police to board the plane, before realising their mistake. A spokesman said that from now on, officials would notify air-traffic control whenever there was a pilot called Jack on duty. I don't know!

Macmillan Education
Between Towns Road, Oxford OX4 3PP
A division of Macmillan Publishers Limited
Companies and representatives throughout the world
ISBN-13: 978 0 333 91740 4
ISBN-10: 0 333 91740 5

Text © Ceri Jones, Tania Bastow, Sue Kay and Vaughan Jones
Design and illustration © Macmillan Publishers Limited 2001

First published 2001

Designed by Keith Shaw, Threefold Design
Illustrated by Gary Andrews pp79, 101, 120; Emma Brownjohn pp16,
51, 62, 99; Martina Farrow pp15, 43, 46, 72, 91, 94, 96, 110; Julian
Mosedale pp5, 7, 9, 17, 18, 19, 22, 23, 27, 28, 32, 38, 40, 43, 59, 61,
76, 80, 87, 90, 111, 114, 122, 123, 126, 129; Peter Richardson pp11,
48, 52, 53.
Cover design by Andrew Oliver
Cover painting © Howard Hodgkin

Authors' acknowledgements
We would like to thank staff and students at IH Madrid Serrano and
The English School of L'Aquila. Special thanks to Bev, Fred and Rich
for their constant support. Also to Fausto Corti, Roberto Giordano,
Anna-Maria Ianni, Gianluca Racano, Dafydd Jones, Mandy Grocutt,
Melody and Nick Sawyer and David and Zena Bastow for their help
in providing and testing material. A big thank you also to Karen
Warner, our editor, for all her help, hard work and patience.
We are especially grateful to Jon Hird for writing the review units
and for his contribution to the teacher's book. His comments, along
with those of Peter Maggs, were much appreciated. Similarly, our
thanks to Russell Stannard (Inside Out Workbook), Helena Gomm
(Inside Out Teacher's Book) and of course everyone involved in the
Inside Out Resource Pack.

The authors and publishers would like to thank the following for
their help in piloting the material and making comments:
Mary Pickett and Ben Darby, International House, London. Tom
Bradbury, London School of English, London. Amanda Smith, Kings
Street College, London. Angus Savory, Lake School of English, Oxford.
Sarah Briscoe, Regent Oxford, Oxford. Alejandro Zarzalejos, EOI Las
Rozas. Elisa Jimenez, EOI Fuenlabrada. Rosa Melgar, EOI Valdezarza.
Henny Burke, British Language Centre, Madrid. Fiona Miller,
International House, Madrid. Angela Tomkinson, British School
Cinecitta, Rome. Tobias Jones, Parma University, Parma. Alison
Hayman, Liceo Scientifico 'G.B.Grassi', Latina. Jennifer Malia and Neil
Tibbetts, British Institutes, Milan. Patrick McCann, Linguaviva, Milan.
We would also like to thank teachers and staff at the Escuelas Oficial
de Idiomas of Spain for their help in the early stages of the project,
in particular at A Coruña, Alcala de Guadaira-Seville, Alcorcón,
Barcelona 1, Barcelona 2, Bilbao, Cartagena, Ciudad Lineal,
Fuenlabrada, Gandía, Getafe, Jesus Maestro-Madrid, Mostoles,
Pamplona, San Blas, San Sebastián de los Reyes and Santander.

The publishers wish to thank Steven Poole and Helen East.

The authors and publishers would like to thank the following for
permission to reproduce their material:
HarperCollins Publishers Ltd for extracts from Men Are From Mars,
Women Are From Venus by John Gray Ph.D.; IMP and EMI for My
Girl, words and music by Michael Barson, © 1979 EMI Music
Publishing Limited, London WC2H 0EA; LondonNet Limited
(http://www.londonnet.com) for adapted extracts from Leicester
Square by David J. Clee, all rights reserved; Lonely Planet Publications
for extracts from Spain, ed. 1, Lonely Planet, 1997 and Central
Europe, ed. 2, Lonely Planet, 1997. Reproduced by permission of
Lonely Planet Publications; Lonely Planet Publications for extracts
reproduced by permission of Lonely Planet Publications from the
Lonely Planet website: www.lonelyplanet.com.au; Anvil Press Poetry
Ltd for Stealing, taken from Selling Manhattan by Carol Ann Duffy,
published by Anvil Press Poetry in 1987. Oxford University Press for
definitions of conversation, conversational, conversationalist and
conversation piece reprinted from The Concise Oxford Dictionary (9th
edition, 1995) by permission of Oxford University Press, © Oxford
University Press 1995; Macmillan Publishers Ltd for definitions of
conversation, conversational, conversationalist and conversation
piece from Macmillan English Dictionary, published by Macmillan
Publishers Ltd, 2001; © Bloomsbury Publishing Plc 2001; Virago Press
for an extract from That's Not What I Meant by Deborah Tannen,
reprinted with permission of Little Brown and Company (UK); Tatler
magazine for the article Life's a Bitch/How I won the Lottery by
Carinthia West, from Tatler, April 1998, Vol 293, No 4. Carinthia West
© Tatler/The Conde Nast Publications Limited; Laurence Pollinger

Limited and the John Wyndham Estate Trust, and David Higham
Associates for extracts from The Day of the Triffids by John Wyndham
published by Penguin Books Limited; The Wylie Agency (UK) Ltd for
an extract from The Man Who Mistook His Wife For a Hat by Oliver
Sacks. © 1985; IMP Ltd and EMI for I'm Going Slightly Mad. Words
and music by Freddie Mercury, Brian May, Roger Taylor and John
Deacon. © 1991 Queen Music Limited. EMI Music Publishing Ltd,
London WC2H 0EA JASRAC 出0008579-001; The Yorkshire Evening Post,
29th January 2000, for Counting Money; Camden New Journal, 3rd
February 2000, for High Drama; The Yorkshire Post, 27th May 1999
for False Hope; The Shropshire Star, 15th July 1999 for Deeply in
Love; The Daily Telegraph, 2nd January 2000 for extracts from A brief
history of the future – an interview with Nigel Farndale; International
Music Publications Limited, BMG Entertainment Limited, Mike Stock
Publishing Limited, and All Boys Music Limited for Love in the First
Degree. Words and Music by Sarah Dallin, Keren Woodward, Siobhan
Farley, Mike Stock, Matt Aitken and Peter Waterman. © 1987
Warner/Chappell Music Limited, All Boys Music Limited, Mike Stock
Publishing Limited and Sids Songs Limited. (50%) Warner/Chappell
Music Limited, London W6 8BS; WGBH Educational Foundation, for
extracts from First Without Oxygen taken from NOVA Online
(http://www.pbs.org/wgbh/nova/everest) © 2000; Times Newspapers
Limited for an extract from The Times Millennium Weekend, 11th
December 1999. © Times Newspapers Limited, 11th December 1999;
Headline for extracts from Debretts New Guide to Etiquette and
Modern Manners by John Morgan; Robson Books for an extract from
Muhammed Ali by Thomas Hauser, © 1991 Thomas Hauser and
Muhammed Ali; Bantam Press, a division of Transworld Publishers for
an extract from If Only by Geri Halliwell, © Geri Halliwell 1999. All
rights reserved; Little Brown & Co Inc, USA for an extract from Long
Walk to Freedom by Nelson Mandela, Copyright © 1994 Nelson
Rolihlahla Mandela; Rosie Burke for extracts from Uneasy Virtue,
from Voyager July/August 2000; Constable & Robinson Publishing Ltd
for an extract from Smarties: All the incredible facts you ever need to
know, edited by Mike Ashley; Corgi, a division of Transworld
Publishers for an extract from The Book of Lists © David
Wallechinsky, Irvine Wallace and Amy Wallace. Extracted from The
Book of Lists published in the UK by Corgi, a division of Transworld
Publishers. All rights reserved; The Telegraph Group Ltd for an extract
from In hindsight, it's easy to scoff at past predictions by Robert
Uhlig in The Daily Telegraph 31st August 2000 © Telegraph Group
Limited, 31st August 2000.

Whilst every effort has been made to locate the owners of copyright,
in some cases this has been unsuccessful. The publishers apologise for
any infringement or failure to acknowledge the original sources and
will be glad to include any necessary correction in subsequent
printings.

Picture research for units 8–14 (inclusive) by Helen Reilly/Arnos
Design

The authors and publishers would like to thank the following for
permission to reproduce their photographs:
Allsport pp89 Grazia Neri, 121(tl); Aquarius Library p4(b); Anthony
Blake Photo Library p20; Chris Bonington Picture Library p92(tr);Tony
Boyle pp98(b); The Bridgewater Book Company Ltd p44(scarab,
peacock feathers, horn, dragon, blue eye); Camera Press p129;
Collections p121(tm); SIN/Corbis p11, Micheal S Yamashita/Corbis
p17(t); Ian Derry/Freediving Association of GB p93(t); Mary Evans
Picture Library p98(all); Eyewire p108(all); Peter Gould p85(t); Ronald
Grant Cinema Archive/ Twentieth Century Fox p50; Robert Harding
pp81, 93(b), 121(bb,bc), 130(ml); David Hoffman p118(fr); Image Bank
pp10, 17(b), 24, 36, 42; Images Colour Library p34(l); Military Photo
Library p14(2); ©The Museum of Modern Art, New York p33(Hopper,
Edward. New York Movie (1939); Network p118 (fl,ml); Ronald
Toms/www.osf.co.uk p63(b); Photonica p44(Japanese cat); Pictor
pp31, 65; Popperfoto pp4(a,c), 68(Playstation 2) Reuters, 107, 117,
127; Powerstock/Zefa pp14(3), 68(palmtop), 85(bl,br), 88(r), 92(bl),
103, 105; Simon Fowler/ ©Queen Productions Ltd p62; Rex Features
pp63(t), 68(wearable computer), 87, 116(m,b); SAMS/Sipa Press p4(d);
Mehau Kulyk/Science Photo Library pp54(scan), 68(ml), 96, 115(l);
Frank Spooner Picture Library pp69, 88(l), 92(r) 116(t), 121(tr); Stone
pp14(1,4), 26, 30, 34(r), 39, 47, 59, 66 73, 78, 118(mr), 121(ba); Tony
Durran©Tatler/The Conde Nast Publications Ltd p44 (Tatler cover);
Dudley Reed©Tatler/The Conde Nast Publications Ltd p45; Telegraph
Colour Library p34(m); The Topps Co.Inc. p70

Commissioned photographs by Gareth Boden pp13, 14(food),
Haddon Davies p55

Cartoons on pp11, 49, 75, 95, 109, 126 reproduced with permission of
Punch Limited; pp21, 29, 35, 106 reproduced with permission of
Private Eye; p83 reproduced with permission of Anthony Kelly.

Printed in China
2006
12 11 10 9